WEST COAST GA S0-AKD-414

WEST COAST GARDENWALKS

ALICE JOYCE

MICHAEL KESEND PUBLISHING · NEW YORK

All rights reserved. No portion of this book may be reproduced in any form or by any means without the prior consent of the publisher.
Copyright 2000 © by Alice Joyce
First Publication 2000
Published by Michael Kesend Publishing, Ltd.
1025 Fifth Avenue, New York, NY 10028

Library of Congress Cataloging-in-Publication Data

Joyce, Alice
    West Coast Gardenwalks: the best gardens from San
Diego to Vancouver, including winery gardens, bed and
breakfasts, and resources for gardeners/Alice Joyce
        p. cm.
        ISBN 0-935576-54-1 (trade paper)
        1. Gardens—Pacific Coast (U.S.)—Guidebooks.
    2. Gardens—British Columbia—Guidebooks. 3. Gar-
    dening—Pacific Coast (U.S.)—Equipment and supplies.
    6. Gardening—British Columbia—Equipment and sup-
    plies. I. Title: West Coast Gardenwalks. II. Title
    SB466.U65 N765 2000
    712.0979–dc21   99-0551146

ACKNOWLEDGMENTS

Since beginning this project more than three years ago, I was uprooted from my home in Chicago. For a time I worked from my office in the Midwest and a temporary apartment in the San Francisco Bay Area. Writing the book required that I travel up and down the West Coast to visit gardens. At the same time, relocating to California became a reality. Eventually I said a final goodbye to the urban garden I had tended for more than 20 years. Tom and I settled into a new place north of San Francisco, where I looked upon a rockhard patch of earth that suffered from years of neglect. We removed all the dense weedy overgrowth with our own hands, and as the months passed, I put in pebble paths, created raised beds with rocks and paving stones, and planted a new garden.

The wonderful gardens in this book inspired me beyond words.

My heartfelt thanks go to all the garden directors, horticulturists, designers, docents, librarians, staff, and innkeepers who found time to talk with me, to read entries for accuracy, and answer my questions. Regretfully, this brief acknowledgment prevents me from naming each and every individual, but I truly appreciate your generosity.

I also wish to thank Art Plotnik, whose guidance was invaluable; Carol Moholt of the Bay Area Gardener web site who helped plant the seed; and Janet Marinelli at the Brooklyn Botanic Garden for her encouraging words early in the project.

A special thank you goes to Karen Wilson for contributing the Orange County/San Diego entries.

I am grateful to my gardening cohorts—Mia Amato, Jolly Butler, Meg Des-Camp, Marcia Donahue, Sean Hogan & Parker Sanderson—for their warm reception to the West Coast; and to my friends and colleagues—Sherry Stansbury, Mary Phelan, Judy Waitz, Peter Hsia, Carolyn Ulrich, Bill Aldrich, and Brad Hooper—for their advice and support.

Thank you to Michael Kesend, Judy Wilder, and Lelia Ruckenstein at Michael Kesend Publishing, Ltd. for helping to see this project to completion.

Thank you to Sean Joyce, my wonderful son, who lifted my spirits whenever they flagged.

Finally, a loving thank you to Tom Frillmann, who accompanied me from one garden, to the next, and the next. . . . There would be no book without you.

CONTENTS

Preface ix
Introduction x

NORTHERN CALIFORNIA

1. San Francisco Gardens 3
2. Winery Gardens of Napa, Sonoma & Mendocino Counties 10
3. North Bay Gardens 22
4. North Coast Gardens 34
5. East Bay Gardens 39
6. The Peninsula & South Bay Gardens 48
Recommended Lodgings 59
North of San Francisco 59
South of San Francisco 67

CALIFORNIA / SANTA CRUZ TO SANTA BARBARA

7. Central Coast Gardens 71
8. Santa Barbara Gardens 79
Recommended Lodgings 92
Central Coast 92
Santa Barbara 94

CALIFORNIA / LOS ANGELES TO SAN DIEGO

9. Los Angeles and Vicinity Gardens 101
10. Orange County Gardens 119
11. San Diego and Vicinity Gardens 125
Recommended Lodgings 136

OREGON

12. Portland & Vicinity Gardens 143
13. Willamette Valley & Southern Oregon Gardens 160
Recommended Lodgings 166

WASHINGTON

14. Seattle Gardens 173
15. Seattle Vicinity Gardens 182
Recommended Lodgings 197

BRITISH COLUMBIA

16. Vancouver & Vicinity Gardens 205
17. Vancouver Island Gardens 217
Recommended Lodgings 221

RESOURCES FOR GARDENERS

Periodicals & Web Sites 227
Garden Sites, Shops, Book Stores & Shows 231
California 231
Oregon 236
Washington 236

GLOSSARY 239

PREFACE

This guide is the result of my quest to discover gardens where plants reign and the art of garden design flourishes. Public landscapes, private retreats, commercial nurseries, suppliers of garden-oriented paraphernalia—all interested me as I became ever more enthusiastic (actually, quite dotty) about cultivating the tiny parcel of urban property to the front and rear of my home.

My husband, Tom, and I were increasingly lured by the sensory pleasures of beautiful gardens. Our all-too-brief vacations revolved more and more around visits to botanical gardens and arboretums, to specialty growers of rare plants, and to well-stocked shops purveying fine garden tools, supplies, and unusual products for gardening buffs.

Our forays extended to countless hours spent in used bookstores, where I perused musty, old garden tomes and botanical illustrations. Tom, a patient man who enjoys bird-watching and revels in examining the myriad insects one encounters in garden settings, generally stalked different aisles, examining bizarre, antiquated medical books, or field guides listing the exotic fauna of whatever region we happened to be visiting.

But before embarking on each of our journeys, I would commence my search for a guidebook—one that would contain a wealth of information on an extensive range of garden locales, together with notable resources of particular appeal to someone like myself who suffers quite contentedly from "gardening fever."

Since I could never find the type of gardener's travel guide I was looking for, I decided to write one myself.

I sincerely hope you will enjoy discovering the inspiring and magical realms that have given me an everlasting appreciation of the natural world and the gardeners, designers, and landscape architects who have worked their wonders. I also hope that you'll enjoy trekking from one garden to another as much as I have.

INTRODUCTION

As this guide began taking shape, Northern California was the initial focus for what I saw as a series of regional travel guides aimed at gardening enthusiasts and garden lovers, alike. Then I happened upon *Gardenwalks,* by Marina Harrison and Lucy D. Rosenfeld. It seemed a logical step to team up with Michael Kesend, publisher of Harrison and Rosenfeld's delightfully informative guide to 101 gardens from Maine to Virginia.

Our talks led to an expanded focus for this project, with the format evolving to include gardens spanning West Coast destinations from Vancouver, British Columbia, to San Diego, California—a companion volume of sorts, to *Gardenwalks.* Basically you'll find the book organized in sections defined by major cities within each West Coast state: California positioned foremost, with subsections arranged by region, and a special chapter on Northern California winery gardens.

In addition to listings of major public gardens and selected private dominions, you'll find specialty plant nurseries, a bevy of inviting places to stay, and an idiosyncratic gathering of resources for gardeners!

Here I must add a special note of thanks to Karen Wilson for contributing the Orange County and San Diego County entries. Karen's familiarity with that region's garden spots offers savvy insights for travelers to the San Diego area and its environs.

SPECIALTY NURSERIES: Gardeners of the West Coast are blessed with a remarkable number of commendable plant nurseries. Garden travelers might easily be overwhelmed by the sheer multitude of nurseries encountered while exploring the area. Rather than attempt to provide a comprehensive listing of them all, you'll find instead a wide range of specialty nurseries which I consider the best among hundreds of first-rate businesses specializing in distinctive plant genera.

Looking for a rare native species? Perhaps you're in pursuit of antique roses, Japanese maples, or uncommon medicinal herbs. Be aware that a journey to any of the primary points of interest this guide covers—Vancouver, Seattle, Portland, San Francisco, Santa Barbara, Los Angeles and San Diego—would be incomplete without touring at least several of the exciting enterprises located within easy driving distance of these cities, or in close proximity to the major highways.

While surveying these diverse offerings, I encourage you to find opportunities to talk with the spirited entrepreneurs responsible for overseeing day-to-day nursery operations. During my travels, chatting with them about plants never failed to prove enlightening. You too can take advantage of such occasions to learn as much as possible about unfamiliar varieties that will frequently be a cut above ordinary nursery stock.

Whether one's passion is for bamboo, bonsai, or heirloom perennials, it's inspiring to meet dedicated horticulturists who earn their living promoting the plants they most cherish. Conversations with accomplished professionals foster new ways of thinking about gardening and can set into motion ideas for renewing or revamping the plantings in your own garden back home.

Plant lovers may expect revelations, and maybe even an epiphany or two when wandering among the magical plant kingdoms of specialty nurseries.

RECOMMENDED LODGINGS: Like many travelers who maintain full, even jam-packed itineraries, I sometimes yearn for a quiet place to unwind at the end of a heavily-scheduled day of trekking from one garden destination to another. It's not the confines of a rented room I seek, but rather a secluded, preferably verdant area for contemplation.

The congenial Bed & Breakfast inns recommended here provide guests with the customary amenities, and then some! In general, you'll find luscious breakfasts and freshly-baked snacks, refreshing complimentary beverages, snug robes to curl up in, private baths, and impeccable furnishings intended for your comfort and pleasure.

Criteria for inclusion, however, extend beyond such desirable attributes. Even more important, a lodging must be distinguished by an authentic connection to the natural environment. Yes, a pleasing garden setting was a prerequisite, but eventually I realized the significance of a thoughtful, considered approach to the overall landscaping. In the end, it was a special sort of aesthetic sensibility, perhaps best described as a naturalistic style of garden design, which I found to be the most inviting and with the most appealing ambiance.

In my attempts to find places that would add an element of enchantment to each day's sojourn, I looked for agreeable proprietors who maintain relaxed settings amid lovely grounds.

The select group of inns listed here stand apart from the majority that offer suitable rooms, but little or no outdoor area where one might commune at will with the local flora and fauna. They share a refreshingly informal attitude toward planting, in sites ranging from a tiny village lot, to an expansive property with woods, meadows, and gardens.

Whether you like a quiet stroll before breakfast, or require a few minutes to breathe in the night air after an evening meal, you will enjoy these serene and private places.

Please note that cancellation policies vary. Always request details when phoning for reservations.

WINERY GARDENS: Northern California's spectacular wine country— Napa, Sonoma, and Mendocino counties—draws travelers from around the world. Unfortunately, many glorious vineyard gardens are not open to public viewing and can only be enjoyed by individuals lucky enough to gain special entrée. There are, however, a number of "must-see" landscapes planned primarily for the pleasure of winery visitors.

Walking the grounds of these gardens, the visitor can observe how winery owners engaged in an aesthetic conspiracy with landscape designers. The best of their imaginative handiwork produces exhilarating design schemes linking the natural terrain with elements of "hardscaping" and inventive plantings.

One should not miss the alluring panoramas and intimate vistas, impeccably maintained formal gardens and eccentrically designed areas of lush informality of the wine country.

RESOURCES FOR GARDENERS: Listed under this heading you will find distinctive products and services such as uncommon garden ornaments and Internet web sites that list up-to-the-minute events; rare gardening books; vintage botanical illustrations; aged chicken manure for your roses or the perfect cultivating tool.

From Vancouver to San Diego, there are hundreds of fine plant nurseries and garden centers. I regret not being able to include each and every laudable establishment I came across in my travels. But don't let that stop you from going further afield. Allow yourself to wander and you're certain to find additional sites that will stir your particular passions.

One thing to keep in mind, it's always important to call ahead to confirm seasonal business hours and to obtain detailed directions. In many cases, gardens or plant nurseries are open to the public on designated days, or may be visited by appointment only. Business hours may be limited during winter, or a garden or nursery may be closed for the season.

Of course, the qualities I find most alluring about a given garden setting may not necessarily delight every garden traveler. Still, I trust that the material compiled here will provide guidance in choosing places that will appeal to your own inclinations and desires.

All the information in these pages has been carefully checked, but, please note that a garden's open hours, admission fees, etc., are always subject to change. In the case of bed and breakfast inns and garden-oriented businesses, ownership can change along with pricing, types of accommodations, and particular offerings. So, whether planning a short jaunt or lengthy vacation, phone first before setting out in order to assure your sojourn is a pleasant one.

Finally, I'd like to hear about your garden adventures: the high points, as well as any plans that may not have turned out as expected. Drop me a line care of Michael Kesend, Publishing, Ltd., and let me know what gardens or activities you found most appealing. From one garden lover to another, here's wishing you the best of times on your gardenwalks!

NORTHERN CALIFORNIA

CALIFORNIA

← Eureka

Carter House

● **Fort Bragg**
Mendocino Coast Botanical Gardens

● **Mendocino** Cafe Beaujolais Garden

● **Albion**
Digging Dog Nursery

● **Hopland**
Fetzer's Bonterra Garden
Fetzer Vineyards B&B

Healdsburg Ferrari-Carano
Madrona Manor
● **Calistoga** Schramsberg

Korbel **Guerneville**
Fulton California Flora

California Carnivores **Forestville**
Occidental
Matanzas Creek
Western Hills Nursery
Santa Rosa Luther Burbank Home & Gardens
Inn at Occidental
Mom's Head Herb Gardens
Sebastopol
Napa Artesa
Sonoma Horticultural Plant Nursery
Hess Collection
McAllister Water Gardens
Tomales
Brookside Vineyard
Mostly Natives
Petaluma
Bed & Breakfast
Garden Valley Ranch
Inverness
Sandy Cove Inn
Ten Inverness Way

Marin Art & Garden Center **Ross**
Las Baulines Nursery **Bolinas**
Gerstle Park Inn **San Rafael**
Golden Gate Park
Sausalito
Green Gulch Farm
● **SAN FRANCISCO**

PACIFIC OCEAN

1

San Francisco Gardens

Golden Gate Park, San Francisco

Encompassing more than one thousand acres, Golden Gate Park is to San Francisco what Central Park is to New York City: a vast, welcoming refuge of greenery. To this day San Franciscans pay homage to William Hammond Hall, the man who in 1872 worked wonders with a barren landscape of desert and dunes. Historians recall how the acclaimed landscape architect Frederick Law Olmsted had suggested that San Francisco would do well to find another site for such an important undertaking, saying that the land was too dismally sandy and windswept to grow trees on.

Following in Hall's footsteps, John McLaren, the park's superintendent at the turn of the century, devoted more than half a century of his own life to developing the park's impressive grounds. Famed for endowing Golden Gate Park with hundreds of uncommon species from around the globe, Scotsman McLaren is said to have planted one million trees. His gifted floriculture skills transformed the park into a landscape of rare beauty in the midst of a large metropolis.

At Golden Gate Park, you can observe a herd of American bison, indulge yourself in golf, handball, tennis and equestrian sports, or if it suits your fancy, operate model boats. With its beautiful lakes, horticultural treasures, first-rate museums, and miles of pathways for jogging, biking, or walking, the park will gratify most any predilection for recreational activity.

INFORMATION AND DIRECTIONS

Golden Gate Park stretches from Stanyan Street west to the Pacific Ocean, and from Fulton Street south to Lincoln Avenue. For general

Golden Gate Park information, contact the San Francisco Recreation and Park Department, McLaren Lodge, Golden Gate Park, 501 Stanyan Street, San Francisco, CA 94117. Telephone 415-831-2700. Open daily; no fee.

Conservatory Of Flowers, Golden Gate Park

The park's opulent Victorian conservatory was severely damaged due to storms some time ago and is closed until further notice. To learn more about plans for restoration of the country's oldest conservatory, contact park planner Deborah Learner at 415-831-2741.

The Japanese Tea Garden, Golden Gate Park

Not just for garden lovers, but certainly a treat for those who appreciate fine garden design, the Japanese Tea Garden is one of San Francisco's most popular tourist attractions. Mature palms line Hagiwara Tea Garden Drive, the road running between the M. H. de Young Memorial Museum and Asian Art Museum, and the California Academy of Science, and into the garden. Graced with a quartet of fountains and row upon row of wonderfully pollarded sycamore trees, the generous plaza in front of the Academy of Science is known as the music concourse. A legacy of the California Midwinter International Exposition of 1894, the concourse facing the de Young Museum features the Spreckels Temple of Music, a bandstand with classical columns and an impressive portico.

Thought to be the oldest Japanese-style garden in the United States, Golden Gate Park's Japanese Tea Garden was constructed in 1893. The individual largely responsible for the garden's initial design and the fabrication of many of its authentic buildings was Makoto Hagiwara, a prominent Japanese landscape designer. In 1979, Hagiwara's part in the garden's unveiling during the California Midwinter International Exposition of 1894 was commemorated by a startling emerald mound of English boxwood, crowned by a peak of variegated Italian buckthorn. Known as the Mt. Fuji hedge, the sculptural planting honors Hagiwara's region of birth. After you go through the garden's lovely main gates, look for it to the right of the admission booth.

Pass by the Mt. Fuji hedge, following along the path until you reach the Hagiwara Gate, which is painted in a palette of harmonious yet distinctly contrasting earthy hues. The garden ornaments adorning the gateway include the full, rounded forms of ceramic vessels glazed in midnight blue, azure, and russet. Pass under the gate through to the red brick terrace overlooking the Sunken Garden, where large koi frolic in the meandering pond. Even in January, when the deep green scenery can be enveloped in gentle mists, camellias offer their colorful blooms as an antidote to gray skies. Continue walking and you'll meet up with a striking example of statuary placed amid clipped Monterey pines. Here, a large bronze Buddha raises one hand in peaceful repose. Cross the long bridge to find stately redwoods, and in the forefront, the stunning red pagoda, built for the Japanese Exhibit of the Panama-Pacific International Exposition of 1915.

Behind the Buddhist pagoda, a modest Zen garden may be viewed from a walkway where bamboo fencing prevents visitors from disturbing its gravel river and stone waterfall.

The garden's tea house is a popular place to rest while sipping tea and taking in the view of various garden vignettes. Be sure to stop and admire the Drum Bridge, located between the tea garden's main gate and south gate. You may wish to climb the bridge's steep curve if it's not overrun by avid photographers at the time of your visit.

Near the garden's south gate, you'll discover Waterfall Hill, the site of a collection of fine dwarf trees planted over many years by Makoto Hagiwara. His descendants, like countless Japanese Americans living in the U.S. during World War II, were forced to relocate, leaving behind their beloved garden, as well as decades of dedicated service and personal history. When the Hagiwara family's home was destroyed as a result of anti-Japanese sentiments, members of the household removed the rare specimens of dwarf trees and entrusted them to a friend. Fortunately, these trees, and elemental pieces such as rocks and lanterns, were eventually sold to Dr. Hugh Fraser, whose widow, Audrey, became the collection's final owner. Upon her death, Mrs. Fraser made certain that Hagiwara's specimens of dwarf trees were returned to the tea garden.

INFORMATION AND DIRECTIONS
The Japanese Tea Garden, Golden Gate Park, San Francisco, California, 94117. Phone 415-831-2700 to confirm hours and directions. Entrance fee. Open daily from 9 A.M. to 6 P.M.

If driving, enter Golden Gate Park heading west on JFK Drive; watch for signs and turn left onto Hagiwara Tea Garden Drive. For San Francisco transit information, call MUNI at 415-673-6864.

Strybing Arboretum & Botanical Gardens, Golden Gate Park

A visit to San Francisco would hardly be complete without exploring the 55-acre Strybing Arboretum & Botanical Gardens located in Golden Gate Park. One of the country's premier urban gardens, Strybing exceeded the goals described in its mission statement: to display "plants from around the world suited to the central coastal region of California and the San Francisco Bay Area"; "offer a place for reflection, enjoyment and relaxation for the public"; and provide enlightening environmental and horticultural programs.

Established in 1870, Golden Gate Park was without an arboretum for many years, although the park's earliest superintendent, William Hammond Hall, had included one in the drawing of the park's master plan. Despite Hall's best intentions, it was not until the tenure of landscape architect John McLaren that the arboretum became a reality.

McLaren envisioned a setting on a par with the Arnold Arboretum of Harvard University, a challenging objective that would require Golden Gate Park's distinguished superintendent to raise considerable funding. In the 1890s, a number of conifers were planted on the site of today's Strybing Arboretum, but the lack of adequate funds made it impossible to go forward.

Fortunately, McLaren's good friend, Helene Strybing, bequeathed a sum of money to the City of San Francisco, and later another ample gift which constituted most of Mrs. Strybing's estate upon her death. Her generous legacy, which she earmarked especially for an arboretum and botanical gardens, made the development of the gardens possible in the 1930s.

Interestingly, Helene Strybing appears to have been quite a forward thinker, who wanted the collections to include indigenous plants, and those with medicinal applications. As planning went forward, McLaren together with Eric Walther (Strybing's director from 1937 to 1957) designed a master scheme for the gardens, with geographically designated sections of extensive communities of plants. Dedicated in 1940, Strybing Arboretum has long been celebrated nationally for its diverse and distinctive plantings.

Today, in what is an effective partnership between the public and private sectors, the City of San Francisco takes responsibility for maintaining the gardens, while the Strybing Arboretum Society provides a community of dynamic volunteers who help preserve many species of plants, and cultivate unusual varieties. Strybing's renowned plant sales, featuring rare and highly desirable specimens, draw avid folks with green thumbs from near and far. Gardeners come to acquire the exciting offerings and, of course, to visit the gardens in order to glean ideas for how they might incorporate uncommon plants in their landscapes at home.

Should your visit fall during the winter months, you'll still find massings of plants that manifest surprising reminders of tropical wonderlands. The New World Cloud Forest highlights plants located in the western hemisphere: spectacular salvias exhibit a range of colors from fire-engine reds and delicate pinks, to the magenta blooms of *Salvia wageriana,* which unfurl to embellish the plant's long arching limbs. Trees of various heights seek out their required quotient of light. In the area's dense understory of plants, a wealth of epiphytes thrive in little or no soil, and bromeliads run riot over tree stumps and living trees. Fuchsias, too, abound, dripping with elongated blooms that lure hummingbirds to the service of pollination.

Generally considered akin to the Mediterranean's mild climate, conditions in the greater San Francisco Bay area rank among the West Coast region's most remarkably fertile environments. Strybing Arboretum & Botanical Gardens successfully grow an incredible variety of plants from all over the globe. Although many plants originating in Asian countries have acclimated to the habitats and climates in the 50 states, Strybing supports one of the most significant selections of flora from Asia to be found in North America. Overall, the arboretum and gardens boast 7,000 plants from multinational pedigrees—a glorious demonstration of the accommodating milieu.

Strybing's Asian gardens, some of the arboretum's most evocative settings, are filled with superb magnolias and camellias, celestial Japanese maples, and *Michelia doltsopa,* a Himalayan relative of magnolias. Conifers are also handsomely represented. Along the path not far from the Helen Crocker Library you'll find a choice example of *Ginkgo biloba,* a broad-leaved 25-year-old conifer. If you cross the lawn heading south then west, you'll come upon a service road. Follow the path there to a stream, until you glimpse a grove of redwoods. Discovered in 1941 in China, these three rare *Metasequoia glyptostroboides* with their magnificent sienna-colored bark are particularly striking.

During your visit, explore the popular Moon Viewing Garden, given to Strybing by the Ikebana International Society. The garden's wooden deck, oriented so that one may look out at the moon, functions sublimely as a momentary resting place where you can revel in the glimmering contrasts between the trees and shrubs.

One of the Botanical Gardens' newest additions, the Old World Cloud Forest, is enchanting, if not in name alone. Its collection of Vireya rhododendrons are unusual for their capacity to rebloom in San Francisco's summers, after putting on a most impressive floral exhibition in the spring. In the Primitive Plant Garden, plants related to more ancient species are displayed. Proceed along the angular, zigzagging wooden walkway to view imposing tree ferns, horsetails, and the enormous presence of *Gunnera chilensis* from Patagonia.

If you like scented gardens, the Garden of Fragrance will lure you with its myriad aromas. The garden has Braille labels designed for the visually impaired. For a wealth of ideas, perennial gardeners may want to study the handsome plantings of the Zellerbach Garden of Perennials, which was developed in 1967.

Savor the special atmosphere of this region by spending time in the arboretum's redwood grove that has been developed into the Redwood Trail. Here, species of plants native to coastal redwood habitats are featured. Discover the John Muir Nature Trail and the Arthur Menzies Garden of California Native Plants, which also display the local flora.

When I reminisce on walks through the Strybing Botanical Gardens, my mind's eye recalls image upon image of arresting plants, in harmonious arrangements. Strolling past the wildfowl pond to the adjoining boggy gardens, I rejoiced in the awe-inspiring apparition of *Gunnera*, with its sprawling leaves and immense form. The upright coral pokers of South African aloes and sensational Cape Province kniphofias are representative of the garden's brilliant displays.

Perhaps you've heard someone say about the San Francisco Bay area, "just take a plant and stick it in the ground, then watch it grow . . . and grow!" A visit to these gardens proves this saying right. Although fire, drought, and frigid weather occasionally wreak havoc on the garden's tenderly nurtured horticultural treasures, Strybing Arboretum & Botanical Gardens admirably demonstrate just how blessed the region is. Before departing the gardens, amble over to the Helen Crocker Russell Library of Horticulture, located just inside Strybing's main entrance on the left. Here you may take advantage of the library's peaceful reading room to peruse extensive compilations of nursery catalogs, periodicals and books, as well as slides and videos. There is no charge to visit. For information and open hours, phone the library at 415-661-1316, ext. 303. Don't fail to explore the new ¾-acre entry garden inside Strybing's main gate. The exciting plantings here include vibrant combinations of plant material such as palms, cycads, bamboo species, and a variety of bananas. Five hundred exceptional plants are featured in this lush garden which is the work of David McCrory and Roger Raiche, a design team from Berkeley known as Planet Horticulture.

Just inside the main gate to the right, look for the kiosk housing the bookstore and gift shop. There, you'll find a fine selection of regional titles, general gardening books, and the *Pacific Horticulture* magazine, an especially stimulating read when visiting the region. Open from 10 A.M. to 4 P.M.

INFORMATION AND DIRECTIONS

Strybing Arboretum, Golden Gate Park, Ninth Avenue at Lincoln Way, San Francisco, CA 94122. Daily walks usually leave from the main gate entrance and the Friend Gate, at the north entrance. No fee, but donations are encouraged for walks. For information on activities, special lectures, classes, and times for garden walks, phone 415-661-1316 or visit the website: *www.strybing.org*. For plant sale questions, call 415-661-3090. Open 8 A.M. to 4:30 P.M. weekdays; 10 A.M. to 5 P.M. weekends. To take public transportation to the gardens, phone 415-673-MUNI for directions.

2

Winery Gardens of Napa, Sonoma & Mendocino Counties

Artesa, Napa

Artesa produces sparkling wines in one of Napa Valley's most dramatic settings—the Carneros region. Situated atop a knoll, Artesa's architecturally intriguing winery is amazing to behold.

This masterpiece of design features a building with smoky quartz windows, and remarkable, slanted grass-blanketed walls planted with native grasses. Luminously contemporary, the low, broad structure of Artesa appears to merge uninterruptedly with the summit's horizontal expanse of lawn. The building and landscaping fit seamlessly into the heavenly Carneros countryside.

A host of water features—the glistening water course, exquisite fountains, and a sensational reflecting pool—add to the setting's memorable impact. At Artesa, the terrace is perfectly situated; you can sip methode champenoise wines, admire the stunning views, and enjoy the winery's blissful surroundings.

INFORMATION AND DIRECTIONS

Artesa, 1345 Henry Road, Napa CA, 94559-9703. Phone 707-224-1668 to confirm visiting hours and to obtain directions to the winery. The visitor center is open to the public Monday through Thursday, 10 A.M. to 5 P.M.; Friday through Sunday, 10 A.M. to 3 P.M.

Located 40 miles northeast of San Francisco.

Ferrari-Carano Vineyards and Winery, Healdsburg

Upon first approaching the gardens at Ferrari-Carano Vineyards and Winery, visitors are overwhelmed by great masses of cheerful annuals, bedded-out in exuberant displays. Take a moment to enjoy these riotous plantings of salvias, marigolds, zinnias and begonias accenting the entranceway to the irresistible Villa Fiore. This fine Italianate edifice, with exquisitely tinted stucco walls, commanding stone columns, and a deep-toned Roman tile roof, houses the winery's handsome tasting room and gift shop.

When you exit the building, you'll think you've landed in one of the grand European gardens of the Renaissance. Arguably the Ferrari-Carano Vineyards and Winery can claim one of the most photogenic gardens Northern California has to offer. Wherever you choose to wander within these five acres of formal gardens, a host of arresting tableaus appear. Ferrari-Carano's endless pleasures include charming water features, orderly parterres surrounded by meticulous lawns, and a fine rose garden. Formidable boulders provide counterpoints to deep emerald copses, and stand out against the spiky mounds of audacious grasses. If you consider the relative newness of the landscape, these remarkably lush plantings are all the more impressive. Undoubtedly, the gardens will become even more striking over time as countless trees, shrubs, and perennials mature.

Further afield, follow the pale undulating curves of a concrete walkway, until you arrive at the gentle arch of a wooden bridge. Cross over the meandering stream, which links one garden area with another, and continue exploring. Everywhere, the distinctive sound of moving water produces a tranquil effect. Almost magically, the moment one begins to think about taking a rest, quiet places of reflection and repose, such as rustic gazebos and arbors harboring attractive benches, emerge. Sheltered from the sun, these appealing resting places provide fine vantage points from which one can bask in the flowers and foliage. Take note of the rare Portuguese cork trees, too, when you're admiring the crape myrtles, bays, and pines.

Bound to enchant garden lovers with its grand sense of style and the sumptuous spaciousness of its gardens, the Ferrari-Carano Vineyards and Winery deserves an unhurried visit.

INFORMATION AND DIRECTIONS
Ferrari-Carano Vineyards and Winery, 8761 Dry Creek Road, Healdsburg, CA. 95448. Phone 707-433-6700 for directions and hours of operation. Tasting room open daily, 10 A.M. to 5 P.M.

The Healdsburg location is approximately 75 miles, or 1 hour and 15 minutes, north of San Francisco in Sonoma County's Dry Creek Valley.

11

Bonterra Garden at Fetzer Vineyards, Hopland

Fetzer Vineyards is widely known for its Bonterra brand of organic wines, but gardening buffs have been increasingly singing the praises of Fetzer's Bonterra Garden at Valley Oaks. This wonderful five-acre garden is worthy of a special side trip even if Mendocino County does not happen to be on your itinerary.

Organically grown grapes used in the production of Bonterra Vineyards wines are but one facet of the Bonterra Garden, which has been recognized as one of the nation's premier kitchen gardens. Call ahead to schedule a tour, or be spontaneous and enjoy a self-guided stroll through the gardens. Either way, get ready to celebrate an inventive, deliciously appealing melange of plants, represented in row upon row of culinary and ornamental varieties. The soil they are cultivated in has been enriched with the pomace remains of the grapes used in the winemaking process.

A breathtaking selection of herbs and flowers are interspersed with shrubs and fruit trees, vegetables and berries. Edibles of all sorts are grown pesticide-, fungicide-, and herbicide-free at the Bonterra Garden. Fairly recently, according to Fetzer's landscape supervisor and gardener extraordinaire, Kate Frey, signs have been placed around in various beds indicating that visitors are invited to "Please Taste" a cornucopia of savory fruits, including raspberries and blackberries, grapes, plums, and cherry tomatoes.

Should you choose to follow the garden's self-guided tour map, you'll find well-marked garden stations with informative signs. Throughout its refined, aesthetically designed grounds, Bonterra Garden emphasizes the education of visitors by underscoring good gardening practices and suggesting exceptional plant selections.

This densely planted, all organic garden counts many heirloom varieties among its diverse assortment of plants. Highlights include a crescent-shaped bed planted with edible flowers with blossoms that are literally good enough to eat! Arrangements of obliquely-angled espaliered apple trees epitomize the Bonterra Garden's savvy garden style. In addition to being visually striking, these trees also produce copious amounts of fruit.

Commingling culinary plants with ornamentals might be quite the rage these days, but the Bonterra Garden has long demonstrated the beauty of this type of planting. The ecological benefits of growing diverse species and ever so many flowers are illustrated by the number of beneficial insects drawn to these environs.

An incredible bounty is produced for the human species, and for the garden's coexisting fauna (hummingbirds and butterflies, in particular). Beds of English lavenders and amaranths are among the more striking ornamentals planted. Although historically amaranth was cultivated for its grain seed, such standout varieties as Hopi Red Dye and Giant Burgundy serve to wow the garden's visitors with showy red plumes.

Fragrant white alpine strawberries fill a whole bed, growing not along runners, but in clumps. Should you visit on a summer afternoon, sample these delectable fruits, and breathe in their perfume.

Propagation of plants is accomplished from within the garden's ranks, one of Bonterra's laudable gardening techniques. From raised beds that encourage aeration and drainage, to a drip irrigation system that both conserves water and deters the growth of weeds, Bonterra Garden offers an exciting contemporary approach to kitchen garden design.

A visit to Bonterra Garden would not be complete without a promenade to the pavilion, overlooking Lake Fumé. Built in 1987, the building is the site of culinary demonstrations and cooking classes taught by chef John Ash. Windows cover three-quarters of the walls, providing entrancing vignettes of swans gliding gracefully across the water's surface. A deck wraps around the building's perimeter, luring visitors on foggy mornings, as well as sunny afternoons. Looking across the mirror-like expanse, one can observe the landscape's gentle rise, and stately trees punctuating the encircling sky.

Amidst this impeccable setting, where ancient oak trees reign over the 95-acre Valley Oaks Ranch, Fetzer's recently reopened reception building now boasts a gourmet delicatessen, featuring fresh pastries, soups & salads, and other delectable picnic fare. Not surprisingly, produce from the garden is used in many deli dishes.

The Mendocino vicinity offers a number of delightful destinations for garden lovers, so if possible, plan to stay a few days in the area and you'll not be disappointed.

INFORMATION AND DIRECTIONS

Bonterra Garden at Fetzer Vineyards, Valley Oaks, 13601 East Side Road, Hopland, California, 95449. Throughout the year, special activities including wine tastings, live music, and food extravaganzas, are planned at the Valley Oaks locale. Phone 800-846-8637 for information on garden tours, specific directions, or to learn more about special events. You can book a particular tour ahead of time, sign up when you arrive at the vineyard, or elect to tour the gardens on your own, referring to Fetzer's self-guided tour maps. The Tasting Room and Visitor Center are open daily from 9 A.M. to 5 P.M. (Fetzer also operates a separate tasting room in the village of Mendocino.)

Note: Folks at Fetzer had an inspired idea when they made bed and breakfast lodgings available to winery visitors. Consult the listing in "Recommended Lodgings" for details on Fetzer's six-room Bed & Breakfast Inn, which is ensconced among the vineyards here at Valley Oaks.

Fetzer's Valley Oaks Ranch is located ¾ mile east of Hopland on Highway 175. Proceed north from San Francisco on Highway 101 to the town of Hopland. You should reach Fetzer Vineyards approximately two hours after crossing the Golden Gate Bridge.

The Hess Collection Winery, Napa

Fine Chardonnay and Cabernet Sauvignon wines may be synonymous with the Hess Collection. Garden lovers, however, are first enthralled with the winery's outdoor environment, designed by the internationally acclaimed landscape architect Peter Walker. Before entering the charming stone buildings of this outstanding Napa Valley winery, survey the formidable wisteria draped arbor, the rectilinear pond, and the sculpture garden.

For art aficionados, the Hess Collection Winery offers galleries filled with Donald Hess' amazing compilation of contemporary paintings and sculptures by such masters as Frank Stella, Robert Motherwell, Francis Bacon, Magdalena Abakanowicz, and Georg Baselitz.

From the third floor of the Visitors Center, you'll enjoy a spectacular view of Mt. Veeder and the winery's vineyards.

INFORMATION AND DIRECTIONS

The Hess Collection Winery, 4411 Redwood Road, P. O. Box 4140, Napa CA, 94558. Phone 707-255-1144 for directions and to confirm open hours. The Visitors Center is open daily 10 A.M. to 4 P.M.

Located approximately 1 hour and 15 minutes north of San Francisco. Proceed north on Highway 29 past the town of Napa, turn left at Redwood Road, traveling west about six miles to the winery.

Korbel Champagne Cellars, Guerneville

The Korbel family first began planting the gardens around the family's summer home in the late nineteenth century. Today, the comfortable Victorian house, with a commodious wrap-around porch, is surrounded by picturesque gardens that continue to fascinate visitors to the Korbel Champagne Cellars.

Towering redwoods, rolling hills, and the coastal mists form the magic landscape. The impressive 1886 red-brick winery building and the adjacent, ivy-draped Brandy tower, with its soaring peaked crown, are architectural treasures that lend a stalwart presence to the Korbel property.

In the 1880s the Korbel brothers—Joseph, Anton, and Francis—played the legendary roles of founding fathers. Adolf Heck purchased the Korbel enterprise in 1954, and after his death in 1984, his son, Gary Heck, became CEO and chairman of the board.

The current management shows its concern for the timeless beauty of the surrounding Russian River landscape by recycling and reusing materials associated with the winery.

Given Korbel's environmental stance, I wasn't surprised to find within the ranks of the Heck family an ardent lover of gardens—Valerie Heck, Gary's sister. Widely applauded for her role in guiding the rejuvenation of Korbel's old-fashioned cottage-style garden, Valerie was instrumental in selecting horticulturist Phillip Robinson, whose exhilarating design work transformed the garden.

The Korbel Garden fulfills Valerie's childhood dream and offers visitors a fine example of the type of garden usually seen only in Britain. Nineteen years ago, when he began the miracle of restoring the garden, Phillip Robinson adeptly cut through overgrowth, uncovering the garden's original layout. Since, Robinson has accomplished a splendid recreation, preserving some of the original varieties used by the Korbels.

It is Robinson's exuberant way with plants, however, that adds breathtaking dimensions to Korbel's lovely setting. Anchored by coastal redwood trees over one hundred years old, the garden's winding paths explode in spring with yearly plantings of countless bulbs. Fuchsias, begonias, and charming Chinese lanterns with their bell-like flowers are among the more tender species used to add lively touches of color. *Abutilon*, 'Canary Bird,' is a tall variety graced with bright yellow blooms. Its new growth contributes dramatic dark stems.

Moreover, the gardens at Korbel are full to bursting with irresistible herbs, interplanted with perennials to provide textural accents year-round. A bevy of traditional ground covers and flowers are standouts, from free-flowering phlox, to hosta with its distinctive foliage and perfumed spikes. Romantic grapevine and Virginia creeper add further lushness. Walkways overflow with bergenia and helichrysum, alstromeria, amethyst agapanthus, and a host of unusual selections.

Tovara virginiana, 'Painter's Palette,' lights up shady spots with its creamy variegated leaves. In late summer, above a dense growth of brightly adorned stems, the hardy perennial sprays the air with extravagant panicles covered in tiny red bead-like flowers.

A rich sense of history permeates the Korbel Garden tour, as the guides point out both a bench and a birdbath that have been there for over 100 years. On my first stroll here, I was smitten by a fetching volunteer that grew up from the base of a rock retaining wall. Although similar in leaf form to its North American relative (*Stylophorum diphyllum*), the plant was, in fact, "greater celandine" (*Chelidonium majus*), an English species. Enjoying great popularity these days with many avid gardeners, old-fashioned celandine with its cheerful yellow flowers stopped me in my tracks. It would have been easy to mistake this species for the one growing in a raised shade bed in my own garden, were it not for the telltale narrow seedpods that are so different from the American species' rotund, bristly, dangling pods.

Robinson has selected many vigorous specimens of shrubs, hydrangeas and daphnes, among them. Undoubtedly, the shining stars of the Korbel tour, the antique shrub roses enchant with their richly fragrant scent and the beguiling hues of their multipetaled blooms.

While Korbel Champagne Cellars and Winery attract busloads of wine-country vagabonds interested in sampling varieties of sparkling wines, the Korbel Garden's spectacular display of roses draws their own fair share of visitors. More than 250 varieties of antique roses are collected here in a layout reminiscent of long-ago gardens. The Rose Garden's specimens include outstanding examples of climbing

'Souvenir de Malmaison,' 'Old Blush,' and a stunning polyantha rose, 'La Marne,' perfectly pink in coloration. The showy floribunda, 'Picasso,' and *Rosa* 'Perle d'Or' work their magic, too.

Teas, chinas, and noisettes are abundantly represented along the Tea Walk, on the south side of the garden, facing the old winery. Nearly the entire arrangement here can be identified as the original design indicated in a map from 1896. Directly in front of the house with its ornate railing that seems to stretch forever, the crisply clipped Japanese boxwood hedges function as curvilinear elements, adding a subtle formality to the clusters of bushes they serve to frame.

Should you find yourself lingering while the tour proceeds, observe a tangle of clematis scrambling through fragrant viburnum, or pause at the gazebo to take your fill of the floral bouquet.

Amidst an irresistible framework, the Korbel Garden exalts garden wanderers with an evocative blend of heirloom plants and stunning new varieties, flanked by established trees of sanctified bearing and unadorned nobility.

INFORMATION AND DIRECTIONS

Korbel Champagne Cellars & Garden, 13250 River Road, Guerneville, CA. 95446-9538. Three tours of the Korbel Garden are offered daily: Tuesday through Sunday at 11 A.M., 1 and 3 P.M., from May through October. Reservations or appointments are not usually required for the complimentary tours, but it's best to phone 707-824-7000 for directions and up-to-date information.

Traveling north from San Francisco on Highway 101, take the River Road turn-off just past Santa Rosa. Cross back over the freeway. Korbel is located 12 miles west of Highway 101; approximately 1½ hours from the Golden Gate Bridge.

Matanzas Creek Winery Estate Gardens, Santa Rosa

Sonoma County's treasure trove of beautiful wineries represent a veritable Eden to garden lovers. Experience the combination of elegant naturalism and robust verdure found at the Matanzas Creek Winery Estate Gardens and you may understand how it came to be my personal favorite.

Situated amid hilly terrain and washed over in luminous hues, Matanzas Creek is an exquisite treasure yet to be discovered. In this

17

sublime setting, majestic, native oaks tower over extravagant plantings in a landscape that might well be unsurpassed by any other vineyard regularly open to the public.

Not so long ago, founders Sandra and Bill MacIver first envisioned the Matanzas Creek garden. Growing up in New Orleans, Sandra was inspired by the Longue Vue House and Gardens, her grandparents'—the Stern family's—nationally acclaimed estate. Reigning over Longue Vue's tantalizing landscape was her grandmother, doyenne Edith Rosenwald Stern. It comes as no surprise that the Matanzas Creek garden is dedicated to Edith, as undoubtedly, she planted the seed for the MacIver's garden of the future.

Landscaping at Matanzas Creek was undertaken in 1990. Apparently, the fine climate and conditions outside Santa Rosa have worked their magic, and Matanzas Creek has already attained a radiant grandeur. Ask anyone who has had the good fortune to venture down Bennett Valley Road and they'll tell you of the lavender fields thriving at this stunning Sonoma winery.

It's difficult not to be swept away by the heady aroma of lavender that greets you during a summer visit to Matanzas Creek. Aside from France's Provence region, where else might you encounter the scent emanating from 4,500 intoxicating plants?

Growing on staggered terraces delineated by charming rock walls, the splendidly cultivated lavender includes 'Grosso' and 'Provence' varieties. The lavender's hues and textures create compelling diagonal patterns, leading you on a gradual ascent up the steps of a central path, toward the main building, which houses the tasting room and gift shop.

Appearing at once anchored to the land and gently integrated with the gardens surrounding it, the visitors' center offers a wealth of estate-grown lavender products for purchase. Among these are sachet, potpourri, and lavender wands; sticks for grilling and fireplace bundles; gift baskets, soaps and bath oil. Award-winning Matanzas Creek wines are savored by wine lovers in the tasting room.

As you leave the building, descend the stairway and look to the left. The precise angles and planes of the rectangular Water Garden provide a refreshing contrast to the lavish plantings contained within it. Papyrus (*Cyperus papyrus*), with its airy terminals, and Giant Scouring rush, a handsome California native that resembles bamboo, are two choice specimens.

Continue strolling through the grounds and you'll enjoy artful drifts of swaying grasses like the tall purple moor grass which produces blooming spikes from June through December, softening hillsides and walkways, alike. In the summer, masses of perennials thrive under Sonoma's bright skies. Flamboyant specimens like the giant seakale (*Crambe cordifolia*) shoot flowering stalks high above mounds of generous cabbage-like leaves.

The resplendent plantings at Matanzas Creek are the work of gifted landscape designer Gary Ratway, known for his contributions to the restoration of the Mendocino Coast Botanical Gardens. Besides stunning compositions filled with grasses and pungent herbs, the gardens feature outstanding selections of ornamental vines, shrubs, and unusual trees. Plantings of *Parrotia persica*, 'Select' (a deciduous tree from Persia), grace the lavender field on all sides with medleys of amethyst and lemon-lime leaves in spring, shifting to shimmering golds and reds in the fall.

Eloquently described in the winery's *Garden Tour* booklet, the governing philosophy at Matanzas Creek is one of "designing to reduce design." This approach is readily apparent throughout the entire grounds, but perhaps the most striking examples are boulders that weigh 21,000 pounds. Set in place near a stairway, these massive forms look as if they have been there forever. With the rocks' crevices planted as if by the hand of nature, these boulders function as conspicuous reminders of a unique garden environment.

Carrying on the Stern family's legacy, Sandra and Bill MacIver created a blissful paradise befitting the spectacular setting.

INFORMATION AND DIRECTIONS

Matanzas Creek Winery, 6097 Bennett Valley Road, Santa Rosa, CA 95404.

Phone 707-528-6464 for further information, detailed directions to the winery, or to confirm open hours. Tasting room open 10 A.M. to 4:30 P.M. daily.

Located approximately 1 hour and 15 minutes north of San Francisco.

Schramsberg Vineyards, Calistoga

You may choose to visit Schramsberg during any season of the year, but stop by the vineyards' lush gardens in early April and you'll witness the extravagant bloom of a sensational Lady Banks rose! Although familiar with the buttery yellow, profusely flowering rose pictured in countless gardening books, I was enraptured when I saw the legendary climber growing at Schramsberg. (Note: The common name, Lady Banks, rightfully belongs to *Rosa banksiae banksiae*, a rose with double white flowers. Nearly as often, it commonly refers to either of the two yellow species of *R. banksiae*.)

At this radiant Napa Valley estate, connoisseurs of sparkling wines luxuriate in sampling some of the most elegant "methode champenoise" wines created this side of the Atlantic! Since 1965, owners Jack and Jamie Davies have been committed to the production of champagne-style wines. Today, Schramsberg Vineyards is renowned for having refined the art of winemaking, creating fine wines imbued not only with sparkle, but with great flair. At the same time, Schramsberg has become a destination point for all who enjoy great gardens.

The Lady Banks rose scaling the heights of the estate's lovely Victorian home is just one of many horticultural delights you'll enjoy on a self-guided tour of Schramsberg. A visit to the vineyard must surely include roaming the beautifully planted, wonderfully designed landscape surrounding the Schramsberg house.

Garden visitors applaud the discerning style and aesthetic sensibilities that led Jack and Jamie Davies to renew the glorious gardens that had graced the expansive 200-acre property during the first golden age at Schramsberg. Back in 1862, German émigré Jacob Schram was a pioneering vintner who planted hillside vineyards and created a below-ground complex of cellars in the compliant volcanic rock, turning Schramsberg into one of the finest wineries in the Napa Valley.

In the latter part of the nineteenth century, Schram had an impressive home built for himself and his wife, Annie, and the grounds covered with the lush plantings associated with the grand fashion of Victorian gardens. The Schrams entertained the likes of Robert Louis Stevenson, who chronicled the winery's idyllic setting in *Silverado Squatters*. The entire Schramsberg estate was declared a California historical landmark in 1957.

Today, the Schramsberg Winery garden enchants visitors with the exquisite fragrances of hedges, ground covers, and a host of aromatic trees. Creeping thymes, lavenders, and sages are among the herbs that grow vigorously here, lending their delicate blossoms to a generous exhibition of mock oranges and star jasmine, roses and spice bushes.

Commence your garden walk along the path leading from the visitor's reception area toward the impeccably maintained house, and you'll notice a magnificent blue oak that looks hundreds of years old. Opposite stands a venerable apple tree, and just beyond, a more recently planted black oak. These trees add character to the bounteous landscape.

Approaching the house, you'll pass a California bay laurel, a Japanese maple, and a southern magnolia that typify taller elements in the garden's design. Situated on gently hilly terrain, the house has an amazing verandah, with clematis scrambling up its pillars, and roses ornamenting the fine wooden columns and gingerbread trim.

Turn away from the house and gaze on the view of Schramsberg's expansive grounds. Like stately sentries, towering fan palms keep watch over free-flowing asymmetrical islands replete with flowers and foliage.

Continue your promenade to the corner of the house, and beyond the Lady Banks rose at the end of the walkway, you'll see a dense array of Douglas fir, olive and madrone.

In the spring, the gardens at Schramsberg are aglow with flowering dogwoods, azaleas, camellias, and Japanese quince. One large rectangular space is devoted to fruitless mulberries, reined in along two sides by flower beds, and moored at one corner by a big leaf maple. Include Schramsberg on your itinerary and experience the charming spell cast by the gardens.

INFORMATION AND DIRECTIONS

Schramsberg Vineyards & Cellars, 1400 Schramsberg Road, Calistoga, California 94515. Visitors are welcome by appointment; to set up an appointment to view the Schramsberg gardens, call 707-942-4558.

Located north of San Francisco, approximately 1½ hours.

3

North Bay Gardens

California Carnivores, Forestville

An impressive collection of carnivorous plants is displayed in the California Carnivores greenhouse, which is ensconced in the Mark West Vineyards. Both a retail nursery and mail-order enterprise, California Carnivores boasts more than 400 intriguing varieties of insect eating plants, with a greater selection available for sale on the premises than in the catalog.

You can learn here about growing the Venus fly trap, pitcher plants, and other astonishing types of flora. Pick up a copy of Cal Carnivores' informative book, *The Savage Garden*, for helpful instructions on plant care and culture, as well as for its descriptions of the intriguing characteristics of numerous varieties.

Be advised, visitors are obliged to bring their own bugs if they intend to feed the plants!

INFORMATION AND DIRECTIONS

California Carnivores at Mark West Vineyards, 7020 Trenton-Healdsburg Road, Forestville, CA 95436. Contact Peter D'Amato or Marilee Maertz. Phone 707-838-1630 to confirm open hours, for directions, or further information. The greenhouse is open just about every day from 10 A.M. to 4 P.M., but visitors are advised to call ahead, especially from December through March when California Carnivores is occasionally closed due to storms and wet weather.

Located about 70 minutes north of the Golden Gate Bridge; 10 miles east of Guerneville. Take Highway 101 north of Santa Rosa to the River Road exit. Proceed left on River Road 5 ½ miles to Trenton-Healdsburg Road. Turn right at the signs, driving ½ mile to the Mark West Vineyards.

California Flora Nursery, Fulton

A bit off the beaten path, "Calflora" started up over ten years ago as a native plant nursery. According to one of the owners, Phil Van Soelen, "we got into flowering perennials . . . before the boom hit." Recently, of course, perennial gardening has galvanized the baby-boomer generation, reaching a fever pitch. The nursery maintains its popularity among gardeners who appreciate an inviting ambiance and many reasonably priced and healthy plants.

In the process of expanding when we spoke, Phil mentioned they will continue "to focus on things that are out of the ordinary," particularly plants well adapted to their climate. Specialties include exceptional natives, new rare varieties and butterfly favorites. California Flora has such wholesale customers as Smith and Hawken, but it also retails to the public, growing the vast majority of the plants you'll find in their nursery and gardens.

INFORMATION AND DIRECTIONS
California Flora Nursery, at the intersection of Somers & D Streets, P O Box 3, Fulton, CA 95439. Phone 707-528-8813 for directions and information. Open hours vary with the season, so make sure you call ahead.

Located just over one hour north of San Francisco. Take Highway 101, exiting just beyond Santa Rosa at River Road. Go west on River Road; around one mile from the highway, turn left on Somers Street and proceed three blocks.

Garden Valley Ranch, Petaluma

Located in a region internationally famous for the production of fine wines and sublime vineyard-blanketed vistas, the Garden Valley Ranch operation revolves around the cultivation of glorious, to-die-for roses. Over 8,000 rosebushes are grown and harvested for the cut-flower trade at this vibrant enterprise.

Although fire destroyed the main Victorian house on the 9½-acre property in 1984, other historic Victorian buildings remain. A charming old belfry houses the Garden Valley Nursery shop and its enticing array of gardening tools, gifts with a floral theme, scented perennials, and rosebushes for sale to the public.

Garden Valley has one of only 25 national "All American Rose Selection" test gardens. Celebrated rose expert and well-known garden writer, Rayford Reddell is one of the judges of the "All American Rose Selections." He calls Garden Valley Ranch home. As you roam through this official test garden, you'll be able to survey unnamed varieties of hybrid teas and floribundas, miniatures, climbers, grandifloras and landscape roses.

To explore Garden Valley's extensive grounds and stunning landscape, you'll first need to purchase a self-guided tour booklet for four dollars. Among the most enchanting of the many beautifully designed garden spaces is a serene one-acre fragrance garden. Here you'll find formal beds that overflow with aromatic flowers and foliage; a wisteria draped pergola; an apple walk; an acid border where rhododendron are interplanted among witch hazel and lilac, magnolia and sweet olive, to name but a few specimens; and an adjoining woodland garden.

Garden Valley's pond garden is complete with frolicking koi, scented water lilies, and surrounding ornamental grasses. This water feature was actually conceived as a unique solution to supplying a water source in case of another fire. After a refreshing respite here, explore the antique and David Austin roses planted nearby.

Rose fanciers, of course, will find incomparable fields of heavenly-scented roses. Garden Valley's countless rose species and cultivars present a unique opportunity for learning about almost every type of rose in cultivation today.

For a particularly inviting vantage point, find a perch within the Victorian Belvedere. According to Garden Valley's tour booklet, this structure "was once a south porch on a neighboring Victorian farmhouse." Take a few moments to muse upon the beauty of the place. It's easy to imagine the setting as a wedding site, and many have chosen to take their vows here. At the same time, Garden Valley Nursery is a terrific place to pick up turkey manure, alfalfa pellets, and other indispensable supplies your roses at home will certainly appreciate.

INFORMATION AND DIRECTIONS

Garden Valley Ranch, 498 Pepper Road, Petaluma, CA 94952. Phone 707-795-0919. Nursery hours: Wednesday through Sunday, 10 A.M. to 4 P.M. Closed for one week between Christmas and New Year's. Garden Valley occasionally closes for special events; phone before visiting to confirm open hours and for directions to the ranch. *Web site: www.gardenvalley.com*

The Petaluma location is about 45 minutes north of San Francisco if you avoid commuter traffic. Take Highway 101 to the last Petaluma exit—Old Redwood Highway/Penngrove. Turn left at end of exit, crossing back over highway to second stop light. Turn right onto Stony Point Road; go 1½ miles, then turn left onto Pepper Road.

Green Gulch Farm, Sausalito

Zen practice meets the pursuit of organic gardening at this remarkable Marin County destination. Green Gulch admirably combines the study of Zen Buddhism with the conscientious nurturing of a farm and gardens. While many guests of the center come for meditation retreats, others visit to partake in a range of classes and special seminars on natural gardening techniques.

In addition to the land cultivated for farming, (their excellent produce is sold to some fine local restaurants), Green Gulch has lovely ornamental flower gardens that are accented with espaliered fruit trees and a circular planting of herbs. Note how the ambrosial noisette roses scramble over the arbors. A short hike across meadow land takes you through sweetly scented paths to the water's edge at Muir Beach on the Pacific Ocean. In all, Green Gulch encompasses more than 100 acres.

"Stalking the Wild Herb" is one example of a recent class offering at Green Gulch Farm. As part of the class, visitors are invited to follow knowledgeable instructors as they explore the valley. After participants have assisted in harvesting edible herbs, they return to the kitchen to create and enjoy soup and salad prepared from the pickings.

The highly regarded annual plant sale supplies gardening patrons with organically grown perennial flowers and shrubs; culinary, ornamental, and medicinal herbs; bamboo; old-fashioned roses; and vegetable starts.

A typical gardening seminar might span topics such as organic gardening principles and practices; plant propagation, irrigation, and integrated pest management; or design, cultivation, and fertilization of the home garden.

INFORMATION AND DIRECTIONS
Green Gulch Farm, 1601 Shoreline Highway, Sausalito, CA 94965. Phone 415-383-3134 to request a schedule of events and to confirm directions. Preregistration by mail is required. Parking is limited; there is a parking fee between 8:45 and 10:30 A.M. on Sundays. Cars with three or more people park free.

Note: Volunteers are welcome to work in the garden Tuesday and/or Sunday from 9 to noon and are invited to stay for lunch. Phone the office at 415-383-3134 before coming, just in case there are special events planned that might preempt garden work. For information on personal retreats at Green Gulch Farm Zen Center, or to reserve a room at the Japanese-style guesthouse, phone 415-383-3134. A stay includes three vegetarian meals made from some of Green Gulch's fresh produce.

Located just north of San Francisco and the Golden Gate Bridge. Take Highway 101 north to the exit for Highway 1, Stinson Beach—Mill Valley. Drive west 2½ miles along Shoreline Highway 1; go past the Panoramic Highway turnoff. Drive another two miles, and look for the Green Gulch Farm sign.

Las Baulines Nursery, Bolinas

Visit picturesque Bolinas for a stopover at this laid-back nursery, where fetching flowering plants consort with deer proof, native, and acclimatized species. In the nursery store, I picked up a bottle of Porter's Lotion, a refreshing, emollient skin care product that blends witch hazel, glycerin, camphor, rosemary oil and other ingredients. Porter's has been made in Montana for over 60 years, but gardeners everywhere have adopted this balm for its soothing properties.

INFORMATION AND DIRECTIONS

Las Baulines Nursery, Star Route, Bolinas, CA 94924. Contact Michael Bernsohn, proprietor. Citizens of Bolinas like to remove the road signs that help direct travelers to their pleasant haven. For directions and to confirm seasonal hours of operation, phone the nursery beforehand at 415-868-0808. They specialize in plants for the coastal climate.

Located about 45 minutes north of San Francisco and the Golden Gate Bridge. Take Highway 101 to the very scenic, winding Highway 1; go past Stinson Beach, north along the Bolinas Lagoon, past the sign for Audubon Canyon Ranch, and look for the turnoff to the town of Bolinas (ask for guidance from someone local, if necessary).

Luther Burbank Home & Gardens, Santa Rosa

Plant-breeder extraordinaire, Luther Burbank developed, and improved upon, a wealth of plant species, leaving behind a tremendously vital legacy of fruit and nut trees, vegetables, and ornamental flowers. Many of these choice varieties are enjoyed and cultivated by modern gardeners.

Born in Massachusetts in 1849, Burbank settled in Northern California, where he pursued more than half a century of horticultural research at a six-acre garden in Santa Rosa and on an experimental farm in the town of Sebastopol. Dedicated to Burbank's accomplishments, the Luther Burbank Home & Gardens currently comprise a 1.6-acre site in central Santa Rosa. Approaching from Sonoma Avenue, visitors see an appealing stone fountain, one of the wonderful elements of this park-like setting. In 1960, at Burbank's widow's request, the gardens were redesigned. A section called the Burbank Memorial Garden, honoring Burbank's role as influential forefather of American horticulture, was completed in 1991. Warmly inviting, the garden has espaliered fruit trees displayed on curved wooden screening.

Consistent with his urge to benefit humanity, Burbank concentrated on breeding plants that would produce greater quantities of food. He even investigated such plants as spineless cacti for their potential to feed cattle in a desert environment. Burbank's research yielded a myriad of beneficial plants, including the 'Paradox' walnut, with its refined wood-grain for use in furniture.

A recent project incorporated more plants related to Burbank's work and updated structural elements to revitalize the gardens. Passing through the main entrance of this Registered National, State and City Historic Landmark, you'll enjoy a fabulous rose garden. Roses introduced by Burbank encircle a bird bath fountain, while parent varieties that were used to breed roses are growing by the fence. You'll also find richly fragrant old garden roses, along with modern roses that were developed by California hybridizers and are here placed along curving lines according to color.

Although edible plants were Burbank's specialty, his reputation flourishes as the breeder of hundreds of shrubs and flowers, including the queen of all blooming plants, the rose. His varieties bear larger, more fragrant or more beautifully colored flowers. The Border Garden in front of the Burbank home features lilacs, spireas, and lavish displays of annuals and perennials grown in Victorian times. Other plantings include a small orchard of fruit-bearing trees located by the Carriage House and along the property's perimeter; raised demonstration beds; bird and butterfly gardens; and a medicinal herb garden.

INFORMATION AND DIRECTIONS
The Luther Burbank Home & Gardens, corner of Santa Rosa and Sonoma Avenues, Santa Rosa, CA 95402. Phone 707-524-5445 for general information, and for the schedule of tours of the modified Greek Revival-style Burbank Home; fee charged to tour the Burbank Home. Carriage House Museum, Burbank Home, and the Gift Shop are open April through October, Wednesday through Sunday from 10 A.M. to 4 P.M. Gardens are open daily 8 A.M. to dusk, year-round; free admission.

Follow Highway 101 north to Santa Rosa; located approximately one hour from San Francisco.

Marin Art And Garden Center, Ross

Hidden within the boundaries of Marin County, the prosperous town of Ross lies near San Anselmo, a short distance west of Highway 101. Preserved by a consortium of community groups as a cultural oasis and horticultural haven for Marin's citizenry, the Marin Art and Garden Center occupies a wooded ten-acre site.

Buildings located on the property are dedicated to various functions: art exhibitions; theater productions; and meeting rooms for ardent garden clubs such as the Garden Society of Marin, one of the center's founding organizations. Built in 1864 and fully refurbished with a gleaming interior, balcony and circular staircase, the picturesque Octagon House now shelters the Jose Moya del Piño Library and Ross Historical Society.

Perhaps best known for its fine array of trees, the Marin Art and Garden Center showcases an enormous Southern magnolia, planted in 1870 by the son-in-law of the town's founding father, James Ross. Centrally located on the property, this monumental specimen presides over the landscape, truly living up to its botanical name, *Magnolia grandiflora.*

Other rarities include: the dawn redwood, relative of the coast redwood (this rare deciduous variety was found in China); the Center's giant sequoia, which exhibits a prematurely aged domed form due to its sunny position; English oak; hawthorn; Atlantic cedar and camphor; silk tree; evergreen ash and dogwood. These are only a few of the excellent specimens found in the sylvan groves of Marin Art and Garden Center.

INFORMATION AND DIRECTIONS
Marin Art and Garden Center, P. O. Box 437, 30 Sir Francis Drake Boulevard, Ross, CA 94957. Before visiting, phone 415-454-5597 for further information on special events. Grounds are open from dawn to dusk. No fee.

Ross is located about 35 minutes north of San Francisco. Take Highway 101 to the San Anselmo exit; follow Sir Francis Drake Boulevard through the towns of Greenbrae and Kentfield, to the Marin Art and Garden Center.

McAllister Water Gardens, Napa Valley

In the heart of Napa Valley, McAllister Water Gardens offers a superior variety of ornamental plants for ponds and landscapes with water features. Whether seeking specimens for a boggy, wetland setting, or attempting to plant a big wooden water bucket to sit on the patio, you should visit Walt and Vicky McAllister's nursery. A great resource for neophytes and impassioned water gardeners, alike, the nursery carries water lilies in a wide spectrum of enticing colors, rushes, grasses, and terrific foliage plants for textural contrast and structure. Enjoy the fine display gardens and take advantage of the McAllisters' expert advice on what to plant in order to control the growth of algae, or to oxygenate the water.

INFORMATION AND DIRECTIONS
McAllister Water Gardens, 7420 St. Helena Highway, Napa Valley, CA 94558. Phone 707-944-0921 to confirm seasonal open hours; fax: 707-944-1850. Open to the public March through September; Thursdays through Sundays, 9 A.M. to 4 P.M.

Located two miles north of Yountville on Highway 29, about 1 hour and 15 minutes north of San Francisco.

Mom's Head Gardens, Santa Rosa

We found Mom's Head Gardens, which is named after a cat named "Mom," on the first try, but this organic herb display garden can be difficult to locate. If you're looking for a free-spirited garden sojourn, a visit to Mom's Head promises a delightfully informal atmosphere. The gardens specialize in over 200 varieties of culinary and medicinal herbs. The proprietors Vivien Hillgrove and Karen Brocco worked in the movie industry for twenty years until, as Vivien explains, they tired of "sitting in dark rooms for ten hours a day."

You'll find a number of gardens to peruse, overflowing with angelica, graceful feverfew, prickly nettle, distinctive salvias, and much more. Signs combined with a plant list aid in identifying annuals, perennials, and biennials; denote culinary or ornamental qualities; and point out historically significant species. Wander through the experimental gardens to look over new plants under cultivation.

Throughout the year, a quirky assortment of workshops and classes are offered at Mom's Head. One recent gardening class led by Vivien included demonstrations of seed starting, taking cuttings, and transplanting methods. In the past, visiting artists have taught fabric design, magical herbalism, and a "Botanica Erotica" workshop that showed how to make aphrodisiacs for body, mind and spirit.

During my visit, Vivien helped me concoct a room-freshener spray based upon scents I selected: rosemary, tangerine, and eucalyptus essential oils. The customized formulation was presented in a pretty blue glass spray bottle.

Always phone first before setting out for Mom's Head. The outskirts of the wetlands setting may be soggy enough to warrant rain boots. Furthermore, because goats and rabbits, ducks and cats meander around the grounds, it's recommended you leave the family dog at home.

INFORMATION AND DIRECTIONS

Mom's Head Gardens, 4153 Langner Avenue, Santa Rosa, CA 95407. Phone 707-585-8575 in order to schedule a visit, obtain detailed directions, or find out about the location of an Herbal Marketplace Vivien is organizing. The marketplace offers Sonoma County fresh and dried herbs, nursery plants, seasonal crafts, gifts, books, and art.

Contact Mom's Head via *E-mail: momshead@ap.net*

Mom's Head is a member of Sonoma County Farm Trails, an organization of specialty growers, wineries, and family-run farms (See "Resources For Gardeners").

Located about one hour north of San Francisco, off Highway 101.

Mostly Natives Nursery, Tomales

If you're driving north of San Francisco on coast Highway 1, be sure to include the town of Tomales in your itinerary. The rewarding detour should deliver you directly to Mostly Natives Nursery, growers of West Coast native species and drought-tolerant plants. Since 1984 this Northern California nursery has been a fine resource for native grasses and a host of plants from the Mediterranean, Australia, Chile and New Zealand.

A majority of plants sold at Mostly Natives—including native annuals, irises, shade plants, and species of sage, ceanothus, and manzanitas—are propagated on the premises. In the spring, you'll also find a good selection of perennials and organic vegetables. The nursery's friendly staff will help you find what you're looking for and answer questions about any unusual species and varieties.

INFORMATION AND DIRECTIONS

Mostly Natives Nursery, 27235 Highway One, P O Box 258, Tomales, CA 94971. Phone 707-878-2009 to contact owners Walter Earle and Margaret Graham for further information. Open daily 9 A.M. to 5 P.M. (closed Tuesday year-round, and also closed Wednesdays during the winter season). Call ahead to confirm open hours.

From San Francisco proceed north. Choose either the leisurely, extremely scenic drive up Highway 1; or opt for the quicker route (about 1½ hours, depending upon traffic), by taking Highway 101 north to Petaluma, then following the Tomales-Petaluma road west toward the Pacific Ocean and the town of Tomales.

Sonoma Horticultural Nursery, Sebastopol

Not-to-be-missed, "Sonoma Hort" (as it is referred to by locals) specializes in abundant varieties of rhododendrons and azaleas, as well as shade-loving plants appropriate for the type of moist environment where "rhodies" thrive. You'll delight in the nursery's extraordinary display gardens amid an expansive 7½-acre property where countless fine specimens are assembled.

As might be expected, the emphasis on rhododendrons at Sonoma Horticultural Nursery makes for a lavish and colorful spring season, but the breadth of companion plantings is just as impressive. A leisurely saunter along 1½ miles of footpaths rewards patrons with visions of towering foxgloves and huge flamboyant clematis flowers decorating vertical posts and pillars along the way. This retinue of complementary blooms magnifies the voluptuousness of the rhododendrons, making for an exhibition that rivals any Northern California garden you might visit.

Indelibly imprinted on my memory is one stopover very early in May during an El Niño season, when I witnessed the heart-stopping performance of a legendary dove tree (*Davidia involucrata*). Thanks in large part to proprietor Polo DeLorenzo's magic touch, these rare beauties are grown, propagated, and offered for sale at Sonoma Hort.

You'll see flourishing examples of the tree in a circular driveway adjacent to the nursery's main parking area. One incomparably handsome, mature dove tree is protected by a special ordinance. Look for the plaque which designates this tree a Sonoma County treasure—Heritage Tree #20. Originally from China, the uncommon species is also known as the "handkerchief tree." Usually, it is late April when dove trees parade their flowing white bracts like fluttering handkerchiefs.

Another revelation in May is the empress tree (*Paulownia tomentosa*), with its spectacular show of purple flowers resembling foxgloves. Still, by no means is spring the only season promising a fanfare. Alluring perennial plantings put on sweeping summery displays, while the delightful woodland setting boasts strapping examples of the primitive-appearing *Gunnera chilensis*, and equally picturesque vegetation. Replete with beguiling vignettes, Sonoma Horticultural Nursery represents a unique sanctuary for plant lovers throughout the year.

INFORMATION AND DIRECTIONS

Sonoma Horticultural Nursery, 3970 Azalea Avenue, Sebastopol, CA 95472. Phone 707-823-6832 to confirm directions and open hours, or to contact owners Polo de Lorenzo and Warren Smith for further information. Open year-round: March 1–May 31, open 7 days a week, 9 A.M. to 5 P.M. June 1–February 28, open Thursday through Monday, 9 A.M. to 5 P.M. Individuals are welcome, but groups of ten or more require reservations.

Located 60 miles north of San Francisco (approximately one hour) in the heart of the wine country. Follow Highway 101 north, exit at Cotati and proceed west toward Sebastopol on Highway 116. Turn left and continue on Hessel Road, onto McFarlane, then right onto Azalea Avenue.

Western Hills Nursery, Occidental

When I asked which nurseries in Sonoma County had the most outstanding settings, many professional horticulturists and avid gardeners recommended Western Hills. Plant lovers have been known to assume a reverent tone and devout attitude when describing this woodland wonderland. Once you've walked its three acres of tranquil paths, you'll most likely join the nursery's legions of admirers.

Founders Lester Hawkins and Marshall Olbrich garnered a good deal of attention more than three decades ago when they introduced plants from the Mediterranean region, as well as from Australia. As many area authorities recount, the stir they created generated wonderful enthusiasm for horticultural pursuits among many people who knew them. When Hawkins and Olbrich died, they passed the mantle to Maggie Wych, a former employee and current proprietor of Western Hills Nursery.

The nursery remains as wondrous a place as ever—a cross between an arboretum, botanical garden, and a commercial establishment. Rare species intermingle with varieties of deciduous trees, conifers, shrubs and perennials. Not only can you get lost in the beauty of the grounds, but you can buy some of the fine plants the nursery propagates.

Situated in the rolling, emerald landscape of Occidental, Western Hills lures serious horticulture buffs from all over to make the pilgrimage to this otherworldly dominion. (I could almost hear the gods playing their melodious lutes in the distance!)

INFORMATION AND DIRECTIONS

Western Hills Nursery, P. O. Box 543, 16250 Coleman Valley Road, Occidental, CA 95465. It is recommended you call 707-874-3731 if you're thinking of visiting during the winter months. During other seasons, Western Hills is generally open Thursday through Sunday, 10 A.M. to 4 P.M., but it's advisable to phone ahead to confirm.

Located approximately one hour or so north of San Francisco. Take Highway 101 from the Golden Gate Bridge to the Highway 116 West exit, driving through Sebastopol, to the town of Occidental. Phone to obtain detailed directions before setting out to visit this very special nursery.

4

North Coast Gardens

Cafe Beaujolais Garden, Mendocino

Cafe Beaujolais combines the charming ambiance of a turn-of-the-century Victorian backdrop with great victuals. Amid a picture-perfect Mendocino setting, superb dinners at the cafe are embellished by organically grown produce. Freshly baked bread is delivered straight from the wood-fired oven of the Brickery, installed next door to the restaurant by Executive Chef Christopher Kump, husband of Cafe Beaujolais' founder, Chef Margaret Fox.

Take a seat in the atrium and in addition to fine cuisine, you'll enjoy looking out on a wonderfully landscaped garden that overflows with spectacular rarities and ingenious plant combinations. Renowned among garden lovers for nearly a decade, the Cafe Beaujolais garden was designed with skill and panache by horticultural consultant and landscape designer Jaen Treesinger.

Investigate the vibrant melange of unusual plants found in the one-acre domain, and you'll see that Treesinger's passion for plant collecting is unsurpassable. In 1994–95, Treesinger received a grant from the California Horticultural Society, a special honor acknowledging her work in researching and testing plant varieties. She has repeatedly pushed the boundaries of how far north a plant will grow. One example of the type of innovative flora Treesinger planted at Cafe Beaujolais is a recently discovered native angelica, which has leaves with a tremendous range of variegation.

The garden features some 2,000 plants, complemented by strategically placed sculptures. Long-blooming antique roses, ornamental grasses, and a dynamic silver border create a rich tapestry of distinctive foliage set off by lush blooms. Explore the Sunken Garden, featuring evocative remnants of an old brick wall from Mendocino's early days.

Or sign up for a garden tour to see how drought-tolerant shrubs are integrated with an incredible selection of herbs, perennials, as well as flowers which are used for cut bouquets and for edible ends. Jaen Treesinger refers to her vivacious gardening style as "abandoned villa" gardening. You'll identity plants from Australia, South Africa, New Zealand, and specimens indigenous to the Pacific Northwest. Above all heed Treesinger's observations in order to glean new ideas for innovative garden planning.

INFORMATION AND DIRECTIONS
The Garden at the Cafe Beaujolais, 961 Ukiah Street, P. O. Box 1236, Mendocino, CA 95460. Phone the cafe at 707-937-5614 for further information or to confirm directions. For information on garden tours, which are generally offered from May through August, call Jaen Treesinger at 707-937-0783

Located 150 miles north of San Francisco; approximately a 4½-hour drive from the Golden Gate Bridge to coastal Mendocino. Take Highway 101 north, then follow signs west to Mendocino. Or plan a leisurely drive up the coast on scenic Highway 1.

Digging Dog Nursery, Albion

A couple of years ago, a Bay Area newspaper article highlighted heaths and heathers, pointing out the current popularity of these plants in Northern California. Gardeners along the North Coast, particularly, seem to have discovered just how satisfying it can be to orchestrate attractive plantings with these versatile, acid loving, evergreen performers. You'll find a lovely array of heaths and heathers among the offerings at Digging Dog Nursery in Albion. Observe these plants' distinctive mounding forms, their small textural leaves, which range from silver and gold to bronze and chartreuse, all set off by cheerful little flowers of white, pink or purple.

Heaths and heathers are but a sampling of the praiseworthy ornamental grasses and perennials, vines, trees and shrubs that the nursery carries. Digging Dog proprietors Gary Ratway and Deborah Whigham have selected their plants for such qualities as easy care, lengthy bloom, and plenty of visual interest throughout the year.

Their wonderful gardening style has attracted an appreciative customer base.

Admired for his work at the Mendocino Coast Botanical Gardens, as well as for his design at the Matanzas Creek Winery, Ratway brings an astute flair to companion plantings. Consider the Digging Dog catalog a rich resource: when engaged in garden planning, read over and reflect upon the many promising plant associations suggested in the catalog's pages.

In upcoming seasons, visitors to Digging Dog can look forward to a new demonstration garden that is being established at the nursery's northern edge. Mixing shrubs and perennials, the area also features a grassy path for visitors to stroll along while investigating two planting beds, a rock garden, and an area earmarked to become a secret garden. Digging Dog invites their patrons to watch this "work in progress," which promises to serve as an enjoyable opportunity to learn by example.

INFORMATION AND DIRECTIONS

Digging Dog Nursery, P O Box 471, Albion, CA. 95410. Phone 707-937-1130 to make an appointment, and to obtain detailed directions. Fax: 707-937-2480. The nursery is closed Sunday and Monday, although, as a retail customer, you are invited to phone to set up an appointment for a visit. If you'd like to order by mail, request a catalog for $3.

Located about 3½ hours north of the Golden Gate Bridge, Albion is just south of the coastal village of Mendocino. If you like a slow, scenic drive, take Highway 1 north from San Francisco.

Mendocino Coast Botanical Gardens, Fort Bragg

Ernest Schoefer was a retired nurseryman with a mission! Founder of the Mendocino Coast Botanical Gardens, Schoefer purchased the land that would become the Botanical Gardens in 1961. Along with his wife, Betty, he built trails and cleared areas for plantings. Admission at the time was $1, but additional revenue from a gift shop and retail nursery helped Schoefer realize his vision.

Using grants received from the California State Coastal Conservancy, the Mendocino Coast Recreation and Park Department purchased the entire property in 1992. Today, countless volunteers and a fairly small staff work tirelessly to maintain the grounds of this outstanding North Coast botanical domain. Presided over by a board of directors, the gardens depend upon admission and membership fees, donations, and sales revenues from their nursery and store.

The Mendocino Coast Botanical Gardens' 47 acres are configured to form a plant lover's dreamscape. Given the region's mild, rainy conditions in winter, and cool, fog drenched summers, the gardens boast impressive collections of rhododendron hybrids. Visitors can admire here more than twenty plant collections, including camellias and dahlias, both hybrid and species fuchsias, heathers, and Pacifica irises.

Especially thrilling are the spectacular ocean vistas revealed as one follows along the garden's Coastal Bluff Trail. Craggy bluffs reach as far as the eye can see, descending to a sparkling cobalt sea that pounds ceaselessly against rough, rocky outcroppings. As grand as the views might be, don't become so absorbed that you venture to the cliff's edge. Known to be unstable, the terrain mandates caution.

In September, the dahlia garden puts on quite a show, with deep borders displaying countless varieties of showy blooms. Also in September, a brilliant panoply of deciduous trees and coniferous specimens provides striking contrasts of color, texture, and form. November through January, the gardens are ablaze with Japanese maples, while ocean views thrill visitors with sightings of migrating gray whales on their way southward. Protected by a forest of native pine, the gardens are awe-inspiring throughout the year.

Having a picnic on the grounds of the Mendocino Coast Botanical Gardens can be a pleasure in itself. You'll find plenty of benches for relaxing where splendid plantings can be enjoyed to full effect. The Cliff House, located just off the Coastal Bluff Trail, provides a sheltered spot from where you can enjoy the Pacific in all its glory.

The gardens' gift store features an intriguing array of garden-related paraphernalia. I brought back a bulbous, hand-held, watering container made of rubber, with interchangeable tips for either a fine spray or a very light spritzing. Plants culled from the gardens' nursery stock are offered for sale, so that you can take home interesting specimens to plant in your own garden.

INFORMATION AND DIRECTIONS

Mendocino Coast Botanical Gardens, 18220 N. Highway 1, Fort Bragg, CA 95437. Handicap accessible. Admission fee charged. Phone 707-

964-4352 for further information. Open daily except Thanksgiving and Christmas, 9 A.M. to 5 P.M. from March through October; and from 9 A.M. to 4 P.M. November through February.

Approximately five hours north of San Francisco and the Golden Gate Bridge. Take Highway 101 north, then go west on Highway 20 to Coast Highway 1. The gardens are located on the west (ocean) side of Highway 1, two miles south of Fort Bragg or seven miles north of Mendocino.

5

East Bay Gardens

Berkeley Municipal Rose Garden, Berkeley

A national canvass of public rose gardens would doubtlessly place the Berkeley Municipal Rose Garden among the country's most fetching settings. Boasting a dazzling structural design replete with thousands of roses, this north Berkeley haven will satiate any ardent rose connoisseur.

Explore the rose garden's spectacular amphitheater. Begin your descent at street level, then stroll beneath the ample curvilinear configuration of connecting arbors and strapping wooden pergola that form the garden's graceful framework. Note how the fragrance of strongly scented climbing roses is intoxicating, especially in May around Mother's Day when blooming peaks.

Discerning garden travelers can swoop down the multitiered amphitheater's dramatic stairways, crisscrossing comfortable horizontal walkways, to bask in the garden's lavish rose beds, arranged to emphasize the varied colors. Berkeley's gentle climate fosters a lengthy cycle of bloom for roses, as well as a wealth of flowers. You can expect to enjoy early blooming varieties of roses that flower in April, and then again throughout the summer months on into October.

The Berkeley Municipal Rose Garden presents a veritable banquet of delights throughout the year.

INFORMATION AND DIRECTIONS

Berkeley Municipal Rose Garden, 1201 Euclid Avenue and Bay View Place, Berkeley, CA 94704. Phone 510-644-6530 for information. No fee; open daily year-round.

Located about 35 minutes east of downtown San Francisco, via the Bay Bridge.

Blake Garden, Kensington

Exquisite Mediterranean-type gardens, a handsome elongated reflecting pool, and breathtaking views of the San Francisco Bay—all are yours to behold when you visit Blake House, the residence of the president of the University of California. Situated in the stunning East Bay section of Kensington near Berkeley, Blake House was given to the university by alumni and benefactors, Mr. and Mrs. Anson Stiles Blake. This lovely house was built in the Mediterranean style by architect Walter Bliss in the early 1920s, and it has functioned as the president's house since 1967.

An avid horticulturist, Mrs. Blake looked to her sister Mabel Symmes, a student of landscape architecture at U. C. Berkeley, for expertise in planning the formal ten-acre garden. From the garden's inception in the 1920s, Mr. and Mrs. Blake encouraged the university to utilize it. Maintained today by the Department of Landscape Architecture, the Blake Garden is a valuable resource for students of the program.

The garden's sun-swept hills and terraced areas feature a remarkable collection of approximately 1,000 species and varieties. In the garden's more sylvan areas, you'll discover dawn redwoods which were started from seeds. Numerous types of oak and pine grow here, along with magnolia and maple, plum, cherry, as well as rhododendrons and roses. There is also a rich profusion of perennials and herbs. Striking floral colors are provided by flowering maples (*Abutilon*) and angel's trumpets (*Brugmansia*), monkey flowers, rockrose, and fragrant climbers such as jasmine and Japanese wisteria.

INFORMATION AND DIRECTIONS

Blake Garden, 70 Rincon Road, Kensington, CA 94704. Phone 510-524-2449 for information and directions, or to confirm open hours. No fee. Open Monday through Friday, 8 A.M. to 4:30 P.M. Garden is closed to the public on university holidays.

Kensington is a pleasant enclave adjacent to and just north of Berkeley in the East Bay; approximately 45 minutes from downtown San Francisco via the Bay Bridge.

Our Own Stuff Gallery Garden, Berkeley

Widely known for her carved stone works, Marcia Donahue creates sculptural pieces of rustic grace that can be found in many a West Coast garden. The artist's own wonderfully eccentric Berkeley gar-

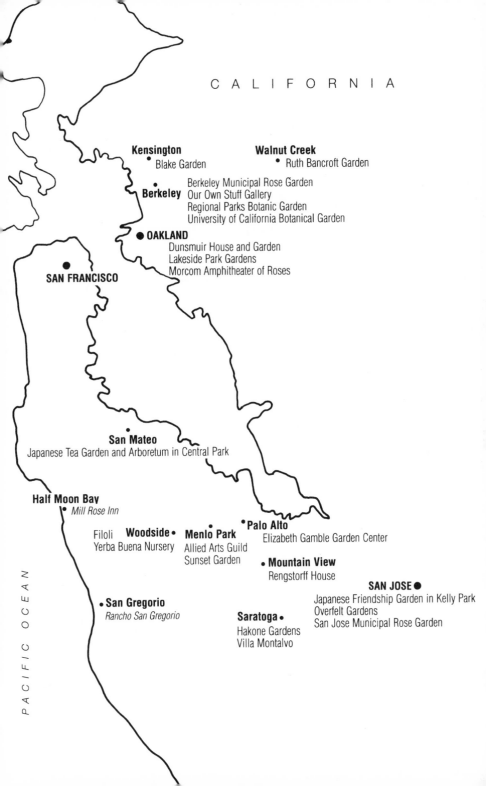

CALIFORNIA

Kensington
• Blake Garden

Walnut Creek
• Ruth Bancroft Garden

Berkeley
Berkeley Municipal Rose Garden
Our Own Stuff Gallery
Regional Parks Botanic Garden
University of California Botanical Garden

● **OAKLAND**
Dunsmuir House and Garden
Lakeside Park Gardens
Morcom Amphitheater of Roses

SAN FRANCISCO

San Mateo
Japanese Tea Garden and Arboretum in Central Park

Half Moon Bay
• Mill Rose Inn

Filoli
Yerba Buena Nursery

Woodside •

Menlo Park
Allied Arts Guild
Sunset Garden

•**Palo Alto**
Elizabeth Gamble Garden Center

• **Mountain View**
Rengstorff House

SAN JOSE ●
Japanese Friendship Garden in Kelly Park
Overfelt Gardens
San Jose Municipal Rose Garden

• **San Gregorio**
Rancho San Gregorio

Saratoga •
Hakone Gardens
Villa Montalvo

PACIFIC OCEAN

den is celebrated for the fantastic juxtapositions of boldly textured, audacious plantings with artwork crafted by Donahue and her partner, Mark Bulwinkle.

Donahue's Berkeley residence consists of a brown shingled Victorian house, wearing a heavy cloak of foliage. The lush outgrowth results from an imaginative grouping of trees, including a 100-year-old cordyline, a distinctive weeping cypress, and a tall, willowy eucalyptus. Also in the front garden space, Bulwinkle's sculptures, with their active forms and richly rusted surfaces, announce the horticultural extravaganza awaiting visitors in Donahue's inner sanctum.

Traveling along a side walkway, you'll enter a sumptuous tropical garden, which is full of exceptional specimens. I was captivated by the conspicuous beauty of *Solanum quitoense*, with its luxuriant purple veined leaves and provocative red-violet new growth. A wooden gate in the shape of a brawny hand is the muscular icon which affords entrée to Donahue's high-spirited, elaborately structured rear garden.

On my initial visit, I felt a delectable sensory overload. Uniquely conceived, Donahue's urban realm is distinguished by a canopy of towering flora combined with a generous understory of rare plants. Add to this the unexpected placement of abundant ornamentation and a surprising assemblage of found objects, and you have horticultural theater at its most expressive. Mind you, all this takes place within the boundaries of an unexpectedly bantam-size realm, which measures 40 by 60 feet!

Note a collection of boisterous bowling balls. This raucous rainbow of lustrous orbs is set against the backdrop of exquisite, pale-hued bamboo varieties. Only here will you witness such an outrageous arrangement of incongruous elements. Certainly the exciting examples of bamboo Donahue has gathered point to the finesse of a savvy plantswoman. But look closely, for some of these stately canes are hand-crafted ceramic forms made by Marcia herself! Glazed clay totems are just one example of the surprises that await you amid the dense plantings.

You'll happen upon sculptural stone pieces, such as a full featured face I discovered during my visit. A tiny leaf had fallen upon the sad countenance of that stone visage, taking on the appearance of a teardrop, and accentuating the garden's theatrical impact. During your visit to Marcia Donahue's bewitching garden, expect to be drenched in colorful contradictions. You'll enjoy encountering the unexpected.

INFORMATION AND DIRECTIONS
Our Own Stuff Gallery Garden, located at 3017 Wheeler Street, Berkeley, CA 94705. Phone 510-540-8544 for information. In the welcoming spirit associated with gardening enthusiasts, Donahue opens her garden to the public on Sunday afternoons between noon and 5 P.M. No fee.

This Berkeley garden is located in the East Bay, approximately ½ hour from downtown San Francisco via the Bay Bridge.

Regional Parks Botanic Garden, Berkeley (Contra Costa County)

Established within the boundaries of Berkeley's expansive Tilden Regional Park, the Regional Parks Botanic Garden presents an exciting environment in which to learn about California's flora. While discovering breathtaking views amid sometimes steep and rocky terrain, you'll find that the garden appears at once cultivated and untamed.

The Regional Parks Botanic Garden specializes in the propagation of the state's trees, shrubs, and flowers. Divided into nine distinctive sections, the garden displays the diverse flora growing in California's various geographical regions—from the desert to the Pacific Rain Forest.

At any time of the year, you'll find compelling plant species to study and admire in the garden's fine collections of conifers and oaks, ceanothuses, and numerous endangered plants. If it's blooming or colorful specimens you're after, you won't be disappointed. In March, the fragile beauty of trout lilies, fritillaries, trilliums, and California poppies usher in spring. The berries of the madrone, the blooms of the Chaparral Currant, and the leaves of deciduous oaks, dogwoods, willows, and hawthorn put on a show of striking colors throughout the fall season. Even a December visit can be a harbinger of things to come: the first manzanita blooms come out at year's end, followed by a riot of flowering manzanitas, silktassels, and currants in January.

The grounds of the Regional Parks Botanic Garden captivate visitors with their natural beauty.

INFORMATION AND DIRECTIONS
Regional Parks Botanic Garden, Tilden Regional Park, Berkeley, CA 94708. Entrance to the garden on Wildcat Canyon Road at South Park

Drive. Phone 510-841-8732 for information and directions. Open 8:30 A.M. to 5 P.M. daily. No fee.

Located in the East Bay, about 45 minutes from downtown San Francisco via the Bay Bridge.

The Ruth Bancroft Garden, Walnut Creek

The first garden in the United States to merit the sponsorship of the Garden Conservancy, the Ruth Bancroft Garden is a great garden in every sense of the word. The Bancroft Garden grows on land located below Mt. Diablo, a parcel of what was originally a 400-acre property Hubert Bancroft set about developing in the 1880s as orchards and ranchland. Carrying on the tradition of the Bancroft family's connection to the landscape, Philip Bancroft's wife, Ruth, began the installation of the gardens in the early 1950s. Soon after gardens sprang up around their house, Mrs. Bancroft started cultivating succulents, her favorite plants, in greenhouses.

The Bancroft Garden's overall framework was created in 1972, with the assistance of designer Lester Hawkins. Mrs. Bancroft proceeded to place and plant the numerous specimens she had been collecting. She eventually devoted 2½ acres to her outstanding "dry garden," where today visitors can discover a breathtaking array of unusually striking succulent plants, with their often peculiar, generally stunning architectural forms, textural foliage, and vibrantly colored and distinctive flowers.

A sterling plantswoman, Ruth Bancroft has thoughtfully selected species and hybrid forms of succulents, emphasizing the wonderful structure of agaves, yuccas, and African aloes, as well as stunning desert cacti, euphorbias and iceplants. Graceful pine, mesquite, and palo verde trees, offer some shade for those plants which require screening from the sun. Stately Australian bottle trees, shapely palms, and *Eucalyptus pauciflora*, with its sensational peeling bark, all lend grandeur to the setting. Visitors can learn here all the fundamentals about creating a garden where water conservation is of primary concern.

The Bancroft Garden demonstrates Mrs. Bancroft's passion for and knowledge of succulents. You will find here one of the country's finest gardens of drought-tolerant species showcased in a splendidly designed landscape.

In 1993, the Ruth Bancroft Garden was incorporated as a non-profit organization. The following summer, Mrs. Bancroft deeded the garden property. The garden now operates through the support of its founder, by contributions from members, and from grants, plant sales, special events, and tour fees.

INFORMATION AND DIRECTIONS

The Ruth Bancroft Garden, 1500 Bancroft Road, P. O. Box 30845, Walnut Creek, CA 94598. Entrance to the garden is by appointment only; fee charged. Tours take about 1½ hours and are given at the following times: early April to early July; mid-July to mid-October; late November to early April. Phone 925-210-9663 for specific dates and times, and reservations. Parking is limited. Plants propagated from the garden are offered for sale at tour times. *Web site: www.ruthbancroftgarden.org*

The Ruth Bancroft Garden is located about 28 miles east of San Francisco, about a 40-minute drive in light traffic via the Bay Bridge. From the bridge, take Highway 24 East until it ends at I-680. Go onto 680 North and take the first exit, Ygnacio Valley Road. Take YVR about three miles to Bancroft Road, then turn left. The garden is one block up on the right.

University Of California Botanical Garden, Berkeley

With its hilly topography and sometimes steep paths, Strawberry Canyon is the perfect setting for Berkeley's University of California Botanical Garden. Stretching over 34 acres, the grounds' geographical arrangement of gardens displays plants from around the world.

The abundant plantings, and the university's educational outreach and research make the U. C. Botanical Garden a thriving horticultural museum without walls. Located across Centennial Drive to the northwest of the garden entrance is the Mather Redwood Grove. Within the garden the large section devoted to California natives is full of color throughout the year: the profuse blooms of spring wildflowers are followed by bright poppies in summer, conspicuous Madia sunflowers in fall, and fetching California lilacs (*Ceanothus*), manzanitas, and currants in winter.

In May, seek out the perfumed air of the garden of old roses. Nearby, the traditional English knot garden, which features Western herbs, is one of the most popular displays. Continue along the path, pass the herb garden's flagstone terrace and handsome stone sundial, and you'll find a section devoted to Chinese medicinal herbs. In the summer season, savor the fragrance of blooming herbs. In other sections of the garden, fine collections of diverse flora from South America, the Mediterranean and Asia are exhibited.

The Mesoamerican section pulses with the animated activity of hummingbirds as they flash and shimmer among summer's abundant flowers. The birds' ostentatious enterprise, however, is not the only thing to rivet one's attention. The view across the bay will enchant all who wander through here.

Indoors in the Desert and Rain Forest House, you'll find succulents and epiphytic orchids. Ferns and insect-eating plants grow in a building nearby, and tropical crops such as bananas and coffee in the Tropical House.

There is always something in flower at this wonderful garden. Especially noteworthy are fragrant wintersweet (*Chimonanthus*) that bloom in January and February. March and April are ablaze with blooming rhododendrons and other spring-flowering plants. And throughout the summer and fall, until frost arrives in December, the Mexican and Central American collections are abloom.

Each time I visit, I'm grateful to the staff and faculty of years gone by, whose far-flung expeditions contributed exceptional specimens to the garden's plant collections. The horticulturists at the Botanical Garden have created a splendid haven—a place where we can joyfully observe the plant world in all its glory.

INFORMATION AND DIRECTIONS

University of California Botanical Garden, Centennial Drive, Berkeley, CA 94720. Phone 510-643-2755 for directions, to confirm open hours, or for information on special events such as plant sales. Admission fee and parking fee; every Thursday free admission. Open daily from 9 A.M. to 4:45 P.M.

Web site: http://www.mip.berkeley.edu/garden

Located in the East Bay, about 40 minutes from downtown San Francisco via the Bay Bridge.

AND IN ADDITION . . .

Dunsmuir House and Garden: Oakland
2960 Peralta Oaks Park, Oakland, CA 94605.

Phone 510-615-5555 to confirm open hours. Open April to September. Grounds are open to visitors Tuesday through Friday, 10 A.M. to 4 P.M.; no fee. Reservations required for tours of house and garden; fee charged. A historic home amid 40-acre estate, with landscaping originally designed by Golden Gate Park's John McLaren.

Lakeside Park Gardens: Oakland
666 Bellevue Avenue, Oakland, CA 94610.
Phone 510-238-3208. No admission fee. This five-acre Oakland site is incorporated within the Lake Merritt parkland. It features an assemblage of garden areas devoted to herbs and lilies, rhododendrons, fuchsias and more. A popular setting for flower shows and plant society functions.

Morcom Amphitheater of Roses: Oakland
700 Jean Street, Oakland, CA 94610.
Open daylight hours; no admission fee. Hybrid teas (the so-called "modern," repeat-blooming roses that were first bred in the late nineteenth century) are showcased at Oakland's 7-acre arena of roses. Plan to visit around mid-May when the Morcom rose garden presents its most illustrious exhibition of blooms.

6

The Peninsula & South Bay Gardens

Allied Arts Guild, Menlo Park

When you pass through the portals of the Allied Arts Guild's Spanish Colonial-style complex, you will see a flurry of artistic activity, similar to the energy of the Arts and Crafts Movement, which was taking place when the Guild was first launched in 1929.

The Allied Arts Guild was the creation of arts aficionados Garfield and Delight Merner, who together with the foremost residents of San Francisco's peninsula communities, established a superb environment in which the arts could flourish. Here in a courtyard setting, the work of contemporary artists and artisans is exhibited in a series of studios, attractive boutiques, and charming shops. Decorated with murals and frescoes, these enterprises specialize in unique handcrafted clothing, furnishings, pottery and artwork, all displaying floral motifs. "Nature's Alley," a beguiling shop and a picturesque place to browse, sells handsome garden containers and ornaments, gifts, and spectacular topiary creations.

The extravagant sun-drenched surroundings invite garden travelers to explore the Court of Abundance, a Moorish designed orangery with central fountain; the Garden of Delight, a theme garden featuring blue Nile lilies, hydrangeas, and a blue-tiled fountain; and the intoxicating Rose Allée with its stately rose standards.

The fetching pathways, vine-shrouded rustic structures, captivating arches and mesmerizing water features combine to furnish a spectacular framework for the Allied Arts Guild's showcase of Mediterranean specimens.

Since 1932 the guild has sustained an alliance which benefits Lucile Salter Packard Children's Hospital at Stanford University. The guild's philanthropic support for children with chronic illnesses is commendable, and another reason to contemplate spending an afternoon at this alluring locale.

INFORMATION AND DIRECTIONS

Allied Arts Guild, 75 Arbor Road at Cambridge, Menlo Park, CA 94025. For information and detailed directions, phone 650-322-2405. To arrange lunch at the Allied Arts Guild Restaurant, phone 650-324-2588 for reservations. Open Monday through Saturday, 10 A.M. to 5 P.M. No entrance fee.

Web Site: www.alliedartsguild.org

Located approximately one hour south of San Francisco or Oakland, near Stanford Shopping Center; ten minutes from Highways 280 and 101.

The Elizabeth F. Gamble Garden Center, Palo Alto

With its mild climate and generally sunny skies, the pleasant town of Palo Alto boasts a major university, Stanford, and a prominent community-oriented horticultural foundation, the Elizabeth F. Gamble Garden Center. Volunteer gardeners work with the center's resident horticulturist in planting and caring for both formal and working gardens. A restoration effort has beautifully recaptured the original turn-of-the-century gardens. The garden's heirloom roses are especially striking. Its enchanting woodland garden offers a tea house, and handsome collections of viburnum and hydrangeas, camellias and Japanese maples.

A cherry allée and a grotto are located along the garden's Churchill Avenue boundary. One of the most spectacular sights, the bewitching wisteria garden intermingles several varieties that display their pendulous flower clusters during April, in an admirably arranged garden room.

Another springtime phenomenon found in a number of Bay Area gardens is the Lady Banks rose. At Elizabeth Gamble Garden Center the rose's breathtaking ascent adjacent to the parking area dazzles onlookers with a vast cover of vivacious blooms.

Demonstration and working gardens flank the right side of the entrance walkway. Featured here are annuals and perennials, an iris border and a salvia bed, a cutting garden, and espaliered fruit trees. A striking gazebo, the focal point within this section of the former Gamble estate, provides a pleasant place from where one can observe the enthusiastic involvement of the center's multigenerational participants and volunteers.

INFORMATION AND DIRECTIONS

The Elizabeth F. Gamble Garden Center, 1431 Waverley Street, Palo Alto, CA 94301. Phone 650-329-1356 for further information. Funded by contributions, the Gamble Garden Center's cluster of gardens are open to the public every day during daylight hours. The main house, a Colonial/Georgian Revival style building, is open to visitors weekdays from 9 A.M. to 12 noon. No fee. Individuals are welcome. Docent-guided tours for groups of eight or more are $3 per person; call ahead to reserve a place. Since the center is the site of many weddings and receptions, it's always best to phone before visiting to find out whether the formal gardens are taken up with a special event.

Located about one hour south of San Francisco. From Highway 101, proceed down Embarcadero Road to the stop light at Waverley Street. The garden center is on the southeast corner.

Filoli, Woodside

One of the country's most breathtaking estates, the impeccably maintained, lavishly planted formal gardens of Filoli should not be missed on your San Francisco Bay Area itinerary.

As described in one of Filoli's brochures, the motto "Fight, Love, Live" was drawn from William B. Bourn II's personal philosophy that one should "fight for a just cause, love your fellow man, live a good life." It was Bourn who bestowed the acronym, Filoli, upon his beloved country property south of San Francisco.

Owner of the Empire Mine, Bourn became enraptured in the early 1900s by the landscape near another of his businesses, the Spring Valley Water Company, because it reminded him of Ireland's Lakes of Killarney. After purchasing a substantial piece of land, Bourn selected architect Willis Polk to design an elegant English Georgian Revival mansion. Landscape designer Bruce Porter together with Isabella Worn were instrumental in planning and planting the sublime 16-acre gardens styled after grand European landscapes.

Mr. and Mrs. Bourn moved into their magnificent new home in 1917, where they both passed away nearly twenty years later in 1936. The following year, the estate became home to the Roths, who subsequently bequeathed Filoli to the National Trust for Historic Preservation.

Exuding a tremendous joie de vivre, the Filoli mansion and elaborate gardens present an intoxicating feast for the senses. Filoli's garden plan unfolds in a series of beautifully lush, walled garden rooms, with terraces and lawns, parterres and magnificent pools. The mansion itself features a U-shaped floor plan with two axes and a long hallway paralleling the valley beyond. The garden's overall design with its north-south axis repeats the line of the mansion's transverse hall.

A grove of olive trees line the front drive. Just north of the house, blue Atlas cedars impart a sylvan grace and coast live oaks ancient splendor. In the spring, Filoli's entry courtyard is fragrant with the scent of magnolias and bolstered by the alluring forms of Japanese maples. Everywhere one can see how the wonderful plan of the house and gardens celebrates the natural vegetation and vistas surrounding the estate.

The renowned Yew Allée exemplifies Filoli's grandeur. Unquestionably, it is these Irish yews, which were so close to William Bourn's heart, that impress all who come here. At Filoli more than two hundred of these yews are grown, all started from cuttings taken from William Bourn's daughter and son-in-law's home in Ireland, Muckross House. Along with yews, espaliered apple and pear trees lead to the High Place, a lovely open-air theater facing south where ancient columns form an inspiring backdrop.

Filoli opens its gates in early spring, when the mansion's clematis and wisteria-draped portico and terrace balustrades bid a riotous welcome. In February, March, and April, the grounds teem with gala exhibitions of tulips and daffodils, azaleas, camellias, wildflowers and blooming shrubs. Late spring brings forth glimmering dogwood and 'Sunburst' honeylocust, flowering cherries and glowing laburnums.

Where the outlines of reflecting pools, lawns, parterres, and brick paths frame perfectly complementary shapes, you will find another exceptional garden room: the Sunken Garden. Dramatic in scale, the Sunken Garden's design is a balancing act between meticulously groomed hedges, soaring trees, containers in profuse bloom, and classic ornamentation in the form of petite, cast lead water maidens. From here you can gaze at the vast hilly terrain visible in the distance.

In the knot gardens at Filoli, Celtic patterns are woven with emerald germander, violet-hued Japanese barberry, lavender, and silvery santolina, with its perky yellow flowers.

Designed by Arthur Brown, Jr., Filoli's tea house serves as an integral part of the estate's distinctive brick enclosure—the Walled Garden. Italian Renaissance in style, the Walled Garden holds a central place among Filoli's gardens. This partitioned realm encompasses three garden rooms, each one characterized by its own indelibly romantic ambiance.

In the Walled Garden, you'll find the Wedding Place and its fifteenth-century red marble Venetian fountain; the Dutch Garden, with rare New Zealand black beech trees and fine latticework; and a dazzling floral scene, the Chartres Cathedral Garden. Here, replicating a stained glass window are boxwood borders, English holly hedges, and flower beds filled with annuals and standard roses.

The property surrounding the estate is a haven of undeveloped woods and fields that can be explored on hikes with Filoli's nature docents. Filoli's Woodside microclimate, 25 miles or so south of San Francisco, is a near ideal environment for a garden of this caliber. Because William Bourn so appreciated this land, the vision of Bruce Porter and Isabella Worn was focused upon the sumptuous gardens visitors enjoy to this day. Interestingly, Isabella Worn remained involved in the plantings to the age of 81. Together with Filoli's owner and benefactor, Mrs. William P. Roth, the two lovingly nurtured the estate's gardens for decades, carrying on in the spirit of Bourn himself.

The glorious house and landscape of Filoli are now preserved and maintained in their estimable present-day condition under the auspices of the National Trust for Historic Properties, Filoli Center, and the Friends of Filoli, a congregation of avid volunteers.

INFORMATION AND DIRECTIONS

Filoli, Cañada Road, Woodside, California 94062. Filoli is open from mid-February through the first week of November. To visit Filoli, phone 650-364-8300, extension 507 for information, directions, and reservations for docent-led tours of the house, gardens, and nature hikes. Guided tours of the house and gardens are given on Tuesdays, Wednesdays, and Thursdays; reservations are required. Friday and Saturday are set aside for self-guided tours, no reservations necessary. Admission fee charged for all tours.

Located approximately 25 miles south of San Francisco and north of San Jose; 12 miles southwest of San Francisco Airport.

Hakone Gardens, Saratoga

Magnificent black stemmed, golden, and Japanese timber bamboo varieties are represented in a two-acre Bamboo Park, first incorporated into Saratoga's beautiful Hakone Gardens in 1987.

The summer residence of the Stine family, Hakone Gardens was established as a Japanese-style retreat in the early part of this century. In the 1930s, a subsequent owner, Major C.L.Tilden, built the gardens' main gate. Restoration work under the auspices of the City of Saratoga began in 1966, and today Hakone Gardens is praised for its estimable plantings and authentic design.

As early as January and February, visitors are treated to the entrancing blooms of flowering plum trees, camellias and azaleas, daphnes and violets. A sublime asymmetry contributes to Hakone's splendid terrain, where a sensitive balance is achieved between the varying dimensional forms and shallow shapes of the garden's design. Unlike the inherent regularity found in a formal Western garden plan, here no specific focal point or center is sought after. From the verandah of the Upper House, perched on the Moon Viewing Hill, you can observe waterfalls, the serpentine pathways of the hill and Pond Garden, and the mossy inclines of the Tea Garden. In the contemplative Zen Garden, patterns are created by bold stone shapes and raked gravel.

Among the gardens' imposing trees, Hinoki cypress, valley oak, Japanese red pine, and California laurel lend a quiet grandeur to the scene. A congregation of flowering cherries put forth abundant blossoms, while Japanese maples contribute rich, hued foliage and elegant forms.

The Bamboo Garden's central section—Kizuna-en—has fascinating woven fences that exemplify the binding of international friendships between the sister cities of Saratoga in the U.S. and Muko-shi in Japan. Be sure to pick up the informative printed brochure offered by The Japan Bamboo Society of Saratoga. It will help you understand the garden's symbolism, as well as learn more about the types and habits of bamboo plants.

INFORMATION AND DIRECTIONS

Hakone Gardens, 21000 Big Basin Way, Saratoga, CA 95070. For detailed directions, to confirm open hours, and for information on docent tours, or tea ceremony demonstrations, phone the Hakone Foundation at 408-741-4994. Or write the Hakone Foundation, P. O. Box 2324, Saratoga, CA 95070. Visiting hours are 10 A.M. to 5 P.M., weekdays; 11 A.M. to 5 P.M., weekends. Closed Christmas, Thanksgiving, and New Year's Day. Gift shop open 12:30 P.M. to 4 P.M. A parking fee is charged. Located approximately 1½ hours south of San Francisco.

Sunset Garden, Menlo Park

Sunset Publishing Corporation produces informative, enlightening garden-design books and how-to manuals. *Sunset* magazine features gardening topics among a wealth of beautifully photographed and illustrated articles on design, decorating, travel, and cuisine. Sunset's various publications function as essential references for serious Western gardeners and neophytes, alike, whether living in Seattle or Southern California.

Headquartered in Menlo Park, the company occupies early-California-style office buildings. Designed by Thomas Church, Sunset's expansive display garden integrates special areas representing various West Coast climates.

While one section acknowledges the wet, cold winters of the Pacific Northwest region, others are planted to reflect Northern California's milder climate, Central California's coastal environment, and the hot Central Valley. Another distinctive garden area celebrates the Southwest Desert and Southern California, concentrating on drought-tolerant perennials, cacti and succulent plants.

Befitting Sunset's laudable profile in the world of horticulture, the company's landscaping is impressive. Flower beds at Sunset Garden are replanted throughout the year with seasonal displays. A sweeping lawn is irrigated with well water. On this sunlit green carpet looms the commanding form of a coast live oak, with its enormous, lopsided limbs supported by steel posts. This tree alone is worth a visit to Sunset. To help maintain the venerable old tree's health, stones encircle its base to the edges of the drip line (a reminder of the live oak's intolerance of extra water once the season of wet weather has passed).

Be sure to investigate what's happening in the Test Garden, a 3,200-square-foot space where plants, garden projects, and new equipment are put to the test by Sunset staffers.

INFORMATION AND DIRECTIONS
Sunset Publishing Corporation, 80 Willow Road, Menlo Park, CA 94025-3691. Phone 650-321-3600 for further information. Visit the garden any workday between 9 A.M. and 4:30 P.M. and pick up "A Walking Tour of the Sunset Garden" pamphlet, for your self-guided exploration of the grounds. No fee.

Located about one hour south of San Francisco.

Villa Montalvo, Saratoga

Named for Garcia Ordoñez de Montalvo, a Spanish writer of the sixteenth century said to be responsible for naming California, Villa Montalvo exudes a rich historical presence in the midst of serene, pastoral surroundings. Situated near San Jose, at the base of the Santa Cruz Mountains, the villa is a fine example of Mediterranean design. On the property are also a guest house containing artist residency apartments, and an octagonal-shaped Carriage House and Art Gallery.

Built by James Duval Phelan in 1912, Villa Montalvo is currently home to a joyous flurry of artistic, musical and literary activity. Support for Villa Montalvo is gleaned from members' donations, corporate sponsorship, rental of facilities, special fundraising events and volunteers from the community. Encompassing 175 acres, the bucolic estate contains magnificent natural woodlands of oaks, redwoods, firs and eucalyptus, and miles of nature and hiking trails of varying difficulty. Spectacular views await hikers who pursue the fairly steep Lookout Trail to its final destination.

Reaching out to the community at large, Villa Montalvo offers readings, visual arts exhibitions mounted in a handsome gallery space, and a notable Performing Arts Season which draws an appreciative audience from throughout the Bay Area to its lovely outdoor amphitheater. Concerts are held at four locations: inside the Carriage House Theatre; outside in the Garden Theatre; on the large front lawn; and at the nearby historic Mountain Winery on Pierce Road.

Thrice mayor of San Francisco and a United States senator, Phelan reveled in the arts and enjoyed hosting talented friends and providing them with places to work and a stimulating intellectual climate.

He shared the tranquil beauty of his estate with many of his day's most celebrated writers and thespians. Phelan's legacy continues to this day with Villa Montalvo's thriving Artist Residency Program of international renown.

A timeless gardenscape graces Villa Montalvo's main building, where the picturesque design features classical statuary and manicured emerald lawns. Curving hedges trace discreet walkways, while low, mounded rock walls embrace fragrant lavender plantings. Visit in spring and be mesmerized by the villa's divine pergola lavishly draped in wisteria.

Explore the sprawling lawn and garden areas laid out to the front of Villa Montalvo and you'll arrive at a breathtaking vista, the Love Temple. Take a pause and contemplate this tiny, jewel-like pavilion, set among towering trees.

Whatever season you choose to visit, Montalvo will enchant you with Saratoga's forests' bracing bouquet, at once fresh and fragrant.

INFORMATION AND DIRECTIONS

Villa Montalvo, 15400 Montalvo Road, Saratoga, California, 95071-0158. Villa Montalvo Arboretum and County Park also comprise an Audubon Society bird sanctuary. Park open 7 days a week: Monday through Friday, 8 A.M. to 5 P.M.; Saturday, Sunday and Holidays, 9 A.M. to 5 P.M. No Fee. As Villa Montalvo is sometimes closed for special events, it's recommended that visitors call ahead. Phone 408-961-5800 for recorded information.

Located approximately 1½ hours south of San Francisco. Approach Villa Montalvo from the Saratoga-Los Gatos Road/Highway 9.

Yerba Buena Nursery, Woodside

Specializing in California native plants and ferns, Yerba Buena was founded by Gerda Isenberg in 1960, a true pioneer and proselytizer of the beauty and usefulness of natives. Current owner Kathy Crane carries on Isenberg's tradition of growing and propagating native species, and has also added all sorts of exciting plants to the nursery's 40 acres. Kathy's admirable, high-energy personality makes visiting Yerba Buena something special.

The nursery's two-acre Gerda Isenberg Native Plant Garden features accessible information cards, allowing visitors to identify plant origins (regions spanning California's shoreline to the Sierra range) and garden uses. Lathe houses, greenhouses, and venerable old buildings grace the Yerba Buena property, while the Garden Shop and the Tea Terrace offer respite from trekking about the beautiful Woodside landscape.

With more than 600 species represented, Yerba Buena is the perfect setting to learn about California's communities of resilient native plants. The helpful nursery staff will answer questions and provide explanations.

INFORMATION AND DIRECTIONS
Yerba Buena Nursery, Kathy Crane, owner, 19500 Skyline Blvd, Woodside, CA 94062. Nursery is open seven days a week, 9 A.M. to 5 P.M. Phone 650-851-1668 for information, directions, or to confirm open hours. Call ahead to make an appointment for weekday High Tea, or for guided tours of the nursery. The Tea Terrace is open weekends.

Approximately 1 hour and 15 minutes south of San Francisco, Yerba Buena is situated in the coastal hills above Woodside. It is within easy reach from the Filoli Estate, and not far from the Saratoga area, if you're planning a visit to Villa Montalvo and Hakone Gardens.

AND IN ADDITION . . .

Japanese Friendship Garden in Kelly Park: San Jose

1300 Senter Road, San Jose. Phone: 408-277-4191. Open every day; daylight hours from 10 A.M.; no admission fee. Visit this multi-leveled, Japanese stroll garden and enjoy its picturesque waterfalls and koi pond.

Japanese Tea Garden and Arboretum in Central Park: San Mateo

50 West 5th Avenue, San Mateo. Phone 650-377-3345. Open 10 A.M. to 4 P.M. weekdays; 11 A.M. to 4 P.M. weekends. No fee. Traditional Japanese garden landscape with tea house. Signs are provided to aid in identifying an appealing collection of trees in the Central Park Arboretum.

Overfelt Gardens: San Jose

2145 McKee Road at Educational Park Drive, San Jose. Phone 408-251-3323. Open every day from 10 A.M. to sunset. Mildred Overfelt bequeathed her property to the city of San Jose as a serene haven for nature lovers. A landscape of some 30 acres offers garden travelers a host of cultivated gardens and natural areas set amid lovely hilly scenery. Overfelt Gardens includes a wildlife sanctuary, as well as gardens devoted to fragrance and the state's native flora. A Chinese Cultural Center features a pavilion and distinctive landscaping.

Rengstorff House: Mountain View

Shoreline Park, Mountain View; located one mile off Highway 101 at the north end of Shoreline Boulevard. Grounds are open daily during daylight hours; no admission fee. Historic Victorian Rengstorff House was moved in 1980 from its original location to the present spot in the park. Mountain View's oldest home, the now splendidly restored house is surrounded by inviting gardens, all part of the Shoreline Park recreational area. In the park you'll find hiking trails, marshland and wildlife habitats, and a saltwater lake.

San Jose Municipal Rose Garden: San Jose

Naglee Avenue, between Dana Avenue and Garden Drive, San Jose. Open daylight hours; garden closes just before dusk. No admission fee. A particularly enticing landscape encircled by redwoods, San Jose's lovely rose garden has brought joy to the community for nearly seven decades. Surrounding the garden's pool and fountain are beds that burst into bloom as early as April.

RECOMMENDED LODGINGS

NORTH OF SAN FRANCISCO

Brookside Vineyard Bed & Breakfast, Napa

Traveling Napa roadways often means assuming your place in a motorcade of pilgrims determined to sample the products of every winery en route. Given correct directions and an advance reservation, however, you'll find a peaceful respite at this California Mission-style retreat tucked away outside the town of Napa in the heart of the wine country.

By the time we learned about Brookside Vineyard Bed & Breakfast, its three rooms were already booked. I had to content myself with strolling the grounds of the inn's intimate, sequestered setting, and chatting with the owners, Susan and Tom Ridley. (We made certain to reserve a room the next time we passed through the area!)

As you approach the inn along a tree-lined entry road, the home's sprawling form emerges amid regular rows of grapevines in the warmly colored Napa soil. Like a welcoming vision, it is an integral part of the pattern created by the linear plantings.

In their working vineyard, the Ridleys raise fine quality Chardonnay grapes which are sold to local wineries. Nestled in this intriguing landscape, Brookside Vineyard B&B offers guests quite a few surprises. Once settled into one of three spacious rooms, wander out back to glimpse the swimming pool area with its terraced gardens and lavish display of roses.

Lovingly tended grounds here invite repose. Whether you choose to sit by the pool and look out over towering oak and bay trees, or prefer to explore Brookside's grassy lawns, you'll find nothing contrived about Brookside Vineyard's landscape.

A hidden bench may persuade you to pause for a while, but take time to wander through the formidable stand of Douglas fir adjacent to the fruit orchard. The setting is simply wonderful for regrouping from the day's activities. Here you can take pleasure in gazing out over land that reaches back toward a meandering creek planted with native specimens.

While staying at Brookside you may decide to drop by McAllister Water Gardens, in nearby Yountville. The B&B's proximity to garden destinations, makes many wonderful day trips feasible.

INFORMATION AND DIRECTIONS

Brookside Vineyard Bed & Breakfast, 3194 Redwood Road, Napa, CA 94558. Contact Susan and Tom Ridley, innkeepers. Phone 707-944-1661; Fax 707-252-6690. The B&B offers three comfortable rooms with private baths. One features a fireplace, sauna, and private patio. Full breakfast served. Rates $105–135.

Brookside Vineyard is located about one hour north of San Francisco, just north of the town of Napa and west of Highway 29.

Carter House, Eureka

Celebrated for majestic ancient redwoods found both to the north and south, the seaport town of Eureka provides an invigorating rest from a scenic motor tour through the region's splendid forests and seashore.

Overlooking Humboldt Bay, the Carter House consists of a group of restored historic buildings. The antique furnishings and luxurious amenities make tasteful, unstuffy accommodations. It comes as a surprise that one of these handsome Victorians, the Hotel Carter, was actually constructed not so long ago by Mark Carter. A Eurekan by birth, Carter stayed true to Eureka's vernacular architecture in building this lovely complement to the original Carter House, located just across the street. The newly-renovated Bell Cottage presents a third alternative should you decide to book a room.

Carter House's highly praised gourmet cuisine draws countless callers to Humboldt's county seat. Weary travelers disembarking in Eureka applaud the mouth-watering repasts of Restaurant 301, open to the public and to hotel guests.

Touring the inn's bountiful organic kitchen gardens, a stone's throw away from the bay itself, is yet another pleasure of a stay here. Quite likely the largest garden of its kind, the Mediterranean-style plantings are harvested daily for fresh ingredients to be used in abundance by the hotel's chefs. Perusing the imaginative fare on a typical Restaurant 301 menu, you are likely to find a sumptuous assortment of edible flowers.

Over 30 species are cultivated in the Carter House garden, where an inviting symmetry distinguishes the garden's design. With centrally aligned birdbaths and fountain, the display features a sweeping rainbow of edible blooms that includes black pansies and signet marigolds, pinks and rose-scented geraniums, primroses and day lilies. The merry blooms of tubular nasturtiums and runner beans scale the heights of trellises, while jasmine drapes a beautiful arbor. In season, masses of flowers and irrepressible greens overflow their beds. Garden aficionados who are guests of the Carter House may inquire about assisting in harvesting the fruits and vegetables, blossoms and herbs that are used daily by the hotel restaurant.

INFORMATION AND DIRECTIONS

Carter House, 301 L Street, Eureka, California 95501. Contact Mark & Christi Carter, innkeepers. Phone 707-444-8062 or 800-404-1390. Rates: $165–$305 for a suite of rooms. All with private baths; full breakfasts served. To arrange a tour (April to December) of the Carter House garden with landscape designer, Dawn Rypkema, contact Carter House prior to visiting.

E-mail: carter52@carterhouse.com Web site: www.carterhouse.com

Carter House is located 300 hundred miles north of San Francisco and 75 miles south of the Oregon border. Highway 101 runs directly through Eureka, so whether journeying north from San Francisco, or south through Washington and Oregon, plan a stop-over at the Carter House.

Fetzer Vineyards Bed & Breakfast At Valley Oaks Ranch, Hopland

As if the area's stunning coastline and convenient access to the picturesque town of Mendocino are not attraction enough, Fetzer Vineyards presents garden travelers with the renowned Bonterra Garden (see Chapter 2, "Winery Gardens" for details), as well as Bed & Breakfast accommodations. Rooms at the Fetzer Vineyards' inn are located in the property's original carriage house, which has been recently converted with modern amenities.

A fabulous spot to unwind, Fetzer's B&B offers guests a comfortable, relaxed decor, and a pool in season. All rooms have patios from which you can admire the adjacent vineyards. The sublime five-acre, organically farmed Bonterra Garden will certainly prove to be a high point of any visit to the Valley Oaks Ranch.

Other delights include sampling Fetzer wines at the nearby Tasting Room and Visitor Center where picnicking on the center's terrace is the order of the day. Select from luscious gourmet fare available at Fetzer's deli, opened in 1996.

Alluring, landscaped grounds are a hallmark of Fetzer Vineyards.

Surrounding the Bed & Breakfast building and nearby Tasting Room and Visitor Center, are plantings of fragrant herbs such as lavenders, rue and artemisia varieties, thyme, marjoram and oregano, together with olive and fig trees, and superb pomegranates cloaked in lime green, burnished oval leaves.

INFORMATION AND DIRECTIONS

Fetzer Vineyards Bed & Breakfast, Hopland, CA 95449 (Mendocino County). For reservations, phone the Hospitality office at 1-800-846-8637. Seven rooms with private baths, continental breakfast, sequestered seasonal pool, patios with vineyard views. Room rate $120, suites $175.

Fetzer Vineyards Bed & Breakfast is located approximately two hours north of San Francisco and the Golden Gate Bridge.

Gerstle Park Inn, San Rafael

A gracious inn featuring elegant, yet unpretentious accommodations, Gerstle Park opened for business in December of 1995. Although the 1½-acre property in Marin County is within walking distance of downtown San Rafael, Gerstle Park's superb setting makes one feel miles away from the bustle of the town. Situated on a quiet cul-de-sac, the historic mansion and carriage house adjoin wooded parklands that are part of Marin County Open Space.

Built before the turn of the century, the inn's beautifully restored buildings are surrounded by giant oaks, cedars, and redwoods. The main house, which measures 6,800 square feet, contains eight spacious guest rooms, elegant parlors, a dining area, and a hospitable kitchen where guests will find delicious treats day and night. The appealing, fully-equipped one-bedroom suites located in the carriage house are ideal for an extended stay.

In this unexpectedly tranquil setting, brick walkways connect patios to garden areas where you can stroll undisturbed. Many rooms have decks or patio access that open onto the inn's interior gardens and beguiling hillside pasture. Deer are frequently seen in the upper orchard.

What makes Gerstle Park Inn so convenient is that one can retreat from the bustling activity of nearby tourist locales to enjoy this quiet haven, and still take advantage of day trips to coastal destinations, winery gardens, specialty nurseries, and public gardens that may be included in your itinerary. From here, San Francisco is readily accessible by car or ferry, Berkeley's gardens are within easy reach of the Richmond/San Rafael Bridge, and Sonoma's treasures are but a short drive north.

INFORMATION AND DIRECTIONS
Gerstle Park Inn, 34 Grove Street, San Rafael, CA 94901. Contact Jim and Judy Dowling, innkeepers. Phone 800-726-7611 or 415-721-7611. 12 rooms, including cottages with kitchen facilities for extended stays. All with private bath; full breakfast included. Rates $139–$199.
E-mail: innkeeper@gerstleparkinn.com Web site: www.gerstlepark inn.com
The inn is located approximately 20 minutes north of San Francisco's Golden Gate Bridge.

The Inn At Occidental, Occidental

Snuggled amid densely wooded terrain surrounding the town, the Inn At Occidental is a classic example of a restored Victorian Bed & Breakfast. This Victorian inn is at once elegant, yet pleasantly genial in feeling and decor. Innkeeper Jack Bullard has planted a colorful cottage garden that's a perfect spot for languishing when the mood strikes.

Approaching the inn's entryway, I paused to admire a magnificent variegated snow-on-the-mountain, *Euphorbia marginata*, with its dense, bright tangle of foliage spilling over the stairway. On the coral-stone paved border around the lush green lawn, you'll find commodious lawn chairs and chaises. Standing center stage is a moss covered fountain. Lavishly planted containers add further color and bloom to the scene.

INFORMATION AND DIRECTIONS
The Inn at Occidental, 3657 Church Street, P O Box 857, Occidental, CA 95465. Contact Jack Bullard, innkeeper. Phone 707-874-1047 or 800-522-6324; Fax 707-874-1078. Eight rooms with private baths; full breakfast served. Rates $180–$270.
E-mail: innkeeper@innatoccidental.com Web site: www.innatoc cidental.com
The inn is located north of San Francisco, about one hour drive from the Golden Gate Bridge.

Madrona Manor, Healdsburg

Listed as a National Historic District, Madrona Manor offers wonderfully genteel accommodations in an elegant country atmosphere. The inn consists of the main building—a distinctive Victorian mansion built in 1881—and the adjacent Carriage House, the Garden Cottage, and the Meadow Wood Complex. Madrona Manor's guest rooms are adorned with Persian carpets, and stately rosewood tables, chairs, and architectural trimmings from Nepal, which were custom-ordered by the former innkeepers while they were living in the Middle East. Guests are liable to become enamored with the widely acclaimed three-star restaurant housed in the mansion.

The garden setting here is especially irresistible, with eight acres of well-groomed lawns, a palm terrace, formal flower beds decorated with fountains, dignified woodlands, urns and winsome ornamentation. Surrounded by a noble balustrade, the manor's swimming pool presents a restful spot from where one can view the landscape's orderly citrus orchard and lively floral displays. Daffodils herald the coming of spring, along with fragrant sweet peas, fields of mustard, and tulips that encircle a group of camellias.

Head gardener, Geno Ceccato can be counted on to provide the innkeepers with ample material for indoor arrangements. Continually cultivating new species, Geno plants prominent annuals such as cleome and amaranthus to add character, verve, and a rather playful element to flower beds. Scarlet and lavender salvias, multicolored cosmos, morning glory vines, and impatiens are all used at times to adorn slopes, free standing fences, and borders.

Appetizing herbs are interspersed with various edibles in a lovely terraced culinary garden, another laboratory of sorts for Ceccato. In the fall, he might cultivate 15 varieties of lettuce for salads served at the manor's restaurant, along with baby carrots, beets, snow peas, and greens. Regardless of the season, the manor's splendid kitchen garden and grounds are a pleasure to behold.

Madrona Manor presents an excellent vantage point for touring the acclaimed Korbel Garden located in nearby Guerneville, and the stunning Ferrari-Carano Winery landscape in Dry Creek Valley.

INFORMATION AND DIRECTIONS

Madrona Manor, 1001 Westside Road, P. O. Box 818, Healdsburg, CA 95448. Contact Joseph and Maria Hadley, innkeepers. Phone 707-

433-4231 or 800-258-4003 (Fax 707-433-0703). 21 rooms; full breakfast included. Rates $195–$330.

E-mail: info@madronamanor.com Web site: www.madronaman or.com

Located 65 miles north of San Francisco in Sonoma County's Wine Country.

Sandy Cove Inn, Inverness

In business for the past six years, Sandy Cove Inn adjoins Tomales Bay in Marin county's secluded hamlet of Inverness. A "green" philosophy rules at Sandy Cove, where the Coles have built their home and inn on land that has never been sprayed with any form of pesticide or herbicide. Priding itself on maintaining a smoke-free environment, Sandy Cove Inn entices stressed-out urbanites "to get in tune with nature" in a garden landscape that neither dominates area wildlife, nor attempts to overpower native vegetation.

The inn's Cape Cod style buildings are surrounded by perfectly poised meadows and pasture lands. Here you'll find a horse barn for Chewy, and the pony, Truffles, gardens, and wooded areas that create a buffer zone between the road running outside the property and the peaceful inn. You can also enjoy the company of the resident sheep, Bummer and Beep. A handsome pair, they're especially adept at following Kathy around, and efficiently vacuuming up weeds as quickly as she tosses them aside.

Gardeners will be able to appreciate the proprietors' efforts to establish a peaceful coexistence with the area's healthy deer population. Kathy told me that they had a good degree of success planting deer-proof herbs and flowers, pointing out vigorous borders of "rabbit-ear" lavender, a long-blooming variety selected by a neighbor from across the bay, and beds overflowing with a profusion of calla lilies.

In a circular ornamental garden begun in 1996, a double, four-foot high fence protects a selection of showier flowers for indoor bouquets, and assorted vegetables and herbs that deer like to eat. Ash from fireplaces, seaweed, manure and other organic plant matter are composted and used to enrich the property's soil which is made up of decomposed granite.

Before breakfast or at twilight, glance out your window or just step outside and you'll observe deer roaming about Sandy Cove's

65

four acres. You can walk through the grassy meadows down to a sandy stretch of Tomales Bay to beachcomb or investigate the heron rookery found close by. Luminous views promise to clear the mind.

In the immediate area of Sandy Cove, you'll find easy access to kayaks, canoes, whale-watching, and some of the best birding in the country. I found watching the California quails cavort particularly charming. Coveys of California's native quail often appear in a grassy clearings on the grounds of the inn, only to dart off into the scrub when a human interloper approaches. Their presence is an exhilarating reminder of the pristine nature of Sandy Cove's bucolic refuge.

Garden travelers are drawn to the inn's proximity to Point Reyes National Seashore, with its scenic, unspoiled hiking trails. Wildflower enthusiasts can spend hours engaged in identifying a wealth of flowering species and native grasses. Sandy Cove is also an idyllic base for exploring a variety of garden destinations—from Garden Valley Ranch (Petaluma's paradise for rose fanciers), to mellow nurseries in Bolinas and Sebastopol.

INFORMATION AND DIRECTIONS

Sandy Cove Inn, Box 869, 12990 Sir Francis Drake Blvd., Inverness, CA. 94937. Contact Kathy and Gerry Coles, innkeepers. Phone 415-669-2683 or 800-759-2683; Fax: 415-669-7511. The inn has three warmly decorated private suites, with a woodburning stove or fireplace; valley views; refrigerator, coffeemaker, and music system. Rates $130–$250; lower without breakfast. Note that breakfasts served at the inn include fresh organic flowers, herbs, produce from the Sandy Cove gardens, as well as locally purchased, hormone-free dairy products. The philosophy behind the room decor is to "leave some room for the person." Although maximum comfort is offered, you will not be overwhelmed by a highly decorated design scheme or unnecessary flourishes.

E-mail: Innkeeper@sandycove.com Web site: www.sandycove.com
Located approximately one hour north of San Francisco.

Ten Inverness Way Bed & Breakfast, Inverness

Delightfully cozy, Ten Inverness Way calls itself the perfect inn for people who like books, long walks, and cottage gardens. Located in the enchanting environs of Marin County's village of Inverness, the inn is a civilized hostelry, which displays a lush, if diminutive, garden in the rear.

For a relaxing soak after a day spent wandering around the Point Reyes Seashore, try the hot tub found in the garden cottage located just a few yards up the walkway.

INFORMATION AND DIRECTIONS

Ten Inverness Way, P O Box 63, Inverness, CA. 94937. Phone 415-669-1648. Contact Teri & Scott Mowery, innkeepers. Four rooms plus one small suite; queen beds, private baths, full breakfast served. Rates $145–$185.

Web site: www.teninvernessway.com E Mail: inn@teninverness way.com

Located about one hour north of San Francisco.

SOUTH OF SAN FRANCISCO

Mill Rose Inn, Half Moon Bay

Esteemed for its lovely beaches and arty ambiance, the seaside town of Half Moon Bay entices garden lovers to its charming main street where frequent flower markets overflow onto the town's walkways. A stay in Half Moon Bay also affords easy access to Woodside and the ravishing estate, Filoli, with its grand house and extraordinary gardens.

A visit to The Mill Rose Inn promises fetching flower beds and borders, indoor vases, and outdoor planters filled with a frequently changing array of scented, showy blooms. Rooms are appointed in a romantic style, with a delicious breakfast served in your suite if you so choose. To cap off your day, sumptuously rich desserts are provided in the evening.

INFORMATION AND DIRECTIONS

Mill Rose Inn, 615 Mill Street, Half Moon Bay, CA 94019. Contact Eve and Terry Baldwin, innkeepers. Phone 650-726-8750 or 800-900-ROSE (7673); Fax 650-726-3031. Six rooms with private baths, full breakfasts, feather beds, and garden views. Rates $165–$285. *Web Site: www.millroseinn.com*

Located about 35 minutes south of San Francisco; 25 minutes from San Francisco International Airport.

Rancho San Gregorio Bed & Breakfast, San Gregorio

Located just five miles inland from the Pacific ocean, this homestyle inn with wood stoves and cozy quilts offers a comfortable, quiet re-treat from civilization. Many flowering potted plants and a profusion of herbs decorate Rancho San Gregorio's lovely patio. Beyond are 15 idyllic acres adorned with pineapple guava and a wealth of fruiting trees, wild blackberries, native plant species, and fields brimming with wild flowers.

Visit in late spring and you may be fortunate enough to behold the wild red trilliums appearing down by the creek. Whenever you visit Rancho San Gregorio, the enthralling countryside setting of this rural valley provides a tranquil counterpoint to nearby sites such as the majestic Filoli, the Heritage Redwood Grove, or Pescadero Beach with its tidal pools and marshlands.

INFORMATION AND DIRECTIONS

Rancho San Gregorio, 5086 La Honda Road (Highway 84), Rt 1 Box 54, San Gregorio, CA 94074. Contact Bud and Lee Raynor, Innkeep-ers. Phone 650-747-0810. Fax: 650-747-0184. Four rooms with private baths. Country breakfasts feature home-made jams, and seasonal home-grown fruit. Rates $85–$145.

Located approximately one hour south of San Francisco.

CALIFORNIA

SANTA CRUZ TO SANTA BARBARA

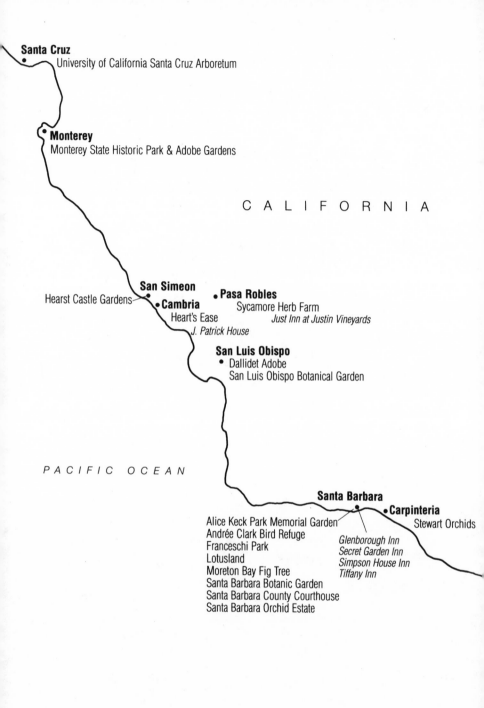

Santa Cruz
University of California Santa Cruz Arboretum

Monterey
Monterey State Historic Park & Adobe Gardens

C A L I F O R N I A

San Simeon
Hearst Castle Gardens
Cambria
Heart's Ease
J. Patrick House

Pasa Robles
Sycamore Herb Farm
Just Inn at Justin Vineyards

San Luis Obispo
Dallidet Adobe
San Luis Obispo Botanical Garden

P A C I F I C   O C E A N

Santa Barbara
Carpinteria
Stewart Orchids
Alice Keck Park Memorial Garden
Andrée Clark Bird Refuge
Franceschi Park
Lotusland
Moreton Bay Fig Tree
Santa Barbara Botanic Garden
Santa Barbara County Courthouse
Santa Barbara Orchid Estate

Glenborough Inn
Secret Garden Inn
Simpson House Inn
Tiffany Inn

7

Central Coast Gardens

Hearst Castle Gardens, San Simeon

The heir to an immense fortune, newspaper tycoon and art collector William Randolph Hearst is perhaps best remembered for creating one of the world's foremost private estates. Christened "La Cuesta Encantada" ("The Enchanted Hill") by Hearst, the palatial estate generally referred to as Hearst Castle, or San Simeon, endures as one of our nation's best known landmarks.

Among private estates, Hearst Castle is arguably unequaled in grandeur. Its extravagant architecture has, at times, been labeled excessive by past critics. However, Hearst Castle is now being reexamined by historians who see it in the appropriate context of the era in which it was created—America's Gilded Age. Since 1958 Hearst San Simeon has been a State Historical Monument operated and maintained by the California State Parks. Perched atop a lofty knoll in the Santa Lucia Mountains of California's Central Coast, the estate actually comprises 165 rooms and 127 acres of gardens, terraces, and pools. Astounding dimensions and eclectic design reflecting Italian, Spanish, and Moorish traditions are hallmarks of Casa Grande, the main building, and the property's equally dramatic guest houses. These so-called "cottages," named Casa del Mar, Casa Del Monte, and Casa Del Sol, pay homage to the sea, the mountains, and the sun.

Esteemed San Francisco Bay Area architect Julia Morgan worked with Hearst for nearly three decades of never-ending construction and landscaping to realize this extravagant dream. Specialized craftsmen and innumerable laborers toiled from 1919 until 1947 building, as well as continually evolving Hearst's fascinating Mediterranean Revival estate.

Still bedazzling visitors today are Hearst's vast collections of venerable art; stunning antique furnishings from Spain, Italy, and France; commissioned works such as ornate, decorative ceilings; and the castle's exalted grounds. Planning a visit involves selecting one of five separate tours that focus on various areas in the castle, grounds and cottages. Tour 4 is of special interest to garden lovers. Presented from April through October, it gives an overview of San Simeon's landscape, along with selected highlights of the estate. All tours offer views of two remarkable swimming pools: the outdoor marble and tile Neptune Pool; and the exquisitely designed indoor Roman Pool, with its luminescent Venetian glass tiles, and accent tiles of opulent gold leaf.

On Tour 4, when you view the magnificent esplanade, terraces, and elaborate walkways, the guides explain how W. R. Hearst placed particular emphasis on planning and planting the gardens of La Cuesta Encantada. Unquestionably, Hearst believed the landscape was of equal importance to the estate's majestic exteriors and sumptuous interior decor.

Although Julia Morgan devised the garden's planting plans, various distinguished landscape architects and designers were also called upon. Horticultural authorities and advisers involved in San Simeon's landscaping include Bruce Porter, who suggested ideas for layouts and plantings, and Isabella Worn, who contributed ideas for stylish color schemes. William Randolph Hearst, of course, requested his personal preferences for flowers, as well as for specific shrubs and trees.

Historical documents indicate reams of correspondence between Hearst and Morgan, concerning issues involving the gardens of his hilltop sanctuary. Before any planting of the estate's fabulous gardens could go forward, tons of topsoil had to be imported to the site's rocky hilltop. Because Hearst wanted the semblance of a forested surround, thousands of trees were planted Often, laborers had to dynamite a hole before planting could even take place.

Hearst was known to have spent $18,000 (a truly exorbitant sum at the time) to move a revered old native oak tree to a prominent position. When Morgan suggested planting Mexican fan palms to bring a soaring, picturesque quality to the setting, her employer, who was already 56 years old, decided to purchase 25-foot specimens rather than wait for smaller trees to grow.

In contrast to the commanding mature trees, note the charming cascades of jasmine mingling with pink polyantha roses; delightful purple lantana spilling over retaining walls; and heritage varieties of old-fashioned annuals. Hearst had a penchant for hollyhocks and sweet peas, and enjoyed a lush, informal style of planting. Lantana coupled with the blushing, pansy-like flowers and trailing foliage of ivy geraniums was one of his favorite combinations.

The Garden Tour (Tour 4) also offers unforgettable impressions of the landscape's formal framework The dashing forms of Italian cypresses are particularly striking, as the trees' evenly-spaced columnar appearance essentially mirrors the Neptune Pool's breathtaking backdrop—a Greco-Roman temple facade glorified by six dynamic vertical columns. Decorating a circular walk are mixed hedges of clipped boxwood and fragrant myrtle which enclose a collection of roses grown as standards. The Fuchsia Walk, dubbed "Lover's Lane" by Hearst's friend Cary Grant, displays numerous varieties of ornamental fuchsias with dangling blooms.

After visiting the gardens of Italy, Hearst wrote Julia Morgan that he wanted to expand the terraces. Today, walks along the promenade, terraces and walkways of Hearst's gardens hold the promise of wonderful memories. You'll behold classical sculpture, radiant statuary, and unique fountains ornamenting the artistically arranged flora at Hearst's incomparable La Cuesta Encantada.

INFORMATION AND DIRECTIONS
Hearst Castle—Hearst San Simeon State Historical Monument, San Simeon, CA 93452. Reservations are recommended and may be made by calling 800-444-4445, seven days a week from 8:00 A.M. to 5:00 P.M. PST. Tickets are sold for specific tour times. Garden tours (Tour 4) are offered from April 1 through October 31, and again, reservations are recommended because tours often sell out in advance. Fee charged. The castle is open year-round, seven days a week, except Thanksgiving, Christmas, and New Year's Day.

Hearst Castle is located on California Highway 1, approximately midway between San Francisco and Los Angeles, six hours from either city.

Heart's Ease Herb Shop & Gardens, Cambria

Founded by garden writer and illustrator Sharon Lovejoy, Heart's Ease Herb Shop and its adjacent gardens are currently owned and operated by Susan Pendergast. Susan admirably carries on the traditions and educational goals of this delightful enterprise.

Located in the village of Cambria, on California's Central Coast, the Heart's Ease Herb Shop is housed in an original Victorian cottage. Well-known to devotees of herb culture and crafts, Heart's Ease stocks a bounty of herbal gift items, along with gardening implements, and a number of books for gardeners and nature lovers. The shop also carries a wealth of products and preparations made from both dried and fresh herbs. Alongside the charming blue building, you'll find the Heart's Ease Nursery. Here new plant stock is propagated from cuttings taken from the gardens' own mother plants, or procured from local growers of rare herbs and perennials. Then, the stock is either sold or planted in the gardens. Featured are California natives, cottage garden flowers, and many herbs.

The Heart's Ease Gardens were successfully recouped from parking lots when the property was purchased by Sharon Lovejoy. On the lilliputian ¼ acre they occupy, you can explore traditional theme gardens: the Bee Garden and Grey Garden, a tiny Knot Garden, Culinary & Medicinal gardens, and a Tot's Garden. The earliest garden beds were designed and planted about 14 years ago. Since then, another parcel of property was acquired, on which now stands a permanent children's sunflower house, cloaked in lively seasonal vines.

Heart's Ease offers a stimulating environment where kids can learn about the natural world. There's a worm bin to fascinate young visitors, and the new Peter Rabbit Garden to encourage future gardeners.

Annual events include both a Faerie Festival and a Rosemary Festival. To commemorate these celebrations, Sharon Lovejoy wrote and illustrated booklets that continue to be sold at the shop. With their melding of fantasy, plant lore, and hands-on projects, the booklets thrill youngsters and intrigue older readers.

If planning a tour of the Central Coast region, or a visit to Hearst Castle and its gardens, don't fail to stop at the delightful Heart's Ease Gardens in nearby Cambria.

INFORMATION AND DIRECTIONS

Heart's Ease Herb Shop & Gardens, 4101 Burton Drive (the town's main historic street), Cambria, CA 93428. Susan Pendergast, proprietor. Phone 800-266-4372 or 805-927-5224 to confirm open hours or for further information. Shop and gardens are open to the public at 10 A.M., seven days a week.

Located approximately four hours from San Francisco or Los Angeles. Take Highway 46 West from Highway 101. Cambria is located at Pacific Coast Highway 1, just south of Hearst Castle San Simeon.

Sycamore Herb Farm, Paso Robles

A Basil Festival and a Mozart concert are just a few of the events sponsored by the Shomlers' four-acre Sycamore Herb Farm. Established seven years ago, the farm has a large display garden devoted to culinary and medicinal herbs. Aromatic herbs such as sage and thyme, rosemary, lavender, and Mediterranean Bay grow contentedly here. An extensive retail nursery features over 350 varieties of potted herbs. Fresh cut herbs, generally ten or so varieties, are available throughout the year.

Overall the property encompasses 40 acres of rolling and terraced hills. In addition to the herb farm, there is a large irrigation pond and a 30-acre vineyard where roussanne and syrah grapes are grown and harvested for the Bonny Doon Winery of Santa Cruz. A tasting room on the premises features Bonny Doon wines. A gift and garden shop is located in the barn building.

Two seasons of classes and workshops instruct participants in the culinary and medicinal uses for herbs. There always seems to be something to sample and savor for visitors who stop by to purchase plants, or to pick up tips on growing and cultivating herbs.

Put your name on the Sycamore Herb Farm mailing list in order to receive their entertaining *Gazette,* which covers events and provides recipes and descriptions of the special products you can order from the farm (i.e., comfrey healing balm, culinary herb seeds and vegetable seeds). The newsletter also features interesting articles, such as a recent one titled "Ancient Herbalism," which discussed the importance of herbs in societies as diverse as ancient Greece, Rome, and the New World.

In the *Sycamore Gazette,* you'll also find lists of herbs for specific theme gardens. For example, for a Butterfly Herb Garden, the *Gazette* recommends planting catmint, butterfly bush, golden butterfly bush, hyssop, licorice mint, and bee balm.

INFORMATION AND DIRECTIONS

Sycamore Herb Farm, 2485 Highway 46 West, Paso Robles, CA 93446. Bruce and Sandy Shomler, proprietors. Phone 805-238-5288, or 800-576-5288 for further information. Fax 805-238-2187. Open 10 A.M. until 5 P.M. daily; closed major holidays.

Located approximately 30 miles north of San Luis Obispo; three miles west of Highway 101 on State Highway 46 West (leading to Cambria and Hearst Castle).

University Of California Santa Cruz Arboretum, Santa Cruz

Located on the grounds of the University of California at Santa Cruz, the 135-acre arboretum displays significant and extensive collections of species from the Southern Hemisphere. Here you'll find geographically arranged sections devoted to the flora of Australia, New Zealand, South Africa, South America, and California natives.

Begun in 1964 with some 90 species of eucalyptus, the arboretum is now a showcase for Australian plants. Important genera such as grevilleas not only flaunt their showy flower clusters but—to the delight of area gardeners—they are some of the few plants deer don't eat. So odd and unlike the shrubs and trees of North America, the plants one sees in the arboretum's Slosson Gardens are a study in botanical contrasts. Look for eye-catching exhibitions of spectacular banksias. These evergreen species often bear countless small flowers that blanket large cone forms. Seek out the grevilleas, too. Varying from low-growing, spreading types to trees 20-feet tall, this large group of sun-loving species sports attractive finely-textured foliage. You'll find numerous shrubs in flower all year long in the Elvenia J. Slosson Garden, and in particular from January through April.

Discover one of the arboretum's highlights in the Dean & Jane McHenry Garden, where an outstanding collection of ancient proteas from South Africa astonish visitors with their stunning colors and silky, floss-like textures. Queen proteas are familiar to many who search florists shops for unusual flowers for arrangements. Oleander-leaved proteas also known as pink minks (*Protea neriifolia*), and ray-flowered proteas (*Protea eximia*) will charm you with their other-worldly beauty. Look also for the colorful, long, dangling blooms and delicate bells of Cape heaths in the fantastic displays of the South Africa section.

In the arboretum, you'll find many more wonderful gardens: the Primitive Flowering Plants, an Aroma Garden, a Cactus and Succulent Garden, and a Eucalyptus Grove. Here, too, Mediterranean regions offer instructive presentations of drought-tolerant plants. Fortunate California gardeners can both appreciate the aesthetic pleasures of the UCSC Arboretum and glean tips for growing attractive species that lend themselves to a regimen of water-conservation. Garden lovers from other areas or climes who cannot hope to grow many of the arboretum's species will still feel blessed to explore a landscape overflowing with such rare and wondrous flora. Superb vistas of the Pacific Ocean and Monterey Bay are yet another incentive to visit the UCSC Arboretum.

INFORMATION AND DIRECTIONS
University of California Santa Cruz Arboretum, 1156 High Street, Santa Cruz, CA 95064. Phone 831-427-2998 for information. Open every day from 9 A.M. to 5 P.M.; closed Thanksgiving and Christmas Day. No admission fee; donations gratefully accepted. Norrie's Gift Shop is open Tuesday through Saturday, 10 A.M. to 4 P.M.; Sundays, 1 P.M. to 4 P.M. *Web site: www2.ucsc.edu/arboretum*

Located off Highway 1, five minutes north of downtown Santa Cruz. From town, follow Bay Street up to the UCSC campus; go left on High Street about ½ mile to the arboretum.

AND IN ADDITION . . .

Dallidet Adobe: San Luis Obispo
1185 Pacific Street near Santa Rosa Street, San Luis Obispo, CA. Phone the San Luis Obispo County Historical Society for information on Wednesday through Sunday, 10 A.M. to 4 P.M. at 805-543-0638. Visit a vivacious garden surrounding the historical (circa 1850) adobe dwelling of French vintner Pierre Hyppolite Dallidet, bequeathed to the Historical Society by his descendant, Paul Dallidet. Open during summer Sundays from 1 P.M. to 4:30 P.M.

Monterey State Historic Park & Adobe Gardens
of Old Town Monterey: Monterey
Monterey State Historic Park, Custom House Plaza, Monterey, CA 93940. Open daily from 10 A.M. to 4 P.M.; closed Thanksgiving, Christmas, and New Year's Day. Tours through the historic adobes and walking tours of old Monterey are offered daily at various times; fee charged. Garden tours are given every Tuesday and Saturday, May through September at 1 P.M.; $5 fee. Phone State Historic Parks at 831-649-7118 for details regarding tours of Monterey's Secret Gardens

(tour times may change; call to obtain up-to-date information). The walking tours offer insight into the significance and history of the gardens and surrounding adobe homes. Visitors can wander around the gardens that are part of the Monterey State Historic Park without taking a tour and at no charge.

Monterey Peninsula *Web sites: www.mty.com & www.monterey. com* Monterey State Historic Park *Web site: www.mbay.net/~mshp*

San Luis Obispo Botanical Garden: San Luis Obispo

Located at El Chorro Regional County Park, on State Highway 1, between San Luis Obispo and Morro Bay, the botanical gardens are halfway between Los Angeles and San Francisco and about seven miles from the ocean. At the time of this writing, the San Luis Obispo Botanical Garden was in its Preview Garden stage. The one-acre site suggested the wonderful things to come in future years. Overall, 150 acres have been slated for the development of a world-class botanical garden, which will highlight plants from five Mediterranean climate zones. Special events are scheduled on the second Saturday of each month from April through November, 1 to 4 P.M. Phone 805-546-3501 for updates and information; or write to Friends of San Luis Obispo Botanical Garden, P. O. Box 4957, San Luis Obispo, CA 93403. *Web site: www.fix.net/~cdills/slogarden/*

8

Santa Barbara Gardens

Alice Keck Park Memorial Garden, Santa Barbara

Donated to the city of Santa Barbara by Alice Keck, the land of the Memorial Garden that bears the benefactress's name is surely one of the most charming city park settings imaginable. Occupying one square city block in a town recognized for its exuberant gardens, Alice Keck Garden is a horticultural haven with an imposing collection of trees. The garden's idealized landscape incorporates an inviting pond, complete with a fantasy island and beckoning palms. Low-water gardening is advanced in a series of abundant plantings that demonstrate various types of microclimates found in the semi-arid Santa Barbara region.

On my first view of the Alice Keck Memorial Garden while driving by the corner of Micheltorena and Garden streets, I was astonished to see a spectacular sprawling Australian tea tree (*Leptospermum laevigatum*).

When I returned to contemplate this fantastic gnarled form, I found a wealth of flowering trees, including Hong Kong orchid (*Bauhinia blakeana*) and Brazilian orchid (*Bauhinia forficata*) trees; sweetshades (*Hymenosporum flavum*); and Natal coral trees (*Erythrina humeana*), a South African native with brilliant orange-red flowers from August through November.

One particularly strange apparition in this garden of arboreal delights is the floss-silk tree (*Chorisia speciosa*). A South American species characterized by thorny trunks and branches, the floss-silk tree produces vivid flowers resembling hibiscus in fall, with seed pods that contain kapok.

Highlights of the garden include the Dry Creek Bed, where during May for example, the section sparkles with the foliage and flowers of rockrose and snow-in-summer. Also growing in this alluring area are lamb's ears, salvia, and mounds of heliotrope, which are set off by the contrasting textures of ornamental grasses, yellow trumpet vine, and a graceful Gold Medallion tree (*Cassia leptophylla*).

The garden's perennial borders exhibit profusely blooming pincushion flowers and Jupiter's beard, intermingled with outrageous angel's trumpet and climbing roses. In another garden section, after the freesias, bluebells, and winter irises die back, a fragrant herbal melange of catmint, thyme and lavender, enhanced by trailing white gazania and the dainty flowers of ground morning glory, follows.

In another garden realm that celebrates sunny sites, you can admire the pale silvery foliage of artemisia, which appears luminescent against a low-growing form of rosemary. Pindo, triangle, and Mediterranean fan palms add elements of dramatic structure to this garden's visually arresting framework.

INFORMATION AND DIRECTIONS

Alice Keck Park Memorial Garden is on the 1500 block of Garden Street, between Micheltorena and Arrellaga streets. For further information write to: City of Santa Barbara, Parks & Recreation Department, P. O. Box 1990, Santa Barbara, CA 93102-1990. Open sunrise to sunset. No fee.

Located in central Santa Barbara.

Andrée Clark Bird Refuge, Santa Barbara

Birds are often found to congregate in, or at least pass through, places of abundant plant life. Originally a tidal marsh, the 42-acre Andrée Clark Bird Refuge was purchased by the city of Santa Barbara in 1909 for public enjoyment. By 1928, Mrs. Huguette Clark gave the city funds to create an artificial lake as a bird refuge dedicated to the memory of her late sister.

Today, the Andrée Clark Bird Refuge is one of Santa Barbara's most agreeable parks, with its sparkling lagoon and inviting footpath that wraps around the water's perimeter. While the south shore of the lagoon emphasizes Santa Barbara's diverse horticulture, the north shore shows a more naturalistic style of landscaping. You'll find that, as part of Santa Barbara's Parks Department's revegetation project, north shore habitats such as a freshwater marsh, a coastal sage scrub, riparian and oak woodlands, have been planted with a variety of native species.

Enjoy the serene setting at the Andrée Clark Bird Refuge, and spend some time observing a variety of freshwater birds. At the city's request, signs have been posted for visitors not to feed the ducks or other birds, because it severely degrades the water quality.

INFORMATION AND DIRECTIONS

Andrée Clark Bird Refuge, 1400 East Cabrillo Boulevard, Santa Barbara. Parking on the north side of the lagoon. Open daily, sunrise to sunset; admission is free.

Located near the intersection of Cabrillo Boulevard and Highway 101.

Franceschi Park, Santa Barbara

High in the hills of Santa Barbara, a segment of property originally purchased in 1904 by Italian botanist Dr. Francesco Franceschi is now the site of Franceschi Park. Offering breathtaking panoramic views of the pristine coastline, this Santa Barbara city park attracts both horticulture buffs from out-of-town, and locals who appreciate the park's magnificent locale.

The one-time proprietor of a plant nursery, Dr. Franceschi is famous for introducing new plants to the area, and continues to be celebrated for the botanical collection of rare specimens surviving in the park that carries his name. When you visit, look for signs pointing out the many handsome trees, including Australian species such as the lemon-scented Gum tree (*Eucalyptus citriodora*), the Grass tree (*Xanthorrhoea arborea*), as well as Canary Island date palms (*Phoenix canariensis*).

Visitors can enjoy the park's brick patio and use the picnic tables overlooking the city. From here, one sees phenomenal vistas extending from the Colonnade of Palms lining the Ocean drive, to the surrounding communities, and distant Channel Islands.

The glory days of Dr. Franceschi's estate are past, but the City of Santa Barbara Parks Department, along with members of the Santa Barbara Horticultural Society, continue to care for the important flora assembled at the park. One semicircular overlook embellished by a wrought iron railing can still transport a garden traveler like myself to an elegant era when the park was an aesthetic proving ground for Dr. Franceschi's experimental plantings.

INFORMATION AND DIRECTIONS

Franceschi Park, 1510 Mission Ridge Road, Santa Barbara, California. The park is a pleasant place to have a picnic, but note that picnic areas are subject to advance reservation. If you plan on picnicking, call the City Parks and Recreation Department at 805-564-5418, to find out whether picnic sites are still available. Open sunrise to sunset. No fee.

Located in the hills of Santa Barbara.

Ganna Walska Lotusland, Santa Barbara

The images of a sensual kingdom invoked by the "Lotusland" name can only pale in comparison to the actual realm created by Madame Ganna Walska. Unquestionably one of the country's great gardens, Lotusland stretches over 37 acres located in Montecito, adjacent to Santa Barbara. The origins of the gardens trace back to 1882 when nurseryman R. Kinton Stevens began planting exotic subtropical trees, palms, and rare specimen plants at his nursery and home, known by the early 1890s as Tanglewood.

Subsequent landowners Mr. and Mrs. E. Palmer Gavit called their estate "Cuesta Linda." On this property, they had Reginald Johnson design a handsome Spanish Colonial Revival style residence in 1919. Not long afterward, Santa Barbara architect George Washington Smith remodeled the house and built the estate's swimming pool and pink perimeter wall. The horticultural history of Lotusland recommences with the landscape design efforts of Peter Riedel, the horticulturist engaged by the Gavits to plan the gardens.

Opera singer and world traveler Madame Ganna Walska purchased the estate in 1941, and devoted the remaining 40 odd years of her life to creating a botanical wonderland. Madame Walska's Lotusland is distinguished by a matchless, dramatic style. Upon her death in 1984, the Ganna Walska Lotusland Foundation (a nonprofit educational institution) was funded by Madame Walska's estate to care for and preserve these uncommonly beautiful gardens, and to provide visitors with access to Madame's incredible retreat.

Lotusland's main house and surrounding grounds include a formal parterre garden, the Neptune fountain, and hedged allées. The lemon arbor is designed along straight and axial lines, while the paths weaving through areas devoted to plant collections are pleasingly curvilinear. With her own acute sense of design and enthusiasm for plants, Madame Walska worked at various times with distinguished landscape architects. Lockwood de Forest and Ralph T. Stevens helped to create the intriguing plan that dazzles today's visitors with its surprising transitions and stunning settings. In later years, Ganna Walska called upon horticulturists Charles Glass and Robert Foster, who were instrumental in the renovation of aloe plantings, the cactus garden, succulents, and the installation of a new cycad garden.

Formerly a eucalyptus grove, the parking lot now provides entrée to the Visitor Center, where the Lotusland tour commences. Pass through the Australian Garden, a recent addition, and you'll cross a sweeping gravel entryway. Continue along on the bark paths edged with burnished glass slag which is used lavishly throughout the gardens. As in Madame Walska's day, the blue-green fragments catch the light as you meander through sultry tropical areas planted with gingers and ferns. Forested sections are decorated with blooming begonias and bromeliads, and an epiphyllum garden is draped in hanging orchid cacti.

Lotusland's eccentric character and uniqueness are revealed most notably in an overabundance of bristly, barbed, dramatically jagged vegetation. In the gardens' upper stories, you'll find great masses of the exotic, eye-catching forms, including trees which were planted before the turn of the century. Among the stunning reminders of the garden's early nursery phase are towering specimens, such as bizarre ancient Australian bunya-bunya trees exhibiting odd protuberances on their elongated trunks. Unexpectedly lovely wine palms (*Jubea chilensis*) of magnificent girth are shrouded in somber, pale bark that resembles rhinoceros hide.

Perhaps best known for its cycad collection, Lotusland contains rare examples of *Encephalartos woodii*, a plant that has vanished from the wild. With their sharp, prickly leaves and imperative, architectural forms, cycads are often mistaken for palms by those who are unfamiliar with the genus. Botanically speaking, cycads date back to ancient times, and are related to plants which existed 250 million years ago. Adorning the Cycad Garden, a tranquil koi pond makes a wonderful resting point from where you can observe the exciting botanical specimens. The spiky edges of *Encephalartos horridus* aren't "horrible" at all, as its epithet implies, but a compelling, sculptural illustration of a primitive plant form. Bearing leaves of a remarkably cool shade of silvery blue, with each leaf projecting outward at differing angles, this South African cycad can't help but draw attention to itself. *E. trispinosus*, another sinister appearing species, exhibits leathery leaves in transfixing tones that can vary from light gray-blue to soft blue-green. Although resembling a palm, cycads bear cones and are related to conifers. During one serendipitous visit in early summer, a specimen exhibited a large cone ensconced within its bower of leaves. Another plant alongside had recently dropped a cone of hefty proportions, which splintered, strewing hundreds of bright red and yellow-orange seeds on the ground in bewitching disarray.

Madame Walska's Blue Garden and the impressive Succulent Collection are worthy of their legend. Picture the impact made by combining all sorts of plants with bluish foliage. From blue atlas cedars, to the whimsical tufts of blue fescue grass planted to form a ground-covering carpet, Lotusland's Blue Garden creates a resounding impression with its diversity of glaucous specimens. If upon hearing the term "succulent," you conjure up the image of a small, common houseplant, the array of specimens found in the area devoted to this group of plants will amaze you. Distinguished by their fleshy leaves and stems that hold water, and likewise, an ability to survive in arid conditions, the succulents at Lotusland have been artistically arranged to display the bold beauty of these unusual forms in an optimum situation.

Contrary to Lotusland's reputation for outright eccentricity, you'll find lovely traditional elements in the midst of unconventional displays. Laid out in geometric motifs, beautiful red brick paths from the 1920s follow around the peripheries of garden areas and lead through the plantings. Observe how in Madame Walska's magnificent Water Garden the path follows the contour of a lushly planted lotus pond. Here brilliantly patterned ceramic tiles adorn the benches, while crimson flowering canna lilies light up the boggy plantings nearby. Creating an alluring focal point in the midst of the pond, a stand of papyrus inhabits a crisp circular shape.

When you arrive at the courtyard of Lotusland's residence (where the foundation's offices are now ensconced), you'll find a conspicuous demonstration of cacti and euphorbias—an expression of the departed diva's outlandish temperament. Married six times to a succession of colorful characters, Madame Ganna Walska had a penchant for such bizarre botanical species as *Euphorbia ingens*. The gangly forms and pendulous parts of this tropical plant decorate the house's pink stucco facade.

Prominent among Lotusland's extensive plant collections are more than 100 types of aloes. As they flower, aloes are oddly striking: fantastical flower clusters appear atop tottering unbranched spikes, creating candelabra-like forms and peculiar forked stems. Many aloes bloom throughout the year, but are particularly superb in February. You'll find one of Lotusland's most extravagant water features in the Aloe Garden. Ornamented by two triple-tiered fountains of giant clam shells, the garden's organically shaped pool is a transcendent baby-blue. Its rim is decorated with abalone shells. In this elaborate setting, the precious glimmering seashells offset the animated architecture of the aloe grove for a stunning pictorial effect.

A horticultural adventure of uncommon rapture, Ganna Walska Lotusland is certain to be a thrilling destination point on your itinerary of California's Central Coast.

INFORMATION AND DIRECTIONS

Ganna Walska Lotusland is open to the public on a limited basis, because the number of visitors to Lotusland permitted by the County of Santa Barbara is very low. The garden is open from mid-February to mid-November. All tours are by phone reservation only. Fee charged. Reservations must be booked by phone, at 805-969-9990, one year prior to the month requested. Office Hours: Monday to Friday, 9 A.M. to noon.

Directions to Lotusland are made available once reservations are confirmed.

Moreton Bay Fig Tree, Santa Barbara

Planted in 1874 in Santa Barbara, this gigantic example of a native fig tree from Moreton Bay in Australia stakes a claim as the largest tree of its kind in the U.S.

Officially designated as a "tree of notable historic interest," the spectacular colossus has been granted protected status by the City of Santa Barbara. When I last visited, construction was going on to install a protective post and anchor chain barrier around the tree canopy. Signs were being placed to inform the public of how to fully appreciate and preserve this arboreal gem for future generations.

INFORMATION AND DIRECTIONS

Moreton Bay Fig Tree (*Ficus macrophylla*) has been ensconced at the intersection of Chapala Street and Highway 101 for 122 years, after having survived transplanting from a Santa Barbara location one block to the east.

Santa Barbara Botanic Garden, Santa Barbara

The Santa Barbara Botanic Garden was established in 1926 by Mrs. Anna Dorinda Blaksley Bliss to honor the memory of her father, Henry Blaksley. Dedicated to the study of California's native plants, the 65-acre property features more than 5½ miles of lovely walking trails winding through the garden's regional planting schemes. Here you'll find sections of manzanita, arroyo, desert, ceanothus, chaparral, meadow, island and redwood.

It would be difficult to fathom a setting more pleasing to the eye, or a more thriving collection of the state's vast range of flora. The Santa Ynez Mountains provide a stirring backdrop, and Santa Barbara's splendid climate endows the garden with conditions similar to those of the Mediterranean. The Botanic Garden's landscape encompasses naturalistic meadowlands and craggy canyons; a redwood forest; a historic Mission Dam; and lofty ridge tops from where you can gaze down upon the Channel Islands.

The Desert Section is positioned just beyond the entrance to the garden. Representing countless examples of the agave and cactus families, these plants of dramatic form and texture are presided over by imposing California fan palms (*Washingtonia filifera*), the state's only native palm tree. Formidable boulders rise along the section's paths. Look for the eye-catching Joshua tree, Shaw's agave, and the coast prickly pear, admired for its colorful springtime display of fruit that emerges along the edges of the plant's paddle-shaped stems. After a wet winter, ephemeral species often burst forth with colorful blossoms among the densely arranged spiny specimens. The rewards of the rainy season include such delicate compatriots as dune evening-primrose and thistle sage.

Every month of the year suggests special incentives to visit the Botanic Garden. From February through March the Ceanothus Section is in bloom. At this time garden sojourners take to hiking along the Porter Trail to a place where it begins to ascend the ridge. Here one encounters an especially admirable variety of ceanothus species and cultivars. You'll see ground covering forms to sizable shrubs, and smallish trees. All reveal beautiful blue-hued and white flowers that brighten the rugged surroundings. The Campbell Trail provides another scenic walk, with steep earthen pathways passing through chaparral plantings and leading down to the canyon floor. Here you'll discover the rustic Campbell Bridge which crosses Mission Creek. Where the Campbell Trail meets the Pritchett Trail, you'll observe a transition into oak woodlands and an area of leathery-leaved chaparral vegetation.

Spring brings a bonanza of butterflies drawn to the garden's bounty of blooming flowers. By May, the Meadow Section is awash with ornamental perennial bunchgrasses, and radiant annual wildflowers; California poppies, and the myriad blues of lupines, gilias, phacelias, and blue-eye grass. Along the Meadow Walk, a cluster of age-old coast live oaks provide tranquil sanctuary. Nearby, sunbathing frogs revel in the Sellar and Bessie Bullard brook and pond area, where bright scarlet, water-loving monkeyflowers, azure blue lobelias, and yellow pond-lilies add colorful accents. Observe how the weathered branches used to create low fencing along the edge of the path are structural elements of understated beauty. Such features endow the garden's landscape with a wonderful aesthetic integrity.

The Botanic Garden's Island Section is of particular interest for its display of rare examples of live-forevers. Scientifically classified as *Dudleya*, this distinctive genus is characterized by small gray-leaved and green succulents restricted to Western North America, but found mainly on the offshore islands of Southern California and Baja. June is prime bloom season for *Dudleyas*, as well as for sages and desert willows. Once August rolls around, you'll find the garden aglow with the colors of goldenrods, asters, and California fuchsias. In the fall, the delightfully colored leaves of maples, sycamores and cottonwoods catch the eye and migratory and resident birds seem to be everywhere you look.

Another garden area worth seeking out is the Home Demonstration Garden. What makes it so instructive is the way it showcases water-conserving California natives growing in a residential landscape. Whichever path you follow, whatever time of year you stop over, the Santa Barbara Botanic Garden will charm you with its stimulating walks through diverse communities of native vegetation that are interspersed with noteworthy cultivars.

INFORMATION AND DIRECTIONS

Santa Barbara Botanic Garden, 1212 Mission Canyon Road, Santa Barbara, CA 93105. Phone 805-682-4726 to confirm open hours, and for information on docent tours. Garden is open November through February, weekdays 9 A.M. to 4 P.M., and weekends 9 A.M. to 5 P.M.; March through October, weekdays 9 A.M. to 5 P.M., and weekends, 9 A.M. to 6 P.M. Fee charged.

There is a garden shop and the Garden Growers Plant Nursery, which offers native California and Mediterranean plants for sale. Call for the date of the fall (usually in October) plant sale.

Web site: www.sbbg.org.

To reach the Santa Barbara Botanic Garden located in the foothills above the city, proceed from downtown Santa Barbara, driving past Santa Barbara Mission and continuing north to Foothill Road (Highway 192). Turn right and follow signs to Botanic Garden.

Santa Barbara County Courthouse, Santa Barbara

As you explore Santa Barbara's city center, you'll discover this exemplary public building, with its gleaming white facade, ornamental archways, wrought iron decoration, and expansive, low-pitched red tile roof. Santa Barbara County Courthouse is further enhanced by sweeping lawns and the exuberant plantings which surround it.

To call the courthouse a stunning architectural accomplishment is in no way a hyperbole. The now classic edifice was designed by William Mooser after a severe earthquake in 1925 destroyed a great deal of Santa Barbara's downtown area. Mooser used a studied mix of Spanish Colonial and Mediterranean design themes, combined with rich decorative embellishments that make reference to Moorish and Islamic influences. Today the Santa Barbara County Courthouse building can be looked upon as a definitive example of Southern

Californian architecture, representing all that we have come to equate with that alluring style.

Locate the docent's booth just inside the building and pick up a pamphlet entitled *A Botanical Guide to the Santa Barbara County Courthouse.* On the courthouse grounds, you'll find an amazing collection of exotic palms and trees. This veritable botanical extravaganza represents specimens gathered from twenty-five countries and six continents.

Ample signs will help in identifying rarities such as paradise and umbrella palms, which are found only on one small South Pacific island. Now extinct in its native habitat, the Franceschi palm appears here among more than 40 other varieties of extraordinary palms.

Hearkening back to the days when missionaries first introduced Canary Island date palms to our shores, these auspicious trees once provided fronds for Palm Sunday services. Now, however, they stand as symbols of Southern California's cloudless skies and relaxed lifestyle.

INFORMATION AND DIRECTIONS

Santa Barbara County Courthouse, in downtown Santa Barbara. The courthouse building is open to the public weekdays, from 8 A.M. to 4:45 P.M.; and Saturday, Sunday, and holidays, from 10 A.M. to 4:45 P.M. A small fee is charged for the pamphlet, *A Botanical Guide to the Santa Barbara Courthouse.* The courthouse building and landscaped grounds occupy a city block bordered by Anapamu, Santa Barbara, Figueroa and Anacapa Streets.

Santa Barbara Orchid Estate, Santa Barbara

The lush plantings along the driveway and the palm-lined walkways of Santa Barbara Orchid Estate announce the glorious flora which attracts legions of orchid lovers.

Two acres of orchids await your discovery here, with one acre of plants displayed outdoors, and an acre of exotic orchids found under glass. The general manager, Wayne Ferrell, and an approachable staff gladly answer questions, dispelling some of the mystique surrounding cultivating these gorgeous blooms that have intimidated many gardeners.

Santa Barbara Orchid Estate specializes in cool growing varieties of orchids; 50 percent are varieties of the genus *Cymbidium.* As you walk through the establishment's aisles, you'll see an abundance of orchids growing in various cultural conditions. Signs explain key points about the different types of orchids and provide information on how to care for them in your home, or in an outdoor environment such as that of Southern California, or during the summer season in other parts of the country.

Orchids are always blooming at Santa Barbara Orchid Estate, but note that in March 90 percent of the *Cymbidium* plants are simultaneously in bloom, creating an extraordinary exhibition. Try if possible to plan your visit at this time, so that you can behold this incredible sight.

Cut flowers, as well as plants, are available for purchase at Santa Barbara Orchid Estate. A variety of orchid gifts and blooming plants can be shipped.

INFORMATION AND DIRECTIONS

Santa Barbara Orchid Estate, 1250 Orchid Drive, Santa Barbara, CA 93111.

Phone 800-553-3387 or 805-967-1284 to confirm open hours, for information, or further directions. Fax: 805-683-3405. Visitors welcome Monday through Saturday, 8 A.M. to 4:30 P.M.; Sunday, 11 A.M. to 4 P.M.

Coming from either the north or south, take Highway 101, turn toward the ocean onto Patterson Avenue, which dead-ends at Orchid Drive.

Stewart Orchids, Carpinteria

The internationally renowned Stewart Orchids company has been involved in the orchid business for 90 years. In their impressive greenhouse facilities covering 100,000 square feet, the knowledgeable proprietors, Steve and Mary Jo McNerney, along with a skillful staff, propagate orchids from tissue cultures, as well as from seed.

Best known for countless species and cultivars of *Cattleya* orchids, Stewart Orchids also grows a wealth of other exotic plants. Look for cultivated varieties of lady slipper orchids, for example, of the *Paphiopedilum* genus. According to the company's mail order catalog, lady slippers are generally easy to grow, and often thrive inside the home, on a window sill. Varieties of *Phalaenopisis* are recommended as the easiest orchids for beginners to grow.

Stewart Orchids ships worldwide, offering "Plant-A-Month Plans," and an abundance of rare and unusual orchids through their enticing catalog. Stop by the premises and perhaps you might decide to select an elegant hybrid *Cattleya* in person. Explore Stewart Orchids' extensive collection of intriguing orchid varieties. It will leave you spellbound!

INFORMATION AND DIRECTIONS

Stewart Orchids, 3376 Foothill Road, Carpinteria, CA 93013. Phone 800-621-2450 or 805-684-5448 for further information and to confirm open hours. Fax: 805-566-6609. Open Monday through Friday, 8 A.M. to 5 P.M.; Saturday, 9 A.M. to 4 P.M.; Sunday, 10 A.M. to 5 P.M. Closed major holidays. *E-mail: info@stewartorchids.com*

Located in the seaside town of Carpinteria, 12 miles south of Santa Barbara.

RECOMMENDED LODGINGS

CENTRAL COAST

J. Patrick House Bed & Breakfast, Cambria

Mexican sage, the evergreen blue pea and princess flower shrubs, and countless fuchsias are among the blooming plants that grace J. Patrick House's grounds. Located only several miles from Hearst Castle in charming Cambria, the wooded setting provides a refreshing contrast to the sweeping ocean vistas of Coast Highway 1, and the rolling hills of nearby Paso Robles Wine Country.

An attractive wooden pergola, festooned with enticing jasmine and an unusual deep red-orange flowering passion vine, connects the main log cabin to the Carriage House. The inn's two buildings provide impeccably maintained lodging accommodations. Guests enjoy breakfast in the Garden Room and wine and hors d'oeuvres in a cozy living room, in the main log cabin.

A fairly recent addition to the landscape is a succulent garden, installed alongside a fenced area next to the pergola. Walking around the inn, you'll find water fountains, statuary, birdbaths and a gazing globe, amid the various plantings around the grounds. When you visit, you may want to ask Barbara, the innkeeper, to point out interesting specimens. Or stroll around on your own, searching out colorful flowering maples (*Abutilon*), poor man's rhododendron (*Impatiens oliveri*), Chinese lilac, and other appealing flora surrounding the inn.

INFORMATION AND DIRECTIONS

J. Patrick House Bed & Breakfast, 2990 Burton Drive, Cambria, California, 93428. Contact Barbara and Mel Schwimmer, innkeepers. Phone 800-341-5258 or 805-927-3812 for reservations, information, and directions. Eight rooms feature wood-burning fireplaces and private baths; full breakfast served. Rates $125–$180. *Web site: www.jpatrickhouse.com.*

Cambria is located just south of Hearst Castle, San Simeon, at Pacific Coast Highway 1; approximately four hours from either San Francisco or Los Angeles. From Highway 101, approach the town by following Highway 46 West.

The Just Inn, Paso Robles

On California's Central Coast, the 160-acre family owned and operated Justin Vineyards and Winery runs also the Just Inn Bed and Breakfast Suites. An inviting getaway, the inn is located less than ten miles from the Pacific Ocean, in a rural setting of beautiful hills, imposing oaks, and superb landscaping.

Situated in the wine country region of Paso Robles, the Just Inn gardens combine Mediterranean accents with English-style plantings. Garden elements include a large pergola overgrown with luxuriant vines; stately terra cotta planters embellished with lions' heads; and perhaps the garden's most prominent component, warm-toned, orange-tinted stone retaining walls, which delineate the garden's overall framework.

Flower beds overflowing with lavender and herbs, expansive borders filled with roses and flowering specimens, and a water garden that can be viewed from the balcony of each suite are all encircled with this attractive stonework. The flowing lines created by the rough, low retaining walls integrate the garden into the vineyard landscape.

Near the town of Paso Robles, yet worlds away from any sort of stress or noise, the inn provides convenient access to the neighboring Sycamore Herb Farm; the Hearst Castle Gardens; and the town of Cambria, where you can visit the quaint Heart's Ease Herb Shop & Gardens.

INFORMATION AND DIRECTIONS

The Just Inn, Justin Vineyards & Winery, 11680 Chimney Rock Road, Paso Robles, California, 93446. Contact Justin and Deborah Baldwin, innkeepers. Phone 800-726-0049, 805-237-4150, or 805-238-6932 for information and reservations. Three suites featuring first-class amenities and comfortably elegant country decor, with fireplaces and private baths; full breakfast served. Rates $225–$275 (Justin Wine Society members receive a discount). Staying at the Just Inn is just like luxuriating in a private villa, where you can expect to be pampered. A private chef on staff provides optional gourmet, multi-course dinners at $100 per couple, served in the inn's intimate dining room, where guests can arrange their own special parties. *Web site: www.JUSTINwine.com E-mail: JUSTINwine@aol.com*

The Just Inn is conveniently located midway between San Francisco and Los Angeles. From the intersection of Highway 101 and

Highway 46 East, proceed eight miles west on 24th Street, then onto Lake Nacimiento Road. At Chimney Rock Road continue driving west seven miles to the inn.

SANTA BARBARA

Glenborough Inn, Santa Barbara

A vibrant rose garden bids a cheerful welcome at Glenborough Inn. Lavender and evening primrose, poppies and innumerable other flowers add to the impressive streetside display. Here, also ornamental plum trees enhance and echo the inn's painted trim. This entranceway garden underscores the beauty of the main house, a Craftsman-style bungalow. The inn's other three separate buildings are: La Casa, a private cottage, which is located right next door; and the Victorian Cottage, circa 1886, and the White Farm House, circa 1912, directly across the street.

Offering garden views, private entries, Franklin stoves, and a variety of appealing decor themes, the Glenborough Inn cultivates a gracious, accommodating environment which emphasizes guests' privacy. In keeping with this philosophy, breakfast is delivered to the rooms, rather than served in a common area.

Glenborough's relaxed, informal atmosphere, combined with the generous amenities, make this inn the perfect getaway. One of the proprietors, Steve, like most gardeners, has numerous projects under way: from adding more roses wherever possible, to planting around each building such unusual specimens as Kangaroo Paw (*Anigozanthos*), a native plant found in Australian eucalyptus forests.

INFORMATION AND DIRECTIONS

Glenborough Inn, 1327 Bath Street, Santa Barbara, CA 93101. Michael Diaz and Steve Ryan, innkeepers. Phone 805-966-0589 or 888-966-0589 for reservations and information. The inn has six rooms, six suites, and one cottage. Rates $110–$360 for La Casa, an entire cottage that sleeps up to six people. *Web Site: www.silcom. com/~glenboro E-mail: Glenboro@silcom.com*

Secret Garden Inn, Santa Barbara

Jack Greenwald and Christine Dunstan's Secret Garden Inn conveys the warm, inviting ambiance of an English country style house, and at the same time celebrates the casual, comfortable spirit associated with Southern California at its finest. The friendly innkeeper Jack Greenwald makes guests feel right at home in this cozy Santa Barbara retreat. Of course, cocooning in one of the secluded cottages is always an option if you prefer privacy, but the inn draws a most agreeable group of patrons, and I for one found it a pleasure to converse with the other guests.

Botanical prints decorated my room, in keeping with the inn's garden theme. The actual garden areas are varied and full of surprises. A regal evergreen pittosporum is among the beautiful trees shading the entryway's landscaping. Bright ribbons of annuals flank the sidewalk and handsome terra cotta containers leading the way up the stairs to the inn's front door. After hours of garden hopping in Santa Barbara, I enjoyed unwinding with a glass of wine in one of the wicker chairs on the front porch, The pleasant view encompasses a sea of ivy that covers the ground, and accentuates a variegated pittosporum standing just opposite its handsome relative.

Tall hedges create private spaces throughout the grounds, dividing the Secret Garden property into well defined areas for rest and relaxation. Walking around one side of the main house, you encounter a garden room. Here you'll find an expanse of lawn, and a long sunny border of foxgloves and roses, poppies, ranunculus, and a host of other gay flowers dramatically set off by the richly textured backdrop hedging. Following the sidewalk adjacent to the floral display, you'll encounter an opening through the high clipped shrubbery which leads to the garden at the rear of the main house. With curving paths meandering between the cottages and the inviting pattern of a red brick patio, this idyllic setting will enchant you. Here, breakfast is served in the morning, and wine and cheese await guests at 5 P.M. on an average balmy Santa Barbara day.

A wealth of plants are arranged in such a way as to layer the overall space which encircles the patio. An avocado tree shelters a diminutive tree fern in one of many garden vignettes. Still other levels are created by bushy perennials and blooming shrubs: abutilons and hydrangeas, fuchsias and feverfew, and azaleas and camellias. Completing the picture, a lush ground cover of star jasmine produces a heady perfume. An amiable staff and charming furnishings add to the allure of the Secret Garden Inn's lovely sequestered realm.

INFORMATION AND DIRECTIONS

Secret Garden Inn, 1908 Bath Street, Santa Barbara, CA 93101. Jack Greenwald and Christine Dunstan, proprietors. Phone 800-676-1622 or 805-687-2300. Rates $110–$195. Two rooms in main house and nine rooms in four cottages; private baths, full breakfast served.

Web site: www.secretgarden.com E-mail: garden@secretgarden.com

Simpson House Inn, Santa Barbara

Among its many accolades, the historic Simpson House Inn was recently awarded AAA's coveted Five Diamond Award. The first North American bed & breakfast inn ever to receive the travel organization's highest rating, Simpson House Inn features lavish indoor floral arrangements and an acre of formal English gardens. Highlights include fountains, statuary, and lovely trees—from a 100-year-old English oak, to magnolias, fruit trees, and formidable pittosporums that perfume the air in early spring.

Simpson House Inn has also achieved landmark status. Innkeepers Glyn and Linda Davies accomplished a fine restoration of the 1874 Eastlake-Victorian House, with its beautiful signature verandah. The 1878 barn was also restored. After dismantling the structure in 1992, the owners reconstructed the barn to maintain its architectural integrity, while updating it in grand style.

Obviously not your average bed & breakfast, the Simpson House Inn features an atmosphere where guests may expect to be pampered. Luxurious furnishings and orchids adorn each of the inn's rooms. In the early evening, guests are served Mediterranean hors d'oeuvres accompanied by local Santa Barbara wines

Located in the very heart of Santa Barbara, this very private retreat is just a short stroll from the delightful botanical collections of Alice Keck Memorial Garden, and within easy walking distance of many other attractions.

INFORMATION AND DIRECTIONS

Simpson House Inn, 121 E. Arrellaga St., Santa Barbara, CA 93101. Contact Glyn and Linda Davies, innkeepers. Phone 800-676-1280 or 805-963-7067. The inn offers 14 guest rooms, suites, and cottages, with private baths and full gourmet breakfast served. Rates are from $160 for a room, to $365 for a suite of rooms. *Web site: www.simp sonhouseinn.com E-mail: simpsonhouse@compuserve.com*

Tiffany Inn, Santa Barbara

Charming furnishings and the warmth of gleaming dark woodwork are some of the features that make the Tiffany Inn so inviting. Many rooms offer views overlooking the inn's front gardens, or the patio area, where you'll find a small yet picture-perfect, Victorian rose garden. Encircled by a becoming walkway of red bricks, the garden may be enjoyed from a number of attractive benches.

Guests can also admire an arbor covered with fragrant climbing roses, and eye-catching displays of trumpet vines that put forth enough foliage and flowers to adorn the surroundings and screen the garden from the outside world.

INFORMATION AND DIRECTIONS

Tiffany Inn, 1323 De la Vina Street, Santa Barbara, CA 93101. Carol and Larry McDonald, innkeepers. Phone 805-963-2283 or 800-999-5672. There are six rooms and one penthouse suite occupying the entire third floor, with private baths and full breakfast served. Rates $125–$225. *Web site: www.sbinns.com/tiffany*

CALIFORNIA

LOS ANGELES TO SAN DIEGO

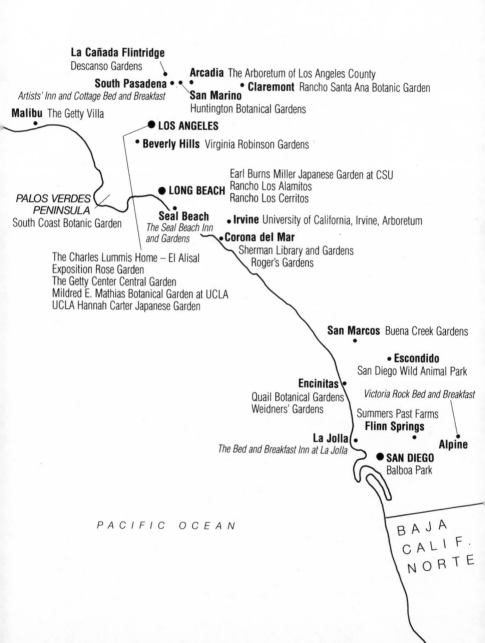

CALIFORNIA

La Cañada Flintridge
Descanso Gardens
Arcadia The Arboretum of Los Angeles County
South Pasadena • • **Claremont** Rancho Santa Ana Botanic Garden
Artists' Inn and Cottage Bed and Breakfast **San Marino**
Malibu The Getty Villa
Huntington Botanical Gardens
● **LOS ANGELES**

• **Beverly Hills** Virginia Robinson Gardens

Earl Burns Miller Japanese Garden at CSU
● **LONG BEACH** Rancho Los Alamitos
Rancho Los Cerritos

**PALOS VERDES
PENINSULA**
South Coast Botanic Garden
Seal Beach • **Irvine** University of California, Irvine, Arboretum
*The Seal Beach Inn
and Gardens* • **Corona del Mar**
Sherman Library and Gardens
The Charles Lummis Home – El Alisal Roger's Gardens
Exposition Rose Garden
The Getty Center Central Garden
Mildred E. Mathias Botanical Garden at UCLA
UCLA Hannah Carter Japanese Garden

San Marcos Buena Creek Gardens
•

• **Escondido**
San Diego Wild Animal Park

Encinitas •
Quail Botanical Gardens *Victoria Rock Bed and Breakfast*
Weidners' Gardens
Summers Past Farms
Flinn Springs
La Jolla • • **Alpine**
The Bed and Breakfast Inn at La Jolla
● **SAN DIEGO**
Balboa Park

PACIFIC OCEAN

BAJA
CALIF.
NORTE

9

Los Angeles & Vicinity Gardens

The Arboretum Of Los Angeles County, Arcadia

A jewel among Southern California gardens, the Arboretum of Los Angeles County offers plant lovers a panoply of demonstration gardens, educational exhibits, and special events throughout the year. Operated jointly by the Los Angeles County Department of Parks and Recreation and the California Arboretum Foundation, the lovely landscape covers 127 acres.

The arboretum is divided into sections arranged according to the geographic origins of species. A Tropical Forest, Redwood and Native Oak Groves, Australian, South American and African sections highlight rare and unusual flora from around the globe. Magnolias, ancient cycads, and acacias are represented in significant plant collections. The arboretum nurtures an assembly of such Australian native trees and shrubs as eucalyptus, leptospermum (commonly known as tea tree), and melaleuca. The considerable presence of these species reflects how well they thrive in the balmy Southern California climate.

The peaceful Baldwin Lake provides a protected refuge for wildlife, affording a pleasing environment for garden travelers. Surrounded by the silhouettes of lofty palms and the dense foliage of innumerable trees, the lake invites repose. Visitors can observe colorful peafowl, migrating ducks and many other birds that congregate here by the lake with the rabbits and turtles living in this sanctuary of the arboretum.

If visiting time is limited, set your sights upon the Meyberg Waterfall, one of the garden's most popular attractions. Locate Baldwin Lake and Circle Road on the visitor map, then proceed past Tule

Pond, following Waterfall Walk into the North American/Asiatic Section. Head toward the Herb Garden, and from there just up the road to the right is the waterfall, situated on the arboretum's western border. The lovely views here are uplifting.

Both of historic appeal, the Hugo Reid Adobe and gingerbread-embellished Queen Anne Cottage are state and national landmarks, respectively. Native Gabrieleno-style Indian wickiups (a type of dwelling), and other restored structures like the Santa Anita Depot provide wonderful glimpses of the region's historical heritage. For history buffs, these buildings offer satisfying encounters with California's bygone days.

The arboretum also boasts the new Sunset Demonstration Gardens. The recently implemented 1½ acre design plan includes eight small gardens: the Water Retreat, the Nostalgia Garden, Gardening under the Oaks, and the Courtyard Garden, to name a few. You'll find them on the way to the Tropical Greenhouse at #30 on the visitor map. Other additional attractions at the arboretum include the Water Conservation Garden and the Tropical and Begonia greenhouses.

INFORMATION AND DIRECTIONS

The Arboretum of Los Angeles County, 301 N. Baldwin Avenue, Arcadia, CA 91007. Phone 626-821-3222 to confirm open hours and directions. Facilities include shuttle tram, reference library, cafe and gift shop. Phone 626-447-8751 for gift shop information. Open daily 9 A.M. to 4:30 P.M.; closed December 25. Admission fee. *Web site: www.arboretum.org*

Located approximately 45 minutes northeast of downtown Los Angeles, just east of Pasadena, and south of the Baldwin Avenue exit of the I-210 Freeway.

Charles F. Lummis Home—El Alisal, Los Angeles

The Historical Society of Southern California maintains its headquarters at the Charles Lummis Home, known also as El Alisal. Celebrated as a City of Los Angeles and State of California Historical Monument, and included on the National Register of Historic Places, El Alisal was once home to the unconventional, multitalented author, journalist, and founder of the Southwest Museum, Charles Lummis. The property is now owned and maintained by the Los Angeles City Department of Recreation and Parks.

Lummis chose the location for his home in 1895. Over a span of some twelve years, the resourceful individualist proceeded to construct a rocky citadel for himself. Deriving inspiration from a majestic sycamore with four huge trunks, Lummis named his new abode El Alisal. The impressive 13-room building possesses a steadfast character and eye-catching appeal.

Visitors to the Charles F. Lummis Home find a noteworthy two acre garden that illustrates the uses and attractions of drought tolerant plants. Designed in 1985 by landscape architect Robert Perry, the Lummis garden plan highlights a low-maintenance approach. Comprised of five distinct sections, the design includes citrus and desert gardens, a regional plant garden incorporating Mediterranean species, a lovely yarrow meadow, and a California native garden. A dry stream bed complements the design. You'll find the landscaping at once educational in its selections of plants and sitings, and a vibrant, aesthetic showcase of interesting indigenous species and cultivated varieties that prosper with lesser amounts of water.

In front of the entry court, the yarrow meadow serves as a creative substitute for a lawn. Among the selection of regional plants are toyon and California lilac, with their seasonal show of blooms and berries. Scent is another important element in the overall garden plan. Lavender, thyme, and sage provide lovely aromas as one walks along the garden's paths of decomposed granite. In early summer, the tall flowering spikes of the pride of Madeira appear, while lovely shade trees like the Western redbud add color in the fall.

When touring the Lummis Home you can explore its museum exhibit of archaeological artifacts that once belonged to Charles Lummis. Among the interior's fascinating decorative pieces, look for the dining room sideboard, with carved doors dating back to 1776. You'll also view framed photographs of writers, singers, artists, and other celebrities that Lummis played host to at one time or another.

INFORMATION AND DIRECTIONS

Charles F. Lummis Memorial Home and Garden, El Alisal, 200 East Avenue 43, Los Angeles, 90031. Phone 323-222-0546. Open Friday, Saturday, and Sunday from 1 P.M. to 4 P.M., except certain holidays. No admission fee.

Located in Los Angeles' Highland Park neighborhood.

Descanso Gardens, La Cañada Flintridge

In 1937, E. Manchester Boddy, businessman and publisher of the *Los Angeles Daily News* purchased property in the San Rafael Hills, north of Los Angeles. He named this land Rancho del Descanso. The enchanting woodland setting endures today as Descanso Gardens, comprising a 160-acre garden with 80 planted acres. Recognized as part of Boddy's extraordinary horticultural legacy, Descanso Gardens features a magnificent camellia forest—one of the largest in North America—that draws visitors from far and near.

Boddy's passion for camellias began early on, when he realized that the mature coast live oak trees growing on the land would provide the perfect filtered shade habitat for the beautiful flowering shrubs. Planting began immediately after Boddy optioned the property, and as the saying goes, the rest is history. The camellia forest comprises an estimated 50,000 plants, with more than 400 varieties of camellias represented, including many unique varieties developed at Descanso. Some specimens are over thirty feet. You'll see the large flowered *Camellia reticulata*, brought to Rancho del Descanso in 1948, and in October an impressive display of the *sasanqua* species. From January throughout March, and October through December, the gardens' serene woodland paths are punctuated with the extravagant flowers of early and late blooming types of camellias. A refreshing host of annuals, planted out among the flower beds, add continual color and good cheer.

Visitors and members of the garden look forward to the informal style and peaceful setting of the Descanso Gardens. Here they can take lovely morning walks along the Nature Trail or explore the restrained beauty of the Fern Canyon. Occasional visitors to the Los Angeles area can also take refuge in these tranquil gardens, which are not far from the city center, but provide a dramatic contrast to L.A.'s unceasing activity.

In the spring, you can enjoy expansive borders chock full of tulips and daffodils, or stroll beneath stately magnolias sheltering fine displays of azaleas. Descanso's Iris Garden displays California's largest collection of breathtaking bearded irises. During April, 1,500 named varieties create a dazzling show. Roses and wildflowers also exhibit their finery at this time, while Descanso's famous lilac grove highlights shrubs which were specifically developed to bloom in Southern California's mild climate. These fragrant, radiant lilacs are a surprising delight.

Eight acres at Descanso Gardens are devoted to a Native Plant collection, with areas of chaparral representing the spirit of a Southern Californian landscape. Devoted bird lovers head for a lake on the property that features a bird sanctuary. An observation station built in conjunction with the Audubon Society provides a restful spot to study the many migrating and permanent species who nest or seek shelter within the sanctuary of the Descanso Gardens.

The International Rosarium enchants rose lovers, with 20 different theme gardens that commemorate various types of roses from antique, to modern. Opened in 1994, the rosarium provides particularly helpful signs that explain different types of flower forms, specific plant traits, origins of plants, and derivations of hybrid roses. A Victorian gazebo, a handsome walled mission garden, a lengthy arbor dubbed Noisette Tunnelle, and *Rosa wichuraiana* arches are a few examples of how garden ornamentation and hardscaping combine to provide wonderful environments for the display of rose collections. Embellishing the rosarium are also exuberant companion plantings of perennials and shrubs, spilling over onto grassy paths.

Not surprisingly, Descanso Gardens features an admirable Japanese Tea House and Garden, inspired by the Asian origins of camellias. Explore the discreet loveliness of the setting with an unhurried stroll through the landscape. The alluring flora—azaleas that bloom in April, Japanese maples ablaze in the fall, and elegant bamboo—encourages a considered awareness of the garden's symbolic elements. Philosophical concepts, such as how the element of moving water suggests one's journey through life, can enrich the garden experience. The sensory delights provided by the pool and waterfalls are, however, admirable in their own right.

During open hours, the public is invited to enjoy art exhibits and the wood-paneled Boddy Library, located in Boddy's former home. Should you choose to amble around the exterior of the 22-room mansion Boddy built in 1938, you'll soon discover a secret garden niche. Here, adjoining the Boddy House and Art Gallery, is a hidden Chinese Garden, established by Boddy years ago.

What a revelation this intimate space proves to be, with age-old relief sculptures from China installed around the upper perimeter of the garden's walls. Note the amazingly vivid glazes which decorate these reliefs, and the skilled craftsmanship reflected in the vigorous modeling of the figures. In this exquisite walled garden my curiosity

105

was stirred. I found myself pondering both the rarefied setting and the narrative revealed by the sculptural relics. Moreover, I wondered what story they might tell about the man who was inspired to build such a secluded garden amid the grand scope of his own Rancho del Descanso.

INFORMATION AND DIRECTIONS

Descanso Gardens, 1418 Descanso Drive, La Cañada Flintridge, California 91011. Phone 818-952-4401 to confirm open hours, or for information, directions, and tram tours. The gift shop, features a fine selection of books, garden accessories, and gift items with garden themes. Admission fee charged. Open daily 9 A.M. to 4:30 P.M.; closed Christmas Day. *Web site: www.descanso.com*

Located 20 minutes north of downtown Los Angeles, just south of Freeway 210, off Glendale Freeway 2.

Earl Burns Miller Japanese Garden, Long Beach

Colorful azaleas light up a hillside during a springtime visit to this traditional Japanese garden, located on the campus of California State University at Long Beach. The 1.3 acre Earl Burns Miller Japanese Garden represents a dream that became a reality for Mrs. Loraine Miller Collins, who wished to create a place that offers rejuvenation to the weary, and aesthetic inspiration for those seeking beauty.

Dedicated in 1981 to her late husband, Earl Burns Miller, the garden is full of fragrant magnolias that provide color in summer, and chrysanthemums and liquidamber trees that light up autumn days in golden tones. Designed by landscape architect Edward R. Lovell, the Earl Burns Miller Garden offers a lovely setting to enjoy diverse flora, with landscaping punctuated by the potent forms of significant objects. Note the exemplary proportions of an arched bridge, the three-tiered pagoda, and stone lanterns. If you stop to regard these important garden elements, your attention will be drawn to the sculpted shapes of trees and the textural interplay of shrubbery. Stroll the garden's paths and enjoy the emblematic streambed of black pebbles. Note, as well, the poetic rustle when you approach the Chinese willow's cascading drapery.

In this Japanese garden, amid the jade green, pale chartreuse and emerald tones of evergreen specimens, you'll find a peaceful feeling and quietude.

INFORMATION AND DIRECTIONS
Earl Burns Miller Japanese Garden, California State University, Long
Beach, 1250 Bellflower Boulevard, Long Beach, CA 90840. Phone the
Garden Office at 562-985-8885 for further information. The garden is
open Tuesday through Friday, 8 A.M. to 3:30 P.M.; Sunday, noon to
4 P.M. Closed Monday and Saturday. No fee to visit the Japanese Garden during public hours. *Web site: www.csulb.edu/~jgarden*
    Located approximately one hour south of downtown Los Angeles;
take Freeway 405 to the Bellflower Boulevard Exit. Use parking lot
#16; on weekdays use metered spaces. Weekend parking is free in
nonmetered spaces.

Exposition Park Rose Garden, Los Angeles

Before the City of Los Angeles leased the land in 1911, Exposition
Park was an agricultural area affiliated with the State of California's
Agricultural Association. At that time, the park was given its current
name, and a sunken garden, measuring 800 by 300 feet, was installed
and enclosed by a masonry wall. The advent of World War I slowed
down progress on Exposition Park's formal, seven-acre garden. It was
1928 before the Rose Garden itself was actually completed.
    On a gardenwalk today through Exposition Park Rose Garden,
you will enjoy some 200 varieties of roses. On view here are 20,000
plants, arranged in 30 by 30 foot beds and embellished with a circular fountain, statuary and sculptures. The garden is awash with
blooms from April on into December. Visitors to the garden can relax
here before carrying on their tour of Los Angeles.
INFORMATION AND DIRECTIONS
Exposition Park Rose Garden, 900 Exposition Boulevard, at Figueroa
and Vermont Streets, Los Angeles, CA. Phone 310-548-7676 for further information. Open seven days a week, from 8 A.M. to 5 P.M. Free
admission.
    Located by the Los Angeles Coliseum, just south of downtown Los
Angeles.

The Getty Center Central Garden, Los Angeles

Breathtaking in its entirety, at a cost of approximately $1 billion, the
Getty Center is the awe-inspiring legacy of one man and the private

foundation established to support and sustain art and culture. After 13 years of planning, the Getty opened its doors to the public in December 1997. Larger-than-life, the center consists of an amalgamation of buildings, including the formidable J. Paul Getty Museum which exhibits Getty's superb art collection, together with institutes devoted to research and conservation, arts education, museum management and a grant program. The center's triumphant design incorporates water features, a tram system, cafes and a restaurant—all of which elaborate on the incandescent architecture. But it is artist Robert Irwin's ravishing Central Garden that functions as the icing on the cake.

The Getty Center is the culmination of the visionary ideas of architect Richard Meier, in association with the J. Paul Getty Trust. With its remarkable synthesis of design, place, and purpose, the Getty salutes the new millennium from its site in the Santa Monica Mountains. Situated on a 110-acre hillside, the Getty's campus is strikingly modernist, yet visitor-friendly. Spectacular terraces offer vistas encompassing the Los Angeles city skyline and sprawling labyrinth of streets, extending to the San Gabriel Mountains, Santa Catalina Island, and the Pacific Ocean. While the view evokes euphoric responses, the building material used also provides a satisfying aesthetic experience: Note the exciting tactile qualities of prominent fossilized remains on the surfaces of the Roman classic travertine covering the 1.2 million square feet of the center's walls and pavement.

Major hillsides of the Getty Center are the landscape design work of Emet L. Wemple & Associates Landscape Architects, while other gardens on the campus have been designed by Olin Partnership, of Philadelphia. The Getty Center commissioned artist Robert Irwin to design the 134,000 square-foot Central Garden as a work of art. Important art commissions often generate conflicting opinions. In the case of the Central Garden, the idea was controversial to be sure. Although his previous expertise was not horticultural, Irwin's skillful touch and satisfying command of space are apparent in the visually engaging Central Garden. His garden scheme is made up of well chosen elements, including a tree-lined walkway, a streambed strewn with boulders, a plaza, a cascading waterfall, and a reflecting pool featuring a maze laid out with azaleas.

Begun in the spring of 1996 and completed in December 1997, the plan of the Central Garden echoes a natural ravine within the existing topography. With the passing of time and the changing seasons, the lush plantings are expected to reveal varying arrangements of plant material. By constantly introducing new plant combinations and schemes, the garden's dominant theme is to surprise and give pleasure to visitors. In the garden, you'll find carved in stone Robert Irwin's statement "Ever Present Never Twice The Same / Ever Changing Never Less Than Whole."

Arriving at the Central Garden on my inaugural visit, I found the rocky watercourse decked out in tall scarlet canna lilies, accompanied by a profusion of herbs and grasses. This exquisite tapestry woven primarily of deep claret and silvery hues had distinct accents of grays and greens. Zigzag walkways, traversing the hillside's gentle descent, lead through the luscious arrangements of plants. Once you reach the plaza, cascading water spills over a stone wall directing the focus down toward the reflecting pool. Here you'll see the configuration of the azalea maze apparently floating within the pool's encircling water. Despite this captivating illusion, the azaleas are planted in soil.

The Central Garden's plaza readily accommodates the bustling, ebullient crowds, as well as solitary pilgrims drawn to the Getty Center. To underscore the exciting dimensions of the plaza landing, Irwin created a number of soaring, splayed sculptural constructions, fabricated of industrial rebar and festooned in bougainvillea. In addition to supporting the colorful vines, the volumetric steel bowers suggest places where you may wish to stop and rest.

I found the horticultural vignettes located around the pool area wildly romantic and totally intoxicating. Curving swaths of steel function as the garden's contoured retaining walls. From one of many benches nestled in secluded niches, I could appreciate the metal's rusty patina, a stunning contrast to the extravagant sensory delight offered by masses of bright blooms and luscious leaf forms thriving in the raised beds. Overall, more than 500 types of plants are found in the Central Garden.

The pool area's terraced gardens create an amphitheater-like setting. In this central space, a cool impression is made by the clipped green shrubbery maze, with its circular frame of gray sedum. In a striking juxtaposition, countless varieties of plants are showcased around the staggered levels above the pool. In one instance, the bold swords of variegated phormiums played off immense and flamboyant dahlias. Arranged according to special themes, the color combinations often go beyond exuberant. If you look in another direction, rose standards, purple coneflowers and uncommon tropical vines work their magic, while everywhere bees and burnished butterflies hover over the fragrant flowers.

After completing your tour of the Central Garden, locate the south promontory on the Getty Center map. The cactus garden planted here offers its own wondrous pleasures. The exalted scale and use of space at the Getty Center simply dazzles. Glistening in the Southern California sun, the center is a haven for art and garden lovers, alike. Don't miss the opportunity to enjoy the beauty of its buildings and priceless artworks, its panoramic views and enthralling gardens.

INFORMATION AND DIRECTIONS

The Getty Center, 1200 Getty Center Drive, Los Angeles, CA 90049-1681. Admission to the Getty is free. If you come by car, please note, however, that parking reservations are required and there is a parking fee of $5. Phone 310-440-7300 to confirm open hours, to make a parking reservation, and for shuttle information. Visitors may also come by public transportation, taxi, or local shuttle service, but may face long lines. Also note that on days when site capacity reaches its maximum, only those with parking reservations are guaranteed admission. Open Tuesdays and Wednesdays, 11 A.M. to 7 P.M.; Thursdays and Fridays, 11 A.M. to 9 P.M.; Saturdays and Sundays, 10 A.M. to 6 P.M. Closed Mondays and major holidays. *Web Site: www.getty.edu*

Located just off the 405 Freeway in Los Angeles; take the Getty Center Drive exit and follow signs to the entrance.

The Getty Villa, Malibu

Scheduled to reopen in 2002, the Getty Villa in Malibu is undergoing a major renovation. The Villa closed in 1997 so that most of the collections could be moved to the new J. Paul Getty Museum at the Getty Center. As this entry was under way, the Villa was closed for renovation. Plans were in place for the Getty Villa to become a center for comparative archaeology and cultures, and a museum for antiquities.

Built in the style of a classical Roman building, the Getty Villa in Malibu features a traditional Roman peristyle garden, a long pool, fabulous colonnades, frescoes and loggias that are hallmarks of ancient villas. The villa features the J. Paul Getty Museum's collection of Greek and Roman antiquities. The collections that were formerly displayed at the Getty Villa are now on view in the museum at the

Getty Center, including major works from the Museum's antiquities collection, and changing exhibitions.

INFORMATION AND DIRECTIONS

The Getty Villa, Malibu, California. To confirm the Getty Villa's re-opening in 2002, contact the Getty Center by phoning 310-440-7300. The Getty Villa is located at Pacific Coast Highway 1, about 20 minutes from downtown Los Angeles.

The Huntington Botanical Gardens, San Marino

H. E. Huntington, creator of Southern California's interurban railway system, and his second wife, Arabella, set up a nonprofit trust to care for their exceptional library of books, fabulous art treasures, and extraordinary gardens. Opened in 1928, the Huntington Library, Art Collections, and Botanical Gardens extended to the public the rare opportunity to view the architectural and horticultural riches of the Huntingtons' San Marino property.

Truly one of the nation's most inspiring landscapes, the Huntington Botanical Gardens makes a wonderful stopover for garden lovers and should be included in any itinerary planned for the Los Angeles area. Once ranch land planted with citrus and fruit trees, grain and other crops, the vast property of nearly 600 acres Henry E. Huntington purchased in 1903 has been remarkably transformed.

Encompassing 150 landscaped acres, the Huntington Botanical Gardens include the renowned Desert and Palm Gardens, a refined three-acre Rose Garden, and a wonderfully untamed Subtropical Garden. Camellias are highlighted in the Japanese Garden and North Vista areas, while the Shakespeare Garden features some of the oldest roses in cultivation, along with such specimens as violets, pomegranate, columbines and pansies, which the English bard alluded to in his writings. An informative booklet is available to facilitate a self-guided tour of the Huntington's fifteen principal gardens.

Distinguished by an elegant formality, the Huntington Botanical Gardens are set amidst imposing classical buildings and statuary, expanses of lawn and aristocratic trees. Rose lover that I am, I was enchanted by the irresistibly opulent exhibition of roses. The lush area devoted to David Austin's English roses, in particular, reveals a marvelous display of the hybridizer's many petaled, exquisitely fragrant flowers. Bordered by luxuriant azure *Agapanthus orientalis*,

'Huntington Blue,' the rose arbor is an admirable landmark to seek out, as is an eighteenth century stone temple featuring the heavenly statue "Love, the Captive of Youth."

Dramatic topography, a grand scale, and fascinating faux wood arbors are some of the striking characteristics of the Japanese Garden. Here, the Japanese House displays and illuminates the Japanese art of flower arranging. Stroll on the camellia lined walkways and wander through towering bamboo groves, enjoying shady havens. Note the intriguingly designed, cast concrete arbors which are known to fool the eye with their skillful emulation of tree trunks and branches.

To discover the Zen Garden, which was completed in 1968, you need to follow the pathway to the left after leaving the Japanese House. In this contemplative courtyard setting, you'll find a garden where the essence of flowing water is suggested by the raked pattern of sand and rock. Just beyond the Zen Garden, you'll find the bonsai court, with its specimens of dwarf trees.

Forty-five full-time gardeners lavish attention on the Huntington Botanical Gardens, helping to maintain the garden's eminent position worldwide. In the 12-acre Desert Garden displays of cacti and succulents offer a thrilling experience to aficionados of rare flora. Handsome coast live oaks indigenous to the property stand watch over more than 5,000 species of plants native to desert regions. Here are handsome aloe trees, and a congregation of barrel-type cactus plants, the roly-poly *Echinocactus grusonii*. When numbers of these robust forms are planted together, passersby are inclined to stop and admire the beautiful, rhythmic composition the plants create.

The Desert Garden features a wealth of thorny plants, including such exotic specimens as the crown of thorns plant (*Euphorbia milii*), with its showy colorful red bracts. Many species found within the succulents and cacti collections display spectacular spiny protrusions, but they are famous also for the bountiful blossoms and brilliant flowers they produce throughout winter, spring, summer and fall. A walk through the Desert Garden underscores the remarkable contrast between the alluring blooms and the bizarre appearance of these thorny plants.

In the second formal garden that H. E. Huntington created, the Palm Garden, you'll find more than 100 species of one of the founder's favorite trees. In a landscape brimming with so many types and specimens of palms, you'll find fishtail (*Caryota* species) and jelly palms (*Butia capitata*). With graceful arching fronds that sway in the breeze, thin elegant trunks reaching skyward, and huge clusters of brightly colored fruit, the dramatic, tropical palms have an extraordinary presence. Don't miss the Jungle Garden, the waterfall, and lily ponds. In these areas you'll encounter delightful displays of gingers, bromeliads, waterlilies, bamboos, and calla lilies scattered throughout. Look for the magnificent giant ombú, with its impressive gnarled trunk. This Argentinean native has unusual, spongy wood that conserves water during periods of drought.

For overall impact, the grandeur of the North Vista is unequaled. Here the perfectly proportioned design brings together such elements as a Renaissance fountain, a seventeenth-century sculpture allée, ornamental shrubbery, an elaborate lawn and a view of the San Gabriel Mountains. Visiting this stately formal garden is like entering a fine seventeenth century European landscape. Although often reproduced, the garden is even more lovely than the image portrayed in photographs.

The glorious grounds of the Huntington Botanical Gardens will inspire you to return again and again to visit the art galleries, the open air collection of sculptural masterworks, and more than 14,000 types of impeccably maintained plants.

INFORMATION AND DIRECTIONS

The Huntington Library, Art Collections, and Botanical Gardens, 1151 Oxford Road, San Marino, CA 91108. Phone 626-405-2141 for information, or to confirm directions and seasonal open hours. The bookstore carries an excellent selection of books. Reservations are suggested for the Rose Garden Tea Room. The Huntington is open Tuesday through Friday, 12 noon to 4:30 P.M.; Saturday through Sunday, 10:30 A.M. to 4:30 P.M. Closed Mondays and major Holidays. Summer hours: Memorial Day through Labor Day, 10:30 A.M. to 4:30 P.M. daily, excluding Mondays. Admission fee charged, except for the first Thursday of every month when it is free. *Web site: www.hunting ton.org*

The Huntington Botanical Gardens are located approximately 30 minutes north of downtown Los Angeles; east of Pasadena Freeway 110, and just south of the city of Pasadena and Foothill Freeway 210.

Mildred E. Mathias Botanical Garden at UCLA, Los Angeles

Situated on the campus of the University of California, Los Angeles, the Mildred E. Mathias Botanical Garden boasts one of the country's largest gatherings of tropical and subtropical plants. The garden's seven frost-free acres display botanical collections of uncommon trees and flora from around the world.

Named for the garden's director from 1956 to 1974, Dr. Mildred Mathias, the Botanical Garden features more than 5,000 species, representing 225 plant families. Special collections include bromeliads, Malesian rhododendrons, ferns, cycads, palms, and the newest one devoted to plants native to the Hawaiian Islands. Another distinctive collection, the lily alliance, highlights the Order Liliales. Incorporated here are a wide spectrum of related plants—from trees and vines, to species demonstrating long periods of dormancy.

A monumental, endangered Torrey pine, and two giant rose gum (*Eucalyptus grandis*) trees exemplify the exceptional tree specimens you'll encounter here. In addition to numerous species of eucalyptus and ficus, the garden's collections include a particularly intriguing array of spectacular flowering trees. Look for many members of the bignon family of plants, particularly the African tulip tree (*Spathodea campanulata*), growing near the corner of South Tiverton and Charles E. Young Drive. Given suitable conditions, the tree produces huge, rounded red flowers from March through November. The Malesian rhododendrons also produce an exhilarating exhibition of blossoms all year-round. Some fine specimens are in flower every day, January through December.

Consult the Botanical Garden map in order to locate the hillside section (number 5), where you'll observe a satisfying collection of palm trees native to both Northern and Southern hemispheres. In the Hawaiian Island section (number 12 on the map), look for colorful, showy species of hibiscus. Lovers of flora will find endless marvels to contemplate and admire at UCLA's Mildred E. Mathias Botanical Garden.

INFORMATION AND DIRECTIONS

Mildred E. Mathias Botanical Garden at University of California, Los Angeles, Hilgard Avenue and Le Conte Avenue, Box 951606, Los Angeles, CA 90095-1606. Phone the garden office at 310-825-1260 for information. Open Monday through Friday, 8 A.M. to 5 P.M. (winter closing 4 P.M.); Saturday and Sunday, 8 A.M. to 4 P.M. Closed on university holidays. Free admission. To park on campus, you must purchase a parking pass at an information kiosk. Or, you can use public parking lots in nearby Westwood.

Located at the southeastern corner of the UCLA campus, in the Westwood section of Los Angeles.

Rancho Santa Ana Botanic Garden, Claremont

Rancho Santa Ana Botanic Garden's 83-acre site deserves exploration for its exceptional collections of native flora, including 2,800 plant species, and hundreds of rare and endangered plants.

Three distinctive areas within the garden feature plants that thrive in the following types of environments: dense clay (in the Indian Hill Mesa); sedimentary, rocky soils (in the East Alluvial Gardens); and a combination of sand, gravel, rocks and alluvial deposits that form the basis of the impressive 55-acre expanse of the California Plant Communities.

The Indian Hill Mesa exhibits numerous types of manzanitas (*Arctostaphylos*), in flower from late November through early March. These winter blooming western natives are characterized by lovely red bark, a sculptural interplay of branches, and charming flowers that dangle like bells. The Mesa section is especially delightful during March and April when masses of California wild lilacs (*Ceanothus*) are blooming.

In the East Alluvial Gardens, you'll find groupings of desert, coastal, and Channel Island plants, and the wonderful Palm Oasis, which features an arrangement of handsome fan palms (*Washingtonia filifera*), the only palm tree native to the state of California. The California Plant Communities, the expansive area devoted to the state's plants, includes among its rich offerings big berry manzanitas, California flannel bushes, and *Nolina parryi*, which is related to the yuccas. Commonly called Parry Nolina, the plants display their stunning flower rosettes on phenomenal stalks ten feet tall in early spring.

Look also for the California Garden, showcasing cultivated varieties of plants, and the Riparian Woodland, located along the banks between the garden's upper and lower pond. You can consult the "Garden Map & Guide for Visitors" to locate any gardens. Remember, although springtime wildflower displays are lovely and colorful, vis-

115

itors can enjoy this haven on any given day of the year.

INFORMATION AND DIRECTIONS

Rancho Santa Ana Botanic Garden, 1500 North College Avenue, Claremont, CA 91711-3157. Phone 909-625-8767 for general information. The California Garden Shop features a host of books, and gift items such as walking sticks and wildflower T-shirts. Open daily from 8 A.M. to 5 P.M., except New Year's Day, July 4th, Thanksgiving and Christmas. Donations are encouraged. *Web site: www.rsabg.org*

Located about 1 hour and 15 minutes northeast of downtown Los Angeles. From the I-10 Freeway, take Indian Hill Boulevard exit north to Foothill Boulevard. Turn right and go east three blocks to College Avenue.

Virginia Robinson Gardens, Beverly Hills

The 1911 Mediterranean Revival mansion of Mr. and Mrs. Harry Winchester Robinson, and the surrounding Italian terraced gardens are one of the earliest homes and landscapes built in this Southern California eden. Cloistered within luxurious Beverly Hills, the Virginia Robinson Gardens exemplifies a graciousness and elegance associated with both its locale and architectural period.

Extending over more than six acres of picturesque hillside, the gardens are divided into five specific garden areas, including the Italian Terrace, the Mall, the Rose, and the Kitchen gardens. Exuberant flower borders, mature cycads, and a stunning patio with decorative balustrades enliven the atmosphere of the Formal Mall Garden. In the Italian Terrace Garden, under the shade of sheltering magnolias and handsome trees, camellias, azaleas, hydrangeas, and bevies of exotics burst forth with their beautiful blooms. Here also, charming brick paths lead garden wanderers to admire the aged patina of stone fountains and elevated ponds.

Mrs. Robinson left her lovely home and beguiling grounds to Los Angeles County. Visitors have continued to admire the unique landscaping, especially the unrivaled grove of Australian king palm trees, planted at the suggestion of well-known landscape architect, Charles Gibbs Adams. Among the gardens' many water features, an ornate pool with exceptional mosaic work is impressive. Accentuated by regal Roman arches, a Renaissance Revival Pavilion rises above the serene pool. This ornamental building takes its inspiration from Italy's Villa Pisani.

A visit to the Virginia Robinson Gardens allows contemporary garden lovers to experience a noble manifestation of wealth, as expressed in the nature of horticultural abundance.

INFORMATION AND DIRECTIONS

Virginia Robinson Gardens, Beverly Hills, CA 90210. Phone 310-276-5367 for information or to make an appointment to visit. Garden open Tuesday through Friday by reservation only; docent tours. Admission fee charged.

Located just north of Los Angeles, in the center of Beverly Hills.

AND IN ADDITION . . .

Rancho Los Alamitos Historic Ranch and Gardens: Long Beach

6400 Bixby Hill Road, Long Beach, CA 90815. Phone 562-431-3541; FAX 562-430-9694. Open Wednesday through Sunday afternoons, 1 P.M. to 5 P.M. Free public events and group tours. On a historic 7½-acre setting, you'll find a ranch house, barns, and four acres of gardens now restored and preserved for the public's benefit. One of the two (see next entry: Rancho Los Cerritos) adobe homes was once owned by members of the Bixby family.

Landscape architect Florence Yoch is still celebrated today for the Oleander Walk she originally designed in the 1920s for a relation of the Bixby clan. Plantings highlight cacti and citrus trees. Among a number of theme gardens, the friendship garden stands out. The Rancho Los Alamitos landscaping is enhanced by a charming fountain and courtyard that resonate with Spanish Colonial influence, while venerable trees of considerable girth add to its historical appeal.

Rancho Los Cerritos: Long Beach

4600 Virginia Road, Long Beach, CA 90807. Phone 562-570-1755. Open Wednesday through Sunday afternoons, 1 P.M. to 5 P.M. Admission is free. This historic two-story adobe, circa 1844, features interiors that represent late nineteenth century life. The grounds stretch over approximately five acres of land once used to raise cattle and sheep. The lovely formal gardens are attributed to Ralph D. Cornell, a prominent Southern California landscape architect associated with Cook, Hall & Cornell. An enclosed courtyard garden, and another spacious area of inviting lawns and charming old brick walkways enhance the restored adobe home. Here, as at Rancho Los Alamitos, towering trees contribute to the atmosphere of a bygone epoch.

South Coast Botanic Garden: Palos Verdes Peninsula

26300 Crenshaw Boulevard, Palos Verdes Peninsula, CA 90274-2515. Phone 310-544-6815. The garden is located about one hour south of downtown Los Angeles, on the Palos Verdes Peninsula. Open daily 9 A.M. to 4:30 P.M.; closed December 25. Fee charged. Here, you'll find an inspiring 87-acre garden built on a sanitary landfill. Visit the successful reclamation project and discover a cultural center, lake and stream, along with some 2,000 plant species.

UCLA Hannah Carter Japanese Garden: Los Angeles

Located one mile north of the UCLA campus in Bel-Air, the garden can be visited by reservation only, on Tuesday, Wednesday and Friday, from 10 A.M. to 3 P.M. Parking is limited. Phone 310-825-4574 to make a reservation for either a self-guided tour of the Kyoto-style Japanese Garden, or to schedule a docent tour. Fax: 310-267-2247. Admission is free.

Affiliated with the University of California at Los Angeles, the Hannah Carter Japanese Garden features a lovely pond with animated koi, and a notable 1000-year-old stone carving. As stated in a pamphlet, the garden's design signifies the cycle from unrestrained youthfulness to sedate maturity, presented in a counterclockwise progression. You'll find a more buoyant spirit in garden areas around the main entrance, while sections to the right reveal a controlled character.

10

Orange County Gardens

Sherman Library and Gardens, Corona del Mar

In contrast to the cornucopia of botanical gardens found in nearby Los Angeles, there are but a handful of public gardens to visit in Orange County. The lack of quantity, however, is more than made up for by the quality of the gardens in this area.

The Sherman Library and Gardens is a case in point. Located in the center of downtown Corona del Mar, the two-acre landscape offers proof that good things come in small packages. Residential in both scale and design, the garden capitalizes on its superb growing climate to offer a near-perfect example of the indoor/outdoor living that California is famous for.

An emphasis on floral color, coupled with a liberal use of garden structures, unite the disparate parts of the garden. Flowering vines, including various colorful *Bougainvillea*, cup-of-gold and *Mandevilla*, 'Alice Dupont,' clamber up walls and trellises. Sturdy wisteria cloaks the arbor-covered walkways connecting the tropical conservatory and shaded lath house areas to the tiled patio and courtyard gardens that flow out from the main house, which is now home to the research library and gift shop.

The overall result is an effortless intermingling of garden "rooms," each with a distinctive theme that highlights its particular group of plantings. Fountains, statuary, hanging baskets, and beds brimming with annual flower color offset the various botanical collections to great effect.

There is a progression to the plantings, as well. The pots of colorful cyclamen and begonias that line the covered path leading away from the lath house shade gardens, for example, gradually give way to a display of tropical orchid cacti (*Epiphyllum*) that reside in the protective shade of an ancient California pepper tree (*Schinus molle*). These, in turn, ingeniously set the scene for the display of rare desert cacti and succulents that follows.

This dry garden of mostly desert plants from the arid regions of the American Southwest and Latin America is among the gardens' most notable plant collections. The small but choice display includes such specimens as the Mexican grass tree (*Dasylirion longissima*), the so-called Madagascar palm (*Pachypodium lamieri*), which is not a palm at all but a relative of the common oleander, and a stupendous six-foot-tall example of *Pedilanthus* sp. an unusual-looking succulent with smooth, pencil-thin stems and reddish, bract-like tips.

Established in 1966, Sherman Gardens offers also remarkable collections of cycads, orchids and tropical foliage plants, the latter two of which are housed inside a conservatory. Entering this tropical greenhouse, one is greeted by an explosion of foliar color: burgundy-leafed *Irisine*; purple-stemmed torch ginger; fiery red and orange bromeliads; cream, rose and maroon-splotched leaves of giant, fancy-leafed *Caladiums*.

It is this consistent attention to detail that elevates Sherman Gardens to a level of excellence unmatched by similar botanical institutions. Any serious lover of horticulture must visit this garden.

INFORMATION AND DIRECTIONS

Sherman Library and Gardens, 2647 East Pacific Coast Highway, Corona del Mar, CA. Tel: (714) 673-2261. Open daily 10:30 A.M. to 4 P.M.; closed on holidays. Amenities include a courtyard café, a gift shop, and a research library. Admission is $3.

From Los Angeles, take Interstate 405 to the Jamboree Road exit. Head west on Jamboree to Pacific Coast Highway, turn left (south) and follow for 1½ blocks. The gardens will be on your right.

University Of California Irvine Arboretum, Irvine

Located off one of Irvine's busiest thoroughfares, the UCI Arboretum's 13 pristine acres offer a refreshing slice of natural beauty in an area better known for its tract-home developments and concrete-and-steel business parks.

As a working research facility attached to a university, the arboretum lacks the frills of an independently financed botanical garden:

there's no gift shop, nor even so much as a public information booth. Maps of the grounds are available from a bulletin board at the arboretum's entrance, although the day I went, the supply was exhausted. If that's the case, you're pretty much on your own. That's less of a drawback than it sounds. The plants are, for the most part, clearly labeled with their botanical name, common name and place of origin, while the plant collections of interest to the public are confined to an area bordering the long, sloping lawn just past the arboretum's entrance.

The day I visited—a weekday afternoon—I had the place to myself, which made for a pleasant sort of private-estate-garden atmosphere that was rather enjoyable. Not only was I able to take in the plantings at a leisurely pace, but I was also able to experience and appreciate the landscape as a whole much better without the human distraction.

Despite its name, the arboretum specializes primarily in South African bulbs, corms and tubers. Its collection, which contains more than 200 endangered species, rates as the largest institutional collection outside of South Africa. Many of the delicate bulb beauties are featured in the planting beds that ring the large sloped lawn area leading down to the San Joaquin Marsh Wildlife Preserve. Stroll on the circular path to explore these beauties.

The delicate flowers of *Gladiolus tristis*, the winter-hardy gladiolus, were among the only bulbs in bloom during my late fall visit, along with some early-blooming freesias. It is in spring that the arboretum reaches its full flowering glory, and undoubtedly is the best time to visit.

While the focus of the arboretum is primarily on South African flowering bulbs, you'll also find here an outstanding aloe collection, probably one of the most extensive anywhere in the world. These large specimen plants make a dramatic display at the top of the sloped site; their large, spiky silhouettes are like punctuation marks in the clear blue sky.

INFORMATION AND DIRECTIONS
University of California Irvine Arboretum, Campus Drive at Jamboree Road, Irvine, CA. Tel: (714) 824-5833. Open 9 A.M. to 3 P.M., Monday through Saturday. Closed on Sunday. Admission to the arboretum is free, but parking in the adjacent lot is metered, so make sure to take plenty of quarters with you.

From Los Angeles, take Interstate 405 south to the Jamboree Road exit west. Follow Jamboree for about a mile to Campus Drive, turn left. The arboretum will be immediately on your right.

AND IN ADDITION . . .

Roger's Gardens: Corona del Mar

Roger's Gardens occupies a prime hilltop site overlooking the Pacific Ocean. Dubbed the Disneyland of nurseries, its 7½ acres of shops and gardens offer a welcoming oasis of horticultural beauty amid the hustle and bustle of busy Orange County. Arboretum-quality display plantings and thousands of the nursery's signature hanging baskets provide brilliant flower color year-round.

Whether your interest lies in heirloom or gourmet vegetables, colorful annuals, flowering vines, or distinctive and unusual perennials, Roger's has them all. Ramble through artful plantings of perennial color, drink in the fragrance of David Austin English roses, or admire a pair of leaping topiary dolphins as you make your way through the various sections of the nursery grounds.

Cooks and herb gardeners will find no less than 24 different varieties of basil in the herb garden section, while flower gardeners looking for inspiration need only visit the color bank of triangular display plots alongside the lower walkway to get a score of ideas on how to combine a variety of different seasonal plantings.

Roger's isn't just limited to outdoor plantings, though; there's a whole indoor world to explore, as well. Stop in at one of the many garden rooms scattered along the pathway leading through the grounds. Each of these separate retail areas has something different to offer, from basic fertilizers and seed packets to garden gifts and one-of-a-kind pieces of garden art. Don't miss the Gallery at the nursery's entrance, which features antique garden furniture, decorative garden items, seasonal and holiday collections, and a definitive selection of garden books.

INFORMATION AND DIRECTIONS

Roger's Gardens, 2301 San Joaquin Hills Road, Corona del Mar, CA. Tel: (949) 640-5800. Open daily, 9 A.M. to 9 P.M.

From Los Angeles, take Interstate 405 south to the Jamboree Road exit west. Follow Jamboree to San Joaquin Hills Road, turn left and go about three blocks. Roger's Gardens will be on your right, just past the intersection of MacArthur Boulevard.

11

San Diego and Vicinity Gardens

Balboa Park, San Diego

Situated on some 1,400 acres in the city's urban core, Balboa Park is one of the most lushly planted city parks in the nation. Given its inauspicious beginnings, that's quite an achievement.

Although land was set aside in 1868 for the establishment of "City Park," as it was then known, several early attempts to develop the rocky, arid, inhospitable terrain foundered, and it wasn't until the close of the century that work got under way in earnest.

Pioneering nurserywoman Kate Sessions is largely credited with landscaping the northwestern portion of the park under a novel lease agreement with the city. In exchange for leasing land for a nursery on the park's northwestern edge, Sessions agreed to plant 100 trees a year throughout the park for the duration of her lease.

She far exceeded that quota, however, planting several thousand specimens in the park during the decade that she operated there. Many of the largest trees on the park's west mesa are her legacy, including the cork oaks, *Melaleucas*, Canary Island pines and Pindo palms. Sessions remains the single largest influence in transforming the park into the forested paradise of 14,000 trees (350 species) it is today.

Planting intensified as the city prepared to host the 1915 Panama-California Exposition, and the park was renamed Balboa, after the Spanish explorer. The Spanish Colonial architecture from which the park gets its old world charm is a legacy of the later California Pacific International Exposition, held in 1935–36.

Today, Balboa Park serves as the cultural heart of the city, housing museums, galleries and performing arts' sites, as well as several notable botanical gardens that offer a cornucopia of horticultural pleasures. Because each of these gardens offers a unique experience, they are detailed separately below.

INFORMATION AND DIRECTIONS

Balboa Park, 1549 El Prado, San Diego, CA. General visitor information: (619) 239-0512.

Located in downtown San Diego, the park's western entrance is at Laurel Street and Sixth Avenue, and its eastern entrance at Park Boulevard and President's Way.

Balboa Park Botanical Building, Balboa Park

Designed by well-known architect Carlton Winslow, this impressive domed building ranked as the largest lath structure in the world when it was built in 1915, and remains among the largest ones today. The building measures 250 feet long, 75 feet wide and 60 feet tall. It took more than 70,000 linear feet of redwood to construct it.

The interior of the Botanical Building houses 2,100 permanent plantings representing more than 350 different species of tropical plants, including an outstanding collection of ferns. Its many niches invite discovery, with a variety of plants chosen to accommodate a broad range of botanical interests. The plantings are augmented by seasonal floral exhibits, making for an ever-changing display of botanical beauty.

Winslow also designed the Lily Pond in front of the Botanical Building, which is actually two ponds separated by a balustrade bridge. The smaller upper lily pond, closest to the Botanical Building, is planted with a selection of popular water lilies (*Nymphaea* sp.), as well as a variety of bog plants, including papyrus (*Cyperus papyrus*), Japanese arrowhead, primrose creeper and water iris.

The lower lily pond, the larger of the two at 193 feet long and 42 feet wide, was designed in the manner of a reflecting pool, but its formal lines are broken up by the colorful water lilies and spectacular Indian lotus plants (*Nelumbo lucifera*) that bloom on the water's surface. Brilliant orange Japanese koi, sun-basking turtles and splashing ducks add a realistic touch of movement to the idyllic scene.

INFORMATION

The Botanical Building is open free of charge from 10 A.M. to 4 P.M., Thursday through Saturday, and from noon to 4 P.M. on Sunday.

Desert Garden, Balboa Park

The Desert Garden, which dates back to 1935, moved to its present location on the east side of Park Boulevard in 1977. Encompassing 2½ acres, this garden showcases some 1,300 drought-resistant cacti and succulents representing more than 150 species from around the world. Plantings include several coral trees (*Erythrina*), giant tree aloes, and surrealistic-looking boojum trees from Baja California.

Inez Grant Parker Memorial Rose Garden, Balboa Park

Lying adjacent to the Desert Garden, the three-acre Inez Grant Parker Memorial Rose Garden contains more than 2,500 roses representing over 200 varieties, including hybrid teas, grandifloras, floribundas, ramblers, shrubs, and Old Garden roses.

Established in 1975, the rose garden is an officially designated All-America Rose Selections Display Garden. It boasts a simple but effective design, with tiered rose beds forming concentric rings around a circular arbor covered with climbing white *Rosa x fortuniana*. Stone benches in the shade of the pergola offer an ideal spot to enjoy a sack lunch or relax. Thanks to San Diego's mild, Mediterranean climate, visitors will find roses in bloom from March through December, with peak bloom occurring from April through early June.

Japanese Friendship Garden, Balboa Park

Located northwest of the Spreckels Organ Pavilion in the park's center, the 11½-acre Japanese Friendship Garden will be the largest Japanese garden in the United States when it is completed.

The garden is named San-Kei-En, or "Three Scenery Garden," for the water, pastoral and mountain landscape themes it encompasses. The master plan calls for the garden to be built in three phases. During the first phase, a small entry garden, an exhibit house, a traditional sand and stone garden, and a viewing platform overlooking a small canyon were completed.

Designed by Japanese architect Takeshi Nakajima, this part of the garden and its structures are distinguished by simple materials and economical design. A wisteria-covered arbor graces the viewing platform, while in the sand and stone garden, the sand is raked in simple patterns of lines and concentric circles around the spare monuments of stone.

Restrained plantings in the entry garden include pines, azaleas, sunburst locust, Japanese maple, saucer magnolia, purple-leaf plum, gingko, camphor and variegated mock orange. Several varieties of bamboo fences serve to connect the disparate parts of the garden.

The second phase of development, currently under way, encompasses the canyon portion of the garden. It is expected to be completed later this year. No date for the final phase of development has been set, since funding has yet to be secured.

INFORMATION

The Japanese Friendship Garden is open from 10 A.M. to 4 P.M., Tuesdays, Fridays, Saturdays and Sundays. Admission is $2 for adults, and $1 for seniors, members of the military and children under 12. For information on group tours, call 619-232-2780.

Marston House and Gardens, Balboa Park

Designed by renowned turn-of-the-century architect Irving Gill, the historic Marston House is located on Seventh Avenue along Balboa Park's western edge. Completed in 1905, the Craftsman-style home served as the residence of the city founding father George W. Marston and his family.

The expansive gardens that surround the house are landscaped, for the most part, in the English Romantic style with California overtones. San Diego horticulture pioneer Kate Sessions was responsible for much of the gardens' design, including most of the mature tree specimens found on the site. Some of the more distinctive of these include the lemon-scented gums (*Eucalyptus citriodora*), deodar cedars, and Canary Island pines.

Sessions also planted the perennial beds that border the long sloping lawn area on the southeastern side of the property, and the cactus and succulent garden that descends down the side of the canyon at the rear.

By contrast, the garden areas on the north side of the house are much more formal in look; they are the work of a succession of various nationally known landscape architects, among them John Nolen and William Templeton Johnson. Here, roses and other flowering plants are confined within geometrically formal planting beds, while a stone balustrade separates the entire area from the wilder landscape beyond.

The concept works best in the semi-enclosed walled patio garden, largely because of the beauty of the tile mural that covers the rear wall. The decorative pattern of the tile recalls the Islamic-style garden, much admired by prominent San Diegans at the time.

A registered historic site, the Marston House and Gardens are managed by the San Diego Historical Society, with the grounds maintained as a public historic garden by the city's Park and Recreation Department.

INFORMATION

Marston House and Gardens, 3525 Seventh Ave., San Diego, CA. Phone 619-298-3142. Guided tours of the house and gardens are offered from noon to 4 P.M., Fridays, Saturdays and Sundays. Cost for the one-hour tour of the house is only $3; the 1½-hour tour, which also takes in the rose and herb gardens of the 4½-acre estate, costs $4. There is no charge for children ages 13 and under. The gardens also are open seven days a week at no charge for self-guided tours.

Palm Canyon, Balboa Park

Palm Canyon lies in the center of Balboa Park, just west of the Spreckels Organ Pavilion. A wooden footbridge crosses over the canyon, weaving between queen palms, blue fan palms (*Brahea armata*), and bamboo-like *Chamaedorea* underplanted with clusters of crinum lilies, ginger and other subtropicals.

The canyon itself contains 450 palms (58 species) within its two acres, including a prominent group of Mexican fan palms (*Washingtonia robusta*) that date to the early 1900s. A wooden staircase to the south of the House of Charm leads to a narrow path that wends its way along the canyon floor, flanked on either side by towering palms that eclipse the sky, creating moist, cool conditions for plants like *Clivia*, philodendron and elephant's ear to thrive in. The dominant palm within the canyon is the pendulous paradise palm, *Howea fosterana*. Sentry palms, pygmy date palms and the graceful feather palms are also in abundance.

The point where the plantings end and the natural canyon continues down toward State Highway 163, is a good place to turn around and head back; the only way out is to retrace your steps back the way you came.

San Diego Zoo Botanical Collection, Balboa Park

Although best known for its animals, the San Diego Zoo has been an accredited botanical garden since 1993. Thanks to San Diego's mild climate, the grounds are always filled with a variety of colorful blooms year-round.

Located in the northeast corner of Balboa Park, the zoo grounds encompass 100 acres and incorporate ten bioclimatic zones in which more than 6,500 different species of plants are showcased.

Included among its several notable botanical collections are more than 400 species of palms, 150 aloe species, and more than 800 types of orchids, as well as 49 coral tree taxa and cultivars. Its cycad collection, which totals some 80 species, contains such unusual examples as *Encephalartos munchii*, the munch cycad, and *E. natalensis*, the Natal giant cycad.

Some plants in the zoo's collection are grown as feed for specific animals. Several of its 31 varieties of bamboo, for example, are integral to the diet of the two giant pandas on loan to the zoo from China, while foliage from its many eucalyptus trees satisfy the appetites of its resident koalas. And its 31 ficus species include those necessary to the survival of the zoo's Sumatran rhino population.

Although some of the plant collections, such as the palms and cycads, are grouped together in a specific area of the park—in the case of the cycads, it's at the top of the trail leading down to Bear Canyon—plants from other collections can be found scattered throughout the grounds. Orchids, for example, can be found throughout the Tiger River exhibit, as well as in Fern Canyon and at the main orchid greenhouse.

Also scattered throughout the grounds are several whimsical topiary animals. The most impressive are the two life-size elephants that grace the zoo's entrance plaza. The ivy-covered beasts incorporate ingenious internal irrigation systems that maintain optimum moisture levels for the growing plant material.

INFORMATION

The San Diego Zoo is open daily from 9 A.M. to 4 P.M., and until 7 P.M. Memorial Day through Labor Day. Admission is $16 for adults, $7 for children ages three to 11; children ages two and under enter free. The zoo is located on the eastern edge of Balboa Park, at Park Boulevard and Zoo Drive. Phone 619-234-3153.

Quail Botanical Gardens, Encinitas

Sitting atop a coastal bluff overlooking the Pacific, this 32-acre plant paradise was first established in the 1940s as the private residence of Ruth Baird Larabee, who filled the garden with collections of rare and unusual plants gathered during her extensive world travels. Cycads, aloes, subtropical fruit trees and several rare dragon trees (*Dracaena draco*) are just some of the original plants that remain on the site today.

Open to the public since 1971, the gardens today are home to more than 10,000 plants representing more than 5,000 species, including over 75 species of bamboo, which make one of the largest and most diverse collections in the country.

Quail's plant collections from all over the globe are grouped by climatic region, with a total of 15 phytogeographic zones, as these groupings are called, represented. The 15 zoned displays—encompassing tropical and dry Australia, tropical and dry South America, the Canary Islands, Madagascar, Southeast Asia, the Himalayas, Southeast Africa, Southwest Africa and South Africa, Central America, Baja California, Oceania and the Mediterranean—form the backbone of the garden layout. Smaller horticultural and demonstration garden areas add thematic displays to diversify the mix.

With less stringent parameters, these thematic display gardens offer a cornucopia of botanical delights, from the spare, dramatic plant forms found in the New World Desert Garden to the exotic Subtropical Fruit Garden, with its more than 75 types of fruit-bearing plants like cherimoya, sapote, macadamia, star fruit and rose apple.

The landscape potential of the region's indigenous flora is the focus of the California Native Plant Display Garden, while the Firescape Demonstration Garden offers homeowners a lesson in wildfire protection through the use of appropriate plant materials and landscaping techniques. Future plans call for the addition of an educational Children's Garden, and a Native Plants/Native People exhibit that will focus on plants used by indigenous Indian tribes, such as the Kumeyaay.

The Bamboo Display Garden, along the gardens' western edge, is home to Quail's first (and, so far, only) commissioned work of art—an organic sculpture/water feature created by well-known local artist James Hubbell.

The Walled Garden, part of the original Larabee estate, displays shade-tolerant plants, including some of the original cycads that were first planted there. Beyond it lies the Herb Garden, with medicinal and culinary herbs, and the Horticulture Display Garden, with old-fashioned roses, perennials, and flowering annuals. Fronting the original residence is a large, sloping lawn area graced by mature shade trees, flowering shrubs, and a Victorian gazebo that is popular for weddings.

From the lawn area, a path makes its way through Monterey cypress and Australian dammar pines toward the sound of water, eventually arriving at a deck overlooking the rocky watercourse and falls that mark the start of the gardens' new Tropical Rain Forest exhibit.

Thanks to its wonderfully mild coastal climate, Quail can create a rain forest experience outside, rather than in a conservatory as most other botanical gardens must. Here you will find plants from the higher rainfall areas of the tropical and subtropical areas of the world: lush green tree ferns, elephant's ear, philodendron, aroids, king palms, epiphytes such as orchids and bromeliads, and a stunning Kashmir cypress whose weeping habit is beautifully offset by the adjacent, large-leafed foliage plants.

INFORMATION AND DIRECTIONS

Quail Botanical Gardens, 230 Quail Gardens Drive, Encinitas, CA. Phone 760-436-3036. Open daily 8 A.M. to 5 P.M. Closed Thanksgiving, Christmas and New Year's Day. Amenities include a gift shop, but no eating facilities. It also should be noted that there are a number of steep inclines to navigate as you make your way through the gardens, which could present a problem for some people. Admission is $5 for adults; $4 for seniors; $2 for children ages five to 12; children under five enter free.

From San Diego, take Interstate 5 north about 20 miles to the Encinitas Boulevard exit. Head east for two blocks; then, turn left on Quail Gardens Drive. The gardens' entrance is a short way up on the left.

San Diego Wild Animal Park, Escondido

Twenty times larger than its sister institution, the San Diego Zoo, the San Diego Wild Animal Park offers a completely different experience from that of its urban sibling.

Largely barren when it opened to the public in 1972, the grounds of the 2,200-acre wildlife preserve today showcase some of the most diverse and unusual plant specimens found anywhere in the United States. An accredited botanical garden since 1993, the park's plant collections encompass some 4,000 species and 1,750,000 individual specimens—including more than 260 endangered species of aloe, cactus, *Euphorbia*, cycads, *Protea*, palms and agaves.

The park's transformation from virtual desert to botanical paradise is the result of a long-term plan known as the "Greening of the Field." Developed by the park's Horticulture Department, the aim of the plan is "to plant and improve (its) botanical collection for the benefit of its animal collection and visitors alike." The project has resulted in the planting of several thousands of trees, as well as the naturalistic landscaping of the massive field enclosure to mimic the native habitats of the animals that roam within.

The department's most ambitious project to date was the landscaping of the park's recently opened Heart of Africa exhibit, a 30-acre "walking safari" that allows visitors to get closer than ever before to the featured wildlife. Horticulturists used primarily plants from central and southern Africa to re-create the many diverse habitats represented in the exhibit.

Traveling by foot, visitors progress from dense forest to flourishing wetlands, sprawling savannas and, finally, open plains. In addition to *Protea*, *Pennisetum* (fountain grass), aloes, rocket pincushions and corn lilies (*Ixia*), the exhibit includes eight different varieties of acacia trees, including *A. abyssinica*, *A. robusta*, *A. caffra* and *A. xantophloea*, the beautiful fever tree.

Besides the landscaped enclosures and other portions of the vast grounds, the park also features ten specialty display gardens, including several unique single-species ones, such as *Protea*, bonsai, fuchsia and conifer. Most of these gardens are maintained, and some were even established, by local plant societies, whose members donate both their time and expertise to the projects.

Clustered together at the northern end of the park, behind the administration building, the first specialty garden encountered is the *Epiphyllum* House which, with more than 600 specimens, is one of the most comprehensive exhibits of epiphytic cacti in the world. This particular collection is best viewed during the plants' bloom season, from March through early fall.

From the Epi House, visitors proceed to the Bonsai Pavilion, which houses about 30 specimens, and then to the Fuchsia House, following a pathway bordered by a small, gurgling stream that wends its way through the lath-covered structure. Numerous hanging baskets and in-ground plantings display the wide-ranging varieties that make up the fuschia collection.

From here, the path leads to the Kupanda Falls Botanical Center, where the 1¼-mile, self-guided tour of the rest of the display gardens begins. The circular hiking trail leads visitors through the Old World Succulent Garden; the Baja (California) Garden, which has the largest global collection of native Baja plants outside of Baja itself; and the extensive, eight-plant-community display of native flora in the California Nativescapes Garden, before ending up back at the center.

From the center, the path descends through the Conifer Arboretum, which boasts over 1,000 plants representing 400 species, including one of the last 12 North African cypresses left in the world. You'll also traverse the Protea Garden before the path wends its way back to the main section of the park.

Display gardens located elsewhere on the grounds include the Herb Garden, with more than 400 varieties of herbs; and the Water-Wise Demonstration Garden, an educational display developed in cooperation with the San Diego Xeriscape Council. Nearby, a recently added Compost Demonstration Site features the latest in composting techniques and equipment.

INFORMATION AND DIRECTIONS

San Diego Wild Animal Park, 15500 San Pasqual Valley Road, Escondido, CA. Phone 760-747-8702. Open daily 9 A.M. to 4 P.M.; and until 8 P.M. Memorial Day through Labor Day. Admission to the park is $19.95 for adults, $12.95 for children ages three to 11, and free for children ages two and under. Parking is $3.

From San Diego, take Interstate 15 north to the Via Rancho Parkway exit, then follow the signs to the Wild Animal Park.

AND IN ADDITION . . .

Buena Creek Gardens, San Marcos

Buena Creek Gardens offers the largest selection of flowering trees, shrubs, vines and perennial plants in Southern California—more than 5,000 varieties altogether. This four-acre retail nursery and display gardens are a year-round flowering mecca for plant enthusiasts.

Featured display gardens include a ½-acre Sun Perennial Garden, a Shade Garden, a Palm Canyon, and a Drought-Tolerant Garden. Of these, the Sun Perennial Garden is the showcase and, as such, is constantly being updated to incorporate the latest and most popular hybrids. Recent additions to the site include several unusual varieties of ornamental grasses—just a small sampling of the more than 20 varieties offered for sale by the nursery!

The nursery is also an officially accredited American Hemerocallis (Daylily) Society Display Garden, with some 2,000 different varieties of daylilies in cultivation year-round. From old classics to the latest modern tetraploids, Buena Creek's daylily selection is geared to both the casual home gardener and the serious hybridizer/collector. Most of the daylilies are grown for sale through the nursery's mail-order division, Cordon Bleu Daylilies, but visitors to the nursery are free to buy any of the selections they find on site that appeal to them.

While the daylily bloom season begins in May and continues through summer and into fall, the three large growing fields are at their best during the month of June, when the daylily bloom reaches its peak.

While the crop's bloom time is generally consistent from year to year, vagaries in the weather can occasionally advance or delay the season. This was the case following the 1997–98 winter weather phenomenon known as El Nino, which delayed the start of the '98 bloom season by a full month and a half! For this reason, daylily aficionados who plan to visit the nursery during bloom time are encouraged to call ahead for a bloom-status report to avoid possible disappointment.

INFORMATION AND DIRECTIONS

Buena Creek Gardens, 418 Buena Creek Road, San Marcos, CA. Phone 760-744-2810. Open 9 A.M. to 5 P.M., Wednesday through Saturday, and 11 A.M. to 4 P.M. on Sunday. Closed Monday and Tuesday.

From San Diego, take Interstate 15 north about 35 miles to the Deer Springs Road exit. Follow Deer Springs to the Y junction at Twin Oaks Valley Road. Turn left onto Twin Oaks, continue about a ¼-mile to Buena Creek Road. Turn right; the nursery will be on your right.

Summers Past Farms, Flinn Springs

Located on four rural acres in San Diego's East County, this highly successful retail herb-and-perennial nursery, which today grows in excess of 30,000 plants, started up as a small herb plot intended only to satisfy the culinary needs of owner Sheryl Lozier. As Sheryl's interest in gardening grew, so did the plot, until seven years ago, she and her husband, Marshall, decided to quit their jobs and devote themselves full-time to their plant-growing endeavor.

The couple set about converting Marshall's longtime family homestead into a retail nursery operation. Today, the former barn houses a gift shop and classroom space for Sheryl's wreath-making and culinary classes, while the former tractor shed has become a full-fledged soap-making factory.

The front yard is now a lath-covered retail area where the assorted pots of herbs and flowers for sale are displayed. Beyond this, a vine-covered arbor houses a small cappuccino bar and a selection of chairs and tables for customers who want to linger a while.

Featured display plantings on the grounds include a potpourri demonstration garden, a flowering perennial garden, a children's garden, a "secret" walled garden of sweet peas, hollyhocks and other cottage garden-type flowers and, of course, an extensive patch filled with fragrant herbs.

INFORMATION AND DIRECTIONS

Summers Past Farms, 15602 Old Highway 80, Flinn Springs, CA. Phone 619-390-1523. Open 8 A.M. to 5 P.M., Wednesday through Saturday, and 10 A.M. to 5 P.M. on Sunday. Closed Monday and Tuesday.

From San Diego, take Interstate 8 east to the Harbison Canyon/ Dunbar Lane exit. Turn left onto Dunbar Lane, then left again onto Old Highway 80. The nursery is located a ½-mile down on the right.

Weidners' Gardens, Encinitas

Owner Evelyn Weidner and her late husband, Bob, initially opened this specialty flower nursery as a "temporary retirement project" back in 1973. But Weidners' Gardens quickly gained fame with its novel "dig-your-own fields" concept, which allows customers to dig their plants straight out of the nursery's growing fields. Now 25 years old, Weidners' currently boasts a mailing list of more than 8,500 customers for its newsletter.

The nursery maintains a seasonal business schedule based on the bloom cycle of its primary field offerings: rainbow-hued, giant-flowered tuberous begonias during the spring and summer months; followed by velvet-petaled pansies and violas in the late fall. A selection of choice potted holiday poinsettias from the nearby Paul Ecke Poinsettia Ranch round out its fall/winter selection.

While the dig-your-own stock fields remain the core of the business, Weidners' has expanded its inventory over the past few years to include a selection of Proven Winners-brand flowering perennials. Proven Winners plants are made up of a select group of unusual new hybrids developed by a group of individual plant breeders based in Israel, Germany, Japan, Australia and the U.S. Proven Winners plants are bred to be fast-growing, vigorous and easy to maintain in the home garden.

Perhaps the best-known plant in the Proven Winners line is the 'Supertunia,' a vigorous-growing (up to an inch a day at the height of the growing season), everblooming petunia that took retail nurseries by storm a few years ago. More recent introductions include a verbena-like ground cover called 'Temari,' and 'Million Bells,' *Calibrachoa*, a type of cascading miniature petunia.

INFORMATION AND DIRECTIONS

Weidners' Gardens, 695 Normandy Road, Encinitas, CA. Phone 760-436-2194. Open seasonally from April 1 to Sept. 15, and Nov. 1 to Dec. 22. Hours during the season are 9:30 A.M. to 4:30 P.M. daily, except on Tuesday, when the nursery is closed.

From San Diego, take Interstate 5 north to the Leucadia Boulevard exit. Make an immediate left onto the eastern frontage road (Piraeus Street). The nursery is located at the corner of Piraeus Street and Normandy Road.

RECOMMENDED LODGINGS

Artists' Inn and Cottage Bed & Breakfast, South Pasadena

The beautiful blooms of mature rose bushes line the entry walkway and flank the entire white picket fence surrounding the Artists' Inn. Situated on a spacious corner property in South Pasadena, the inn acquired a second building, expanding from the five rooms located in its original 1895 Victorian home, to include an additional four rooms and suites in an adjacent cottage circa 1909.

Innkeeper Janet Marangi's eclectic touch and artistic pursuits define the bed and breakfast's general ambiance, as well as the interior decor of each accommodation. All rooms at the Artists' Inn are either named after individual artists or specific art-movements. The color schemes, furnishings and fittings reflect the aesthetic sensibilities associated with Degas, Van Gogh, Gauguin, Grandma Moses and Georgia O'Keeffe. Theme-oriented rooms represent eighteenth century English, Impressionist, Italian, and Expressionist painters.

A distinctly vintage appeal distinguishes accommodations in the original building, while the rooms in the newly restored cottage reflect a more contemporary touch.

Descanso Gardens, The Huntington Botanical Gardens, and The Arboretum of Los Angeles County are a brief drive by car from the Artists' Inn. If you avoid rush hour traffic, the Getty Center is approximately one hour away.

INFORMATION AND DIRECTIONS

Artists' Inn and Cottage Bed & Breakfast, 1038 Magnolia Street, South Pasadena, CA 91030. Contact Janet Marangi, innkeeper. Phone 626-799-5668, or toll free 888-799-5668 for reservations and information. The inn has nine rooms and suites, all with private baths. Full or continental breakfast, and afternoon tea are served. Rates $110–$165.

If you don't travel during L.A.'s commuter hours, the Artists' Inn in South Pasadena is approximately ½ hour northeast of downtown Los Angeles, or about 45 minutes from the Los Angeles International Airport.

The Bed & Breakfast Inn at La Jolla, La Jolla

Built in 1913 by the well-known Southern California architect Irving Gill, the Inn at La Jolla is a registered Historical Site. Its lovely, tranquil gardens were originally planted by renowned horticulturist, Kate Sessions, who was responsible for much of the early landscaping of Balboa Park.

The one-time home of famous American composer John Phillip Sousa and his family, the inn retains many of its original features. Many of the rooms have garden views, and flowers abound inside and out.

INFORMATION AND DIRECTIONS

The Bed & Breakfast Inn at La Jolla, 7773 Draper Street, La Jolla, CA. Phone 619-456-2066. The inn has 15 rooms; nine in the original house, and six in an annex. Room rates run from $109–$279 per night on weekdays; and from $129–$299 a night on weekends.

From San Diego, take Interstate 5 north to the Ardath Road exit. Follow Ardath to Torrey Pines Road, make a left, and continue to Ivanhoe Avenue. Go right on Ivanhoe, continue one block to Kline Street and turn left. Follow on Kline for four blocks to Draper Avenue, and turn right. The inn is in the middle of the block, between the Presbyterian Church and the Woman's Club.

The Seal Beach Inn & Gardens, Seal Beach

One of the country's original tourist courts opened for business in 1923, 25 miles south of Los Angeles. Today that vintage lodging is a beautifully renovated bed-and-breakfast retreat, christened the Seal Beach Inn & Gardens by proprietor Marjorie Bettenhausen Schmaehl.

Situated just a short stroll from the seashore, the inn is tucked away in a peaceful coastal town adjacent to Long Beach. An hour's drive from Los Angeles, yet seemingly a million miles away from the frenzied energy of the city's crowded freeways, the Seal Beach Inn and Gardens is an oasis. You'll find here an exquisite array of antique furnishings, and fascinating architectural elements, from decorative ironwork balcony railings, to inviting gates, elegant benches and cafe tables. Wander through the courtyard and terraces, patio and pathways, and discover the intimate scale of the inn.

Another hallmark of the Seal Beach Inn is the warm and helpful staff who obviously take their cues from Marjorie, an accomplished innkeeper with over two decades of experience. An avid collector with a wonderful eye for antiques, Marjorie has decorated indoor rooms and outdoor areas with remarkable objects of rare beauty. I was enchanted by an antique Parisian fountain ornamenting the swimming pool and patio area. Recently purchased by the innkeepers on one of their European sojourns, the fountain was among the many acquisitions that filled 17 shipping crates!

Garden spaces adorn every secluded nook found throughout the property. Growing in flowerbeds and a profusion of containers, vibrant hibiscus and mandevilla with their incandescent blooms commingle with a wonderful scramble of flowering vines—clematis and honeysuckle, wisteria and bougainvillea, among others. Although threatening to camouflage large expanses of exquisitely patterned wrought iron, the vines are a superb embellishment to the architecture of the inn's buildings.

Delightful foxgloves, delphiniums and a bevy of flowering perennials consort with frilly annuals. Note also the varied shapes and textures of palm trees, delicate ferns, and blooming bushes. The exhilarating sea air combines with scented geraniums, fragrant freesias and nicotiana, extending a cordial greeting to guests of this charming Southern California inn.

INFORMATION AND DIRECTIONS

The Seal Beach Inn & Gardens, 212 Fifth Street, Seal Beach, California 90740-6115. Marjorie Bettenhausen Schmaehl & Harty Schmaehl, innkeepers. Phone 800-HIDEAWAY for reservations or 562-493-2416 for information. The inn has 23 rooms and suites, with private baths, full gourmet breakfast and afternoon hors d'oeuvres served. Rates $155–$325. *Web site: www.sealbeachinn.com Email: hideaway@ sealbeachinn.com*

Located just off the Pacific Coast Highway 1, about one hour south of downtown Los Angeles and the Los Angeles International Airport.

Victoria Rock Bed and Breakfast, Alpine

Located in San Diego's rural East County, this former single-family residence opened for business as a bed and breakfast in mid-1998. Amiable owners/proprietors Darrel and Helga Doliber (she hails from Germany, home of the bed and breakfast) named the establishment after the locally famous rock formation visible from their home, which bears an uncanny likeness to Britain's Queen Victoria, in profile.

The Dolibers' sprawling backyard is an officially certified National Wildlife Federation Backyard Wildlife Habitat. Among its more salient features are a romantic, oak-enclosed wedding grotto, and a butterfly and hummingbird garden that attracts daily visitors, including several different species of hummingbirds. Bird-watchers also have identified several dozen other bird species on the property.

INFORMATION AND DIRECTIONS

Victoria Rock Bed and Breakfast, 2952 Victoria Drive, Alpine, CA. Phone 619-659-5967. Five guest rooms, each with a distinctive decorating theme. Room rates start at $100 a night.

From San Diego, take Interstate 8 east to the Tavern Road exit. Cross over the freeway and make a right onto Victoria Park Terrace. Follow to Victoria Drive and turn left. Continue on Victoria until you reach the 2900 block.

OREGON

WASHINGTON

Scappoose
Joy Creek Nursery •

PORTLAND ●

Troutdale *McMenamins Edgefield*

The Berry Botanic Garden
Crystal Springs Rhododendron Garden
Elk Rock Garden – The Bishop's Close
Hogan & Sanderson Garden
Leach Botanical Garden
Peninsula Rose Garden
Washington Park
Classical Chinese Garden
The Grotto
Ira Keller's Fountain
Lion & The Rose
Terwilliger Vista B&B

Youngberg Hill Vineyard B&B
McMinnville •

The Oregon Garden
Silverton •

Bush's Pasture Park ●
Deepwood Gardens **SALEM**

• **Albany**
Nichols Garden Nursery

PACIFIC OCEAN

• **Springfield**
Gossler Farms Nursery

●
EUGENE
Greer Gardens
Owen Rose Garden
Hendricks Park Rhododendron Garden

•
Coos Bay
Shore Acres State Park Botanical Garden

O R E G O N

Medford
• Siskiyou Rare Plant Nursery

12

Portland & Vicinity Gardens

The Berry Botanic Garden, Portland

Passionate gardener, exceptional plantswoman, and an inspirational figure in the world of horticulture, Rae Selling Berry prevailed over a condition of hereditary deafness and left a remarkable legacy for plant lovers. In the Berry Botanic Garden, the admirable depth and breadth of the plant collections, and the projects the garden carries out today attest to Mrs. Berry's enduring spirit.

In 1938, Rae and Alfred Berry acquired the parcel of land that was destined to become the Berry Botanic Garden. The Berrys purchased this nine-acre property located near the Willamette River to give Rae the sufficient space to pursue propagating and cultivating the myriad specimens she wished to grow.

Seattle landscape architect John Grant assisted with siting trees and laying out the lawn, but Rae Berry took responsibility for planning and planting the areas devoted to exceptional collections of primulas and alpine plants. Mrs. Berry also planted rhododendron species from seeds. Two particularly large types, *Rhododendron decorum* and *R. calophytum* have matured now into what looks like a natural forest.

The Berry Botanic Garden's quarter-acre Rock Garden is most interesting. Represented here are 300 species of alpine plants from around the world, ranging from true alpines to plants that thrive in an alpine bog environment.

Stroll on the Native Plant Trail, and be sure to explore the Demonstration and Water gardens. Awaiting your discovery are nearly 200 Pacific Northwest native plants that make up one of the garden's five major collections. Look for plant labels and interpretive signs to point out examples of lady fern, the lacy leaves of western bleeding-heart, red currant and Oregon grape, skunk cabbage, and pitcher plant.

In June, visitors are left breathless by glorious displays of the mythic Himalayan blue poppy and the Nepalese poppy found growing in the primula beds. I was bewitched by tall—to five feet—stands of dusty pink *Meconopsis napaulensis*. Your attention will also be drawn to simply stunning arrays of the alluringly soft, subtle blue-hued poppies, 'Crewsdon's hybrids!'

The genus *Primula* was one of Rae Berry's cherished favorites, and visitors will revel in the Berry Botanic Garden's profusion of primula species. Aficionados of primroses will be transported by the delightfully colorful, flowering candelabras of *Primula aurantiaca*. Another noteworthy primula, *P. cusickiana*, bears violet-scented flowers and is native to northeastern Oregon. Dubbed "Cooky" by Mrs. Berry, *P. cusickiana* happens to be particularly temperamental to cultivate, and is known to have eluded Rae Berry's skillful attempts to grow it. Today, this plant's delightful image is used as the garden's logo. It symbolizes the Berry Botanic Garden's commitment to promoting a vast kingdom of plants.

Continuing in the tradition set forth by Rae Berry, who carefully planned various microhabitats to preserve numerous rare plants, the Berry Botanic Garden is widely acknowledged for its praiseworthy conservation of endangered plants. The garden maintains a Seed Bank for Rare and Endangered Plants of the Pacific Northwest; engages in research; and participates in studies of imperiled species like the lovely elegant trout lily, *Erythronium elegans*.

When you visit, pick up the hand-out entitled "Plants-of-Note" and follow the numbered map for your own in-depth tour of the Berry Botanic Garden's exhilarating presentation of unusual plants.

INFORMATION AND DIRECTIONS

The Berry Botanic Garden, 11505 SW Summerville Avenue, Portland, Oregon 97219. Garden open daylight hours by appointment only. For further information or to schedule an appointment, phone 503-636-4112 during office hours—Monday through Friday, 9 A.M. to 4:30 P.M. Fee charged. *Web site: www.berrybot.org*

Located in the hills of southwest Portland.

Classical Chinese Garden, Portland

As this book was going to press, exciting plans for Portland's Classical Chinese Garden were under way. Inspired by the classic urban gardens of Suzhou, Portland's sister-city in China, this Chinese garden will have prefabricated buildings and garden materials shipped from China. The groundbreaking for the walled garden took place in June 1999.

Chinese craftsmen from Suzhou will be traveling to Portland, in order to participate in the landscaping and to assemble the garden's buildings. Construction is scheduled for completion in spring 2000. The projected opening for the Classical Chinese Garden is summer 2000. Funding for the garden comes from both public and private sources.

INFORMATION AND DIRECTIONS

The Classical Chinese Garden will occupy the Portland city block bounded by NW Everett & Flanders and NW 2nd and 3rd Avenues, in the city's Chinatown neighborhood.

Before planning a garden tour of the Portland area, phone 503-228-8131 for further information and an update on Portland's Suzhou-style Classical Chinese Garden. *Web site: www.chinesegarden.org*

Crystal Springs Rhododendron Garden, Portland

Rhododendrons have thrived in Portland's temperate climate since England's Waterer Nursery first introduced the plants to the Pacific Northwest in 1905. Crystal Springs Rhododendron Garden presents an inviting landscape, cared for by a group of enthusiastic volunteers affiliated with the Rhododendron Society, and assisted by the Portland Parks and Recreation Department.

Encompassing approximately five acres, Crystal Springs Rhododendron Garden is dedicated to the cultivation of these praiseworthy plants. The garden celebrates the many attributes of rhododendrons, from their fine structure and attractive leaves, to resplendent flowers. Boasting nearly 800 species and hybrid varieties, the 2,500 rhododendrons and azaleas that make up the collection at Crystal Springs include admirable specimens that are nearly one hundred years old.

The glorious display of rhododendron blooms peaks in April and May, and continues into June. Among the more exotic rhododendron species, *R. bureavii* exhibits an enchanting dark woolly covering on the underside of its leaves. Small leaves and a wide mounded shape distinguishes *R. williamsianum;* while *R. macabeanum* is recognized by its remarkably large leaves. Name stakes are placed throughout the garden to help identify noteworthy specimens.

The garden's handsome design employs many prominent features such as rock walls, beautiful wooden bridges, the Paddison Fountain (named for volunteer Fred Paddison), charming waterfalls, and 13 natural springs to further enhance the landscape. Perennials, bulbs, and other companion plantings add seasonal interest and variety, while a wealth of trees—magnolias, maples, and rare varieties—complement the rhododendron collections.

An urban sanctuary with inherent natural beauty, Crystal Springs shelters examples of bald cypress (a deciduous conifer native to the southeastern United States), as well as a rare, deciduous dawn redwood, grown from the seed acquired from the Arnold Arboretum in 1947. In late winter, look for the unusual corneliancherry dogwood, which displays yellow flowers and interesting peeling bark.

Funded by the Portland Garden Club, one of the newer garden sections, the wetland area, incorporates plants and grasses that thrive in boggy conditions. A flourishing duck population and bird life brings another element of charm to the setting. Herons, wild geese, and unusual species of waterfowl are often sighted, to the delight of bird watchers and garden visitors.

The Overlook area provides excellent views of the garden. Take advantage of the benches here for a respite to enjoy one of Portland's most convenient garden settings.

INFORMATION AND DIRECTIONS

Crystal Springs Rhododendron Garden, SE 28th & Woodstock, Portland, Oregon, 97202. Phone 503-771-8386 for information, to confirm open hours, or for further directions. Open year-round, dawn to dusk daily. Admission fee charged.

Located in Portland's Eastmoreland neighborhood.

Elk Rock, The Garden At The Bishop's Close, Portland

Envision a serene cliffside setting high above the Willamette River. Enchanting Elk Rock garden is situated on property purchased in the early 1890s by Peter and Thomas Kerr, together with their partner,

Patrick Gifford. Created over time by Mr. and Mrs. Peter Kerr, the Elk Rock garden was presented as a gift to the Episcopal Bishop of Oregon in 1957. The Elk Rock Garden Committee has supervised the garden since 1986, continuing to maintain the landscape as a peaceful retreat of outstanding beauty.

An important representation of Northwest garden design, Elk Rock encompasses approximately six acres. The formal garden plan incorporates a series of separate, stylized rooms, surrounding the Scottish Manor-style house built for Mr. and Mrs. Kerr. John Olmsted was called on to site the house, and is responsible for its inviting views of Mt. Hood.

Ornamented throughout the seasons with an exceptional collection of magnolias, Elk Rock garden features a bounteous assortment of unusual shrubs and trees, flourishing perennials, and prominent displays of bulbs. Once you've located the visitor's center, pick up a pamphlet for a self-guided tour of the landscape.

March is known as "Magnolia month" at Elk Rock, where species and varieties of that lustrous genus of trees thrive in the beneficial conditions of Portland's climate. During March, the garden's 35 uncommonly diverse magnolia specimens offer a grand floral exhibition.

Begin your Elk Rock tour near the residence, following the paths around the house and chapel areas where a number of established magnolia trees are found. Look also for such other noteworthy specimens as the winter-blooming silk tassel, the summer-blooming golden rain tree, and a fine example of ornamental kiwi vine (*Actinidia kolomikta*). Vigorous and highly decorative, this climber bears extravagant foliage, distinguished by heart-shaped leaves splashed with cream and flushes of deep pink.

Proceed along the Cliff Cottage Walk, where you'll discover madrone, stewartia, and Sitka spruce trees. Here, the shrub Fragrant sarcococca (*Sarcococca ruscifolia*), delights winter visitors with its aromatic proclamation. Explore the Spring Walk, with colorful bulbs interspersed throughout the perennials, and inhale the delicious scents of a host of viburnums, blooming from January through April. Don't miss another seasonal highlight—the sweeping vistas of the garden's elegant lawns carpeted in crocuses from January through April.

Dedicated to Thomas Kerr, the garden's Cascades section is characterized by a fine assemblage of trees that feature a wondrous range of textural bark. A rare variety of birch, the Franklin tree (*Franklinia alatamaha*), and the snakebark maple are selected landmarks. Flowering displays of winter-hazels accentuate the arboreal plantings, while an abundance of shrubs such as camellias and daphnes, fothergillas, hebes, and rhododendrons add noteworthy beauty throughout the seasons.

Investigate the Point, which offers stirring views of the Willamette River. For a tranquil interlude, enjoy the restored Rock Garden. These are just two aspects of Elk Rock that I recall fondly from my last visit. At Elk Rock, limited parking seems to keep the crowds away, making the Garden at the Bishop's Close a peaceful haven.

However, garden lovers who've discovered Elk Rock's verdant greenery and memorable groves of trees, return again and again. I recommend placing Elk Rock, The Garden at the Bishop's Close, prominently on your itinerary of Portland-area gardens. Having contemplated the restrained yet picturesque landscape, I can vouch for the garden's uplifting atmosphere.

INFORMATION AND DIRECTIONS

Elk Rock, The Garden at the Bishop's Close, 11800 SW Military Lane, Portland, Oregon. Phone 503-636-5613 for further information, directions, or to confirm open hours. Individuals are welcome from 8 A.M. to 5 P.M. daily (groups by appointment only). You can write to: Friends of Elk Rock Garden, P. O. Box 69244, Portland, Oregon 97201. Admission is free, but donations are encouraged.

Sean Hogan & Parker Sanderson Garden, Portland

Hogan and Sanderson have become catalysts for a flurry of gardening activity on the 2700/2800 block of NE 11th Avenue in Portland. To date, a number of the homes have thriving gardens, forming richly textured visual links that indicate a unique energy in the neighborhood.

In one beautiful billowy parkway planting of the Hogan/Sanderson garden, the "smokescreen" area is a real eye-catcher. I admired the finely cut leaves and delicate gauzy effect created by tall stands of bronze fennel, and the complementary clear red hues of dahlias found among dozens of other plants.

In the so-called Moon Garden, magnificent canes of the Chinese species rose, *Rosa sericea var. pteracantha*, stretch upward and outward displaying formidable, translucent red thorns that positively glow when backlit by the setting sun.

Rare plants abound, with more specimens than it seems possible to take in at one time. Wherever your gaze might momentarily settle, an impressive species appears. One such plant that caught my eye was *Begonia boliviensis*, which hails from Argentina and has bright, burnt orange blooms that utterly illuminate the garden's abundant flora.

Containers are full to bursting with colorful combinations. Among the extraordinary show-offs, the red leaf banana plant (*Ensete ventricosum rubra*) stands out amid the garden's fireworks of foliage. A stunning specimen with a lush, tropical appearance, it has formidable green leaves accented by deep purple veins and luscious margins.

During my tour of the Hogan/Sanderson garden, I noticed a collection of *Solanum* species potted up (perhaps to keep them from attacking!). Indeed, the array of outrageous forms and textures made me stop in my tracks. *Solanum marginatum* displays scary spikes down the center of its leaves and along the length of its veins. Each entrancing leaf possesses splendidly frosted, curled edges as well. The forbidding thorns exhibited by tangerine colored *Solanum pyracanthum* are equally sinister and exotic.

INFORMATION AND DIRECTIONS

You may wish to scout out the 2700/2800 block of NE 11th Avenue for an overview of the exciting gardening endeavors taking place in this horticulturally vital Portland neighborhood.

Joy Creek Nursery, Scappoose

Gardeners in the Portland area rave about the plants offered at Joy Creek Nursery. During a mid-June stopover, I was bowled over by the horticultural riches, and the invigorating sense of esprit de corps I discovered at Joy Creek's 39-acre operation.

Among the nursery's delights are flourishing demonstration gardens, along with a wealth of hand-crafted sculpture, pottery, and garden ornaments. The Joy Creek test gardens featured rows of exceedingly beautiful delphiniums bursting forth in glorious bloom! Standing erect on sturdy stems, the flowering plants displayed a range of colors from glistening mother-of-pearl and incandescent white, to fusions of blue-violet and dusty rose found among various towering varieties.

A primary goal at Joy Creek is to educate customers and enable them to grow and enjoy beautiful gardens of their own. In business for seven years, Joy Creek was expanding its 3½ acres of display gardens when I visited. New landscaping includes the four seasons garden comprising some 3200 square feet. One half of this garden space is a lovely area designed by Lucy Hardiman especially for classes and special events. A rose garden designed by John Caine is yet another project under way at Joy Creek. It is scheduled for completion in the summer of 2000.

Penstemons are one of Joy Creek's specialties. More than forty species and cultivars of penstemons were available recently, from outrageously showy specimens such as *Penstemon,* 'Raspberry Flair,' to species like *P. barbatus,* with bright green leaves and relaxed spikes bearing red flowers, and firecracker penstemon (*P. eatonii*), with tubular flowers of the brightest scarlet.

INFORMATION AND DIRECTIONS

Joy Creek Nursery, 20300 N.W. Watson Road, Scappoose, Oregon, 97056. Scott Christy, Maurice Horn, and Mike Smith, proprietors. Retail and catalog sales. Phone 503-543-7474 to confirm open hours, for directions, or further information on workshops and classes. Open to the public seven days a week, 9 A.M. to 5 P.M., March through October. Open by appointment at other times. Call in advance to arrange a visit during the winter. Joy Creek Nursery offers free Sunday classes beginning in April. The nursery invites authoritative speakers who present stimulating topics for new and experienced gardeners, alike.

Joy Creek is located approximately 18 miles north of Portland. Take Highway 30 to Watson Road, turning left before entering the town of Scappoose.

Leach Botanical Garden, Portland

The tranquil setting of Leach Botanical Garden was once home to botanist Lilla Leach and her husband, John. Some four decades after the Leaches built their Colonial Revival style Manor House and first established this lovely five-acre garden, the couple donated the house and the surrounding property to the City of Portland in 1979.

According to the terms of their bequest, the Leach Garden became the city's first public botanical garden when it opened in 1981. Currently, the garden occupies a nine-acre parcel of land operated by a group of fervent volunteers known as the Leach Garden Friends, in cooperation with Portland's Bureau of Parks and Recreation. The lovely landscape features 1½ miles of trails emphasizing Northwest native plants.

Explore the garden's established plant collections and you will become acquainted with plants Lilla Leach herself discovered. Among the most notable species associated with Mrs. Leach are plants such as *Kalmiopsis leachiana,* which resembles a small rhododendron, and a native iris, *Iris innominata.* You can refer to the Self-Guiding Nature Trail Map in order to select among the garden's informative and pleasurable walks. You'll enjoy display gardens, and an existing native woodland where the Leaches integrated vast arrays of appealing plants.

Combining unspoiled areas of both moist and dry coniferous woods, streamside plantings, and fern, rock, and bog gardens, the Leach Botanical Garden puts visitors in touch with the varied habitats of the pristine Pacific Northwest. Fifteen hundred plant species carry labels, in keeping with the garden's educational aims and community outreach.

A highlight of the garden, the Leach Collection offers wonderful displays throughout the year. Arranged and planted so that different species of plants in the same genus coexist, this garden area presents a unique opportunity to compare related witch hazels, hollies, hellebores, and viburnums, as well as hybrid rhododendrons and Southeast azaleas. The outstanding plants in this collection exhibit lovely leaf color, aromatic bloom, ornamental berries and sculptured branches.

Even during a summer visit one can't help but notice the generous foliage of the garden's fine collection of trilliums lining the edges of woodland paths. However, I encourage you to visit in mid- to late-March, in order to witness the sight of these magical wildflowers in bloom. They light up the garden's woods! The Leach Botanical Garden's trillium collection includes: *Trillium albidum,* with its exceptionally delicate white flower; *T. Kurabayashi,* a very large species with deep maroon flowers; *T. parviflorum,* native to the Portland area (and easily confused with *T. albidum*); and an exciting addition and recently named strain, *T. ovatum* 'Barbara Welsh.'

INFORMATION AND DIRECTIONS
Leach Botanical Garden, 6704 SE 122nd Avenue, Portland, Oregon 97236. Phone 503-761-9503 to confirm open hours, for information on guided tours, or to obtain directions. Garden is free and open to the public: Tuesday through Saturday 9 A.M. to 4 P.M.; Sunday 1 P.M. to 4 P.M. Closed Monday and some holidays. Visit the gift shop and plant sales.
Located in Southeast Portland.

Peninsula Rose Garden, Portland

Manicured boxwood hedges function effectively as structural elements, at once containing and complementing the luxuriant roses exhibited at Portland's Peninsula Rose Garden. A required stopover on your garden forays in the rose capital, the 17-acre municipal Peninsula Park contains one of Portland's three most beloved rose gardens. The Peninsula Rose Garden is cared for by personnel from Portland Parks and Recreation, as well as local volunteers from the community.

A radiant showcase, the Peninsula Rose Garden presents a wonderful blend of plants and hardscaping. Traditional, yet imaginative, the park's sunken garden plan features a tapestry of color and fragrance within a symmetrical framework. Once the site of patriotic gatherings during the World War I era, the park has a prominently positioned octagonal bandstand dating from that time. Its grand scale, ornate tile roof and decorative metalwork remind visitors of Portland's past and our nation's erstwhile history. From a design standpoint, today the bandstand takes on the appearance of a spectacular gazebo. It's the perfect place from which to view grassy pathways that weave their way like cushiony ribbons through the maze of heavenly scented roses bushes.

Much less visited than the Washington Park Rose Garden, the Peninsula Rose Garden is recognized as a Hidden Treasure of Portland. Here spectacular blooms appear from late May, early June, well on into October. Another distinctive characteristic of the garden is its glassy pool. Centrally placed in the midst of the garden's enthralling geometry, the water feature incorporates a soothing fountain that adds a note of calm to the surroundings.

Plan to linger among the opulent blooms cultivated at the Peninsula Rose Garden. Be on the look-out for Portland's official rose,

'Mme. Caroline Testout.' First bred in France in 1890, the rose's impressive pedigree was established in the days when countless bushes of this type were planted throughout the town, earning Portland its illustrious designation as the City of Roses!

INFORMATION AND DIRECTIONS

Peninsula Park Rose Garden, North Ainsworth and Albina, Portland, Oregon. Phone Portland Parks & Recreation at 503-823-7529 for further information. Roses bloom from early June through mid-October. Open daylight hours, 7 A.M. to 10 P.M. daily, year-round. There is no entry fee, though donations are welcomed, and may be deposited in the donation boxes in the garden.

Washington Park, Portland

If a garden traveler possesses the stamina, an entire day could easily be devoted to investigating the green spaces of Washington Park and its acclaimed International Rose Test Garden, Japanese Gardens, and Hoyt Arboretum.

John Olmsted helped improve Washington Park back in 1903, when he suggested the separation of pedestrian traffic from vehicle roadways, as well as other changes. The park also boasts natural areas and picnic facilities, a children's playground, tennis court, and the Washington Park Zoo.

Linked to Washington Park is Forest Park, a 5,000-acre woodland wonderland. Reigning as the largest municipal park in the U.S., Portland's Forest Park offers access to miles and miles of rustic nature trails for hiking, biking, or running.

Hoyt Arboretum, Washington Park

More than 900 species of trees and shrubs thrive in the invigorating oasis of Portland's Hoyt Arboretum. A handsome, recently constructed visitor center is the result of a successful partnership between the experienced staff of the Portland Parks and Recreation and the spirited membership of the Hoyt Arboretum Friends Foundation. The center represents the energy and commitment of the arboretum's administration.

Equip yourself with a trail map, then proceed to explore the extensive system of trails meandering through the arboretum's 175 acres. Located on an elevated crest barely one mile from the city's downtown neighborhood, the Hoyt Arboretum introduces garden and nature lovers to a forested retreat with wonderful views of one of the Pacific Northwest's most agreeable cities.

Encircled by native firs and cedars, Hoyt Arboretum's ten miles of trails are planted with exciting and diverse arboreal specimens. Labels on trees point out Hoyt's exceptional collections of conifers, heavenly scented magnolias, dogwoods, oaks and maples. Be sure to investigate the Bristlecone Pine Trail. Look, too, for examples of the rare Brewer's weeping spruce.

A gardenwalk at the Hoyt Arboretum will help you understand Portland's reputation as a celebrated horticultural capital.

INFORMATION AND DIRECTIONS

Hoyt Arboretum, 4000 SW Fairview Boulevard, Portland, Oregon, 97221. Phone 503-228-8733 for directions, and to confirm the Visitor Center hours: 9 A.M. to 4 P.M. every day of the week. Call to learn more about free guided tours scheduled on weekends from April through October at the arboretum. Tours begin at 2 P.M.; they are drop-in and go rain or shine. Seasonal tours include the Fall Color Walk, the Flowering Tree Tour and Spring Wildflower Walk. Grounds are open dawn to dark. No admission fee.

From downtown Portland, take TriMet Bus 63 which stops directly in front of the Visitor Center; or ride light rail to the Washington Park stop.

International Rose Test Garden, Washington Park

Rose lovers flock to Portland's three public rose gardens around mid-June, when the queen of all flowers generally reaches peak bloom in "the city of roses." Each of the gardens deserves a visit: the delightful Ladd's Addition Rose Garden, located at SE 16th and Harrison; the Peninsula Park Rose Garden (see separate entry); and by all means, Portland's sublime 4.5 acre International Rose Test Garden.

Located near the entrance to Washington Park, off W. Burnside Boulevard, the International Rose Test Garden holds claim to being the oldest test garden in the U.S. Established in 1917, this rose lover's paradise showcases more than 8,000 roses, representing over 525 varieties.

The garden's design employs a medley of structural supports to artistically display the countless roses. These underpinnings create intriguing contexts that elegantly enhance the abundantly planted, terraced beds. Taken together, the garden's tall steel arches, two-dimensional aluminum structures for espalier, and three-dimensional pyramidal forms accentuate the landscaping's distinctive levels. Ascending the Rose Garden's staircases and walkways, pause beneath archways wrapped in fragrant climbing roses. You'll see clipped green lawns, and observe how their cool expanses bring harmony to the garden's design. As you move from one level to the next, note how the arches become momentary thresholds that entreat you to stop and smell the roses! When planning a stopover, bear in mind that blooming roses continue to flourish throughout the summer months, into October.

A special highlight of the International Rose Test Garden is the Gold Medal Garden. Celebrating 50 years of award-winning roses, the area provides signs to help visitors identify the prized collection on view. As you walk through this national testing ground for new roses, you'll discover rows of unfamiliar roses that have garnered awards bestowed by the city of Portland on exciting varieties not yet released to the public.

Above the Gold Medal Garden, the Royal Rosarian Garden offers beautiful views into the rose garden and the city beyond. Here, planted along the edge of a flat paved walkway, are roses selected by Prime Ministers of the Royal Rosarians—an official Portland group of greeters. Reigning for one year, individual Prime Ministers select a special rose which is then installed in a sequential planting. The roses displayed in this highly accessible garden area can be readily enjoyed by visitors with limited mobility.

Individual gardens within the Rose Test Garden include a pastoral outdoor amphitheater, with inviting seating upholstered in green grass. The arrangement of fastidiously maintained rose beds contains an area known as the Queen's Walk, featuring plaques that recognize every Queen of Rosaria since the early part of the century.

Enjoy a quiet reprieve from your hectic itinerary within the confines of the Shakespearean Garden, where you'll find graceful paved paths of red brick, perennial plantings, and varieties of roses which have been selected for their evident association with England's foremost bard. These include 'Sweet Juliet' and 'Climbing Ophelia.' At the garden's upper level, don't miss the Beach Memorial Fountain, designed by Lee Kelley. Erected in 1974, this contemporary construction honors Frank E. Beach, the gentleman responsible for coining Portland's motto, "city of roses." Look for the stunning contrast between the gleaming stainless steel form and the aged patina of nearby moss-covered rock walls, elegantly draped in lavish cascades of delicate, pale white roses.

From the Rose Garden, you have a much photographed view of downtown Portland and the magnificent Mount Hood. May through August are generally considered peak viewing times, as these are the months when clear blue skies are most likely to reveal terrific vistas that can reach as far as Mount St. Helens. Glorious views aside, you'll surely enjoy a visit to the garden whenever you happen to plan a jaunt through Portland.

INFORMATION AND DIRECTIONS

International Rose Test Garden, 400 S.W. Kingston Avenue, Portland, Oregon, 97201. Phone 503-823-3636 for further information. Open year-round; daily 7 A.M. to 10 P.M. There is no entry fee, though donations are welcomed and may be deposited in the donation boxes in the garden. Note that roses are in bloom continuously from late May, to early June for the earliest bloomers, and through mid-October for the later ones. *Web site: www.parks.ci.portland.or.us*

Japanese Garden, Washington Park

Portland's lovely Japanese Garden is located just beyond the Rose Test Garden in Washington Park. Opened to the public in 1967, this 5½-acre popular garden was designed by Professor Takuma Tono. To discover the intrinsic beauty of the garden's five distinctive garden styles, devote adequate time to each of the five areas: the Strolling Pond Garden, the Tea Garden, the Natural Garden, the Sand and Stone Garden, and the Flat Garden.

As you pass under the wisteria draped arbor, the Strolling Pond Garden will be revealed. Note the rough beauty of the weathered stones at the arbor's base. These aged stones provide a striking contrast to the wisteria's generous flowers and the vine's extravagant foliage. Typically, diverse elements such as plants and rocks are commonly used to heighten one's perception of the garden's aesthetic qualities, and to invoke the mindful resonance associated with Japanese gardens.

The arbor's portal functions as a frame, revealing one of the gardens' most beautiful stone lanterns. Presented as a gift to the City of Portland by its sister city in Japan, Sapporo, the multitiered, eighteen-foot-high traditional pagoda tower appears unexpectedly as you walk through the arbor. The idea of a hidden view like this one embodies an essential aspect of Japanese garden design. The largest of the five gardens, the Strolling Pond Garden presents a succession of lovely vignettes, many of which are accentuated by water features. Water is in fact one of the most significant elements of the garden's overall plan.

In a Japanese Garden the idea of change—day turning into night and the seasons passing—can be demonstrated by a single, transitory experience. During one visit here, I noted how a shifting ray of sunlight created glimmering highlights on the russet leaves of a cut leaf maple. Behind the tree, the recently rebuilt waterfall known as the "heavenly falls" was subtly enhanced by this fleeting play of light. If one takes time to perceive such ephemeral scenes, moments of perfect quietude will be the reward.

Japanese Garden design reveals an infinite number of engaging perspectives throughout the seasons. Opposite the waterfall, the site becomes a springtime haven when a grove of trees produces a sparkling exhibition of cherry blossoms. Enjoy a silent ramble in any corner of the garden; it will gladden the heart and uplift the spirit.

Careful tending of the varied garden settings is readily apparent in the meticulous maintenance of the plantings, as well as in the artistic character of such man-made components as bamboo fencing bound with twine, and the craftsmanship of the garden's buildings. You'll also find here crane sculptures, and the authentic Moon Bridge crossing the garden's Upper Pond. To the south, you'll encounter a creek, and the lower pond. Look for the beautifully crafted Zig Zag bridge to take you through iris beds. A stimulating visual confluence of blues, purples and white materializes here around the third week in June. The lower pond features stones symbolizing the tortoise and the crane; both creatures represent longevity.

Passing a smaller waterfall, note the precisely placed plantings of Japanese maples, the sculptural presence of stones, and the soothing sounds of falling water. Observe the purity of the natural world in the graceful asymmetry of the weeping tree forms, or the low-growing ferns enhancing the edges of rocky hillsides. Together, these elements create a harmonious, tranquil mood.

In contrast, the Sand and Stone Garden presents a walled space where the abstract patterns of raked sand and weathered stone can be contemplated. An overlook provides fine views of this pristine retreat, but in order to experience the garden's solitary, spiritual center, descend a series of steep stone steps and sit and reflect upon the forms placed here to suggest the sea, and the Buddha's sacrifice.

Near the overlook is a hidden alcove, offering a bench set under the cover of trees. This private place of meditation presents a fine vantage point from where to observe the textures of lichens layered over rough rocks, gaze out upon the hilly terrain, or listen to the sounds of a rushing stream. Walk a bit farther and you'll arrive at the Pavilion's rustic deck, where a gleaming cityscape lies sprawling in the distance.

These are but a handful of impressions of Portland's Japanese Garden, where garden travelers delight in the exquisite landscape representing the venerable influences of age-old religions, and the aesthetic concepts integral to Japan's cultural heritage.

INFORMATION AND DIRECTIONS

The Japanese Garden at Washington Park, 611 S.W. Kingston Avenue, Portland, Oregon 97201. Phone 503-223-1321 or 503-223-4070 for further information, to obtain directions, or confirm seasonal open hours. Gift store hours: spring through fall, 10 A.M. to 6 P.M.; winter, 10 A.M. to 4 P.M. The garden is open year-round, seven days a week: April 1 to May 31, 10 A.M. to 6 P.M.; June 1 to August 31, 9 A.M. to 8 P.M.; September 1 to September 30, 10 A.M. to 6 P.M.; October 1 to March 31, 10 A.M. to 4 P.M. Closed on Thanksgiving, Christmas and New Year's Day. Admission fee charged.

Located in the west hills of Portland.

AND IN ADDITION . . .

The Grotto: Portland

The National Sanctuary of Our Sorrowful Mother, on Sandy Boulevard (Highway 30) at Northeast 85th, Portland, Oregon 97220. Located ½-mile west of I-205; ample free parking provided. Phone 503-254-7371 for information. Free admission to the Plaza Level except during special events. Small fee charged for ten-story ride to upper level. The Grotto and Gift Shop are open daily except Thanksgiving and Christmas days; Mother's Day through Labor Day from 9 A.M. to 8 P.M. Winter hours, 9 A.M. to 5:30 P.M.

Comprising a 62-acre retreat of towering fir trees and a wealth of native flora, the Grotto features a rock cave carved into the base of a 110-foot cliff wall, with replica of Michelangelo's Pieta serving as the shrine's central focus. Visitors may take an elevator to the top of the bluff for sweeping views of surrounding mountains and the Columbia River Valley, and to enjoy the upper level's gardens which include streams, reflection ponds, and exultant springtime display of blooming rhododendrons.

Ira Keller's Civic Theatre Forecourt Fountain: Portland

In downtown Portland, between Southwest 3rd and 4th Avenue, and between Market and Clay Streets. Phone Portland Parks and Recreation at 503-823-2223 for information. The centerpiece of this Portland city park space is a joyous unusual fountain completed in 1971. With its terraces and platforms forming a formidable series of waterfalls, the popular gathering spot known as Ira's Fountain was designed by Angela Danadjieva for Lawrence Halprin Associates.

13

Willamette Valley &
Southern Oregon Gardens

Gossler Farms Nursery, Springfield

Gossler Farms' acres of extensive display gardens greet garden travelers year-round with color and bloom. One of the foremost nurseries located in the Pacific Northwest, Gossler Farms has gained a reputation for splendid magnolias. You'll witness in the neighborhood of 500 glorious selections growing in the nursery's garden. Foliage plants with beautiful fall color, fragrant viburnums, and extraordinary dogwood varieties are specialties, as well.

Patrons "in-the-know" call on the Gosslers when seeking an introduction to the eccentric characteristics and enticing design possibilities of witch hazels. *Hamamelis* species and uncommon cultivars are abundantly represented in the repertoire of 5,000 select plant varieties at Gossler Farms Nursery.

Schedule an appointment when you want to purchase praiseworthy specimens for your home garden. You can also place an order to have selections shipped. With its wonderful array of rare flora suitable for gardens found throughout the U.S. Department of Agriculture's hardiness zones, Gossler Farms Nursery is deserving of all its acclaim.

INFORMATION & DIRECTIONS
Gossler Farms Nursery, 1200 Weaver Road, Springfield, Oregon, 97478-9691. Marj, Roger and Eric Gossler, proprietors. Visits to the nursery are by appointment only; phone 541-746-3922 to make arrangements. A catalog is available for $2.00.

Gossler Farms Nursery is located east of Eugene, nine miles from Interstate Highway 5.

Greer Gardens, Eugene

April and May give rise to heavenly visions at Greer Gardens! Stunning collections of azaleas and rhododendrons can be expected to peak around Mother's Day at this fine nursery, but unusual perennials, maples, bonsai and lovely mature trees and shrubs of many kinds endow the premises with radiant foliage, flowers, and intriguing bark textures throughout the year. You'll also find plants displaying a range of branching habits—from upright, to pyramidal, and weeping forms, to prostrate, creeping types—fit for any landscape design plan.

Business is chiefly by mail order at this Eugene, Oregon, establishment, but you'll find the Greer Gardens' sales area open to the public year-round, seven days a week. When you visit, tour the nursery's growing fields for an extraordinary experience. Make sure you investigate the nursery's book department, featuring a laudable selection of gardening books.

Widely appealing to plant lovers, the extensive Greer Gardens' inventory also includes blue Himalayan poppies, rare clematis species and cultivars, uncommon deciduous azaleas, ornamental grasses and bamboo.

INFORMATION AND DIRECTIONS

Greer Gardens, 1280 Goodpasture Island Road, Eugene, Oregon 97401-1794. Harold and Nancy Greer, proprietors. Phone 541-686-8266 for information and directions. To order plants, phone 800-548-0111. Open Hours: Monday through Saturday, 8:30 A.M. to 5:30 P.M.; Sunday 11 A.M. to 5 P.M.

Greer Gardens is a short ten-minute drive from downtown Eugene. From Delta Highway proceed east ⅓ mile on Goodpasture Island Road.

Nichols Garden Nursery, Albany

Glancing at the Nichols Garden Nursery catalog reveals the image of an inviting arbor lavishly draped in hop vine. The trelliswork form beckons you to enter the nursery's herb gardens.

Nichols Garden Nursery welcomes visitors to their Willamette Valley shop and gardens, where ornamentals and edibles are available for purchase as select seeds, bulbs, roots and plants. The catalog photo mentioned above illustrates Cascade hop, an excellent plant to grow for impressive seasonal coverage of a garden structure. This is just one example of the nursery's abundant offerings.

A family business specializing in herbs and rare seeds, the Nichols Garden Nursery features lovely display gardens. Proprietor Rose Marie Nichols McGee explained that the herb gardens are "designed to illustrate the landscape potential of mature specimens." Among the nursery's various garden areas, "the design and plantings are done in a scale and style more reflective of what the home gardener might choose."

On a visit here you'll enjoy a parterred planting, impressive sweet bay hedge, a shade garden, and a flower border designed to attract bees, butterflies and other beneficial insects. The Nichols Nursery is also a great place to consider the exhilarating possibilities for edible gardens. Examine ongoing vegetable trials, and look at the nursery's diverse offerings of unusual vegetables and herbs, true tea plants, horseradish roots, French shallots, and gourds for use in crafts or as garden highlights.

The nursery shop's varied inventory includes spice and potpourri blends, herbal teas, gardening tools, books, and culinary ingredients such as sourdough starter and pectin.

INFORMATION AND DIRECTIONS

Nichols Garden Nursery, 1190 North Pacific Highway, Albany, Oregon, 97321. Keane B. McGee and Rose Marie Nichols McGee, proprietors. Phone 541-928-9280 for information. Shop and gardens are open Monday through Saturday, 8 A.M. to 4:30 P.M.; closed Sundays and holidays. *Web site: www.gardenursery.com*

Nichols Garden Nursery is located on the west side of Interstate 5, midway between Exit 234 Albany and Exit 235 Millersburg, about 20 miles south of Salem.

The Oregon Garden, Silverton

The Oregon Garden was officially initiated with a groundbreaking celebration in June of 1997. Construction is under way to develop the 240-acre display garden which will one day encompass formal theme gardens and natural forests, water features and wetlands, natural meadows, and a home demonstration garden. A gift shop will stock gardening books, paraphernalia, and gifts.

The Oregon Garden's future plans include a restaurant, an outdoor amphitheater, and indoor facilities for special events, lectures, and exhibits. Located just east of Salem in Oregon's lovely Willamette Valley, the garden will draw visitors from near and far to the town of Silverton.

In 1998 excavation and grading on the first phase area took place, and hundreds of trees were planted as well. Nineteen hundred ninety-nine heralded the planting of the A-Mazing Water Garden (formal wetland complexes). Under construction are also the Overlook plaza area, and the Bosc, another plaza on the garden's main walkway.

The year 2000 will be a preview year, while the official opening is scheduled for 2001. The Oregon Garden is the brainchild of the Oregon Association of Nurserymen. This project promises to become a diverse learning environment for anyone interested in horticulture or botany. The public garden will showplace the state's native flora and vast realms of commercially produced plants.

Garden travelers can keep track of the status of the Oregon Garden by contacting the garden's not-for-profit foundation established in 1993 (see details below).

INFORMATION AND DIRECTIONS
The Oregon Garden Foundation, P.O. Box 155, Silverton, Oregon 97381-0155. Phone 503-874-8100 for further information and updates. *Web Site: www.oregongarden.org*

Silverton is 42 miles south of Portland and 15 minutes east of Salem, the capital of Oregon. Located at the edge of the Cascade foothills, Silverton is the gateway to Silver Falls State Park, one of Oregon's most popular natural attractions.

Siskiyou Rare Plant Nursery, Medford

Siskiyou boasts a track record of 35 years devoted to growing rare plants. Nursery owner and manager for the past twenty years, Baldasarre Mineo conveys both an unbridled enthusiasm and discerning eye for unusual garden selections to his nursery's dedicated clientele.

Display gardens highlight the nursery's specialty: exceptional alpine plants. Countless dwarf and miniature plants thrive in refined rock garden settings. You'll also find a verdant landscape of distinctive perennials, ornamental grasses, miniature conifers, Japanese maples, hardy ferns, and uncommon shrubs and trees.

Mid-April through May is generally the peak blooming period at Siskiyou Rare Plant Nursery, which is located in southwest Oregon's

Rogue Valley. Still, you can count upon the area's beneficial climate for displays of exciting, inspiring combinations of plants throughout the year.

INFORMATION AND DIRECTIONS

Siskiyou Rare Plant Nursery, 2825 Cummings Road, Medford, Oregon 97501. Baldasarre Mineo, owner and manager. Phone 541-772-6846 to arrange an appointment to visit, confirm open hours, or to request a catalog. Note: At the time this entry was written, Siskiyou offered open hours to the public on the first and last Saturday of each month, from March through the first Saturday in December, 9 A.M. through 2 P.M. A sale area features thousands of plants at 20 percent off regular prices. *Web Site: www.wave.net/upg/srpn*

Located in Medford, just 30 miles north of the California border after driving through the Siskiyou Mountains. Medford is a six to seven-hour drive from San Francisco, or a five-hour drive from Portland, Oregon.

AND IN ADDITION . . .

Bush's Pasture Park: Salem

600 Mission Street SE, Salem, Oregon 97302. Phone 503-581-2228 for information. Gardens are always open to the public. Greenhouse hours are 9 A.M. to 4 P.M. weekdays; also open weekends in the afternoon. Perennial borders, a renowned collection of old roses, and a Victorian greenhouse are among the attractions of this downtown Salem park, where shrubs and trees bloom as early as January and February.

George Owen Memorial Rose Garden: Eugene

North end of Jefferson Street off 1st Avenue, Eugene, Oregon. Located along the Willamette River; ample parking available. Phone 503-687-5220 for information. Open daylight hours until 11 P.M.. No admission fee.

The five-acre garden boasts 4,500 roses, including species roses, miniatures, polyanthas, and over 100 varieties of modern hybrid teas and floribundas. Borders and beds mingle formal and informal plantings, adorned by perennials, magnolia and silk trees. The second and third weeks of June are generally peak bloom time, but a beacon of bright flowers are on exhibit throughout the summer. In early April, visitors should proceed to the north end of the garden to behold the state's largest cherry tree, the Black Republican Cherry tree, with its spectacular frothy white blossoms.

Hendricks Park Rhododendron Garden: Eugene
1800 Skyline Boulevard at Summit Avenue, Eugene, Oregon
97403. Phone 541-687-5324 for information. Open daylight hours
until 11 P.M. No admission fee.

In a park encompassing 77 acres, you'll find a shimmering eight-
acre Pacific Northwest setting devoted to more than 6,000 rhododendrons, combined with ornamental plantings of bulbs, perennials and
woody specimens. Mid-April signals the beginning of the peak
blooming season for many rhododendron and deciduous azalea, pre-
senting a feast for the senses. In the Main Garden Walk area, shrubs
and trees can be counted upon to bloom from January through July.
Seek out the Del James Walk, where terraced slopes showcase more
than 1,000 plants.

Historic Deepwood Gardens: Salem
1116 Mission Street SE, Salem, Oregon 97302. Phone 503-363-1825
for information. Located downtown in the state's capital, the gardens
are open daily from dawn until dusk (reserved for weddings many
summer Saturdays). No admission fee.

Six acres of gardens embellish the Deepwood Estate's 1894
Queen Anne style house. Created in 1929, the formal gardens are the
work of eminent designers Elizabeth Lord and Edith Schryver, who
established the first female landscape architecture enterprise in the
Pacific Northwest. A nearly 300-foot-long flower border inspired by
England's Gertrude Jekyll is especially interesting. The series of garden rooms at Deepwood Estate are a beautiful sight throughout the
year. You'll enjoy the impressive scale of the Great Room; the decorative ironwork in the Scroll Garden (once known as the Chinese
Garden); and the lush flowers of the Spring Garden.

Shore Acres State Park Botanical Garden: Coos Bay
13030 Cape Arago Highway, Coos Bay, Oregon. Phone 541-888-
3732 for information. Open daily from daylight until dusk. Call to
confirm December's display of lights, when open hours extend until
10 P.M. Admission fee charged for cars.

December is a high point here, with some 200,000 holiday lights
decorating a fine estate garden and house. Located 12 miles from
Coos Bay, the Shore Acres State Park also features a Japanese pond
garden, a formal English garden, a rose garden, and a cliff walk
where you can enjoy exceptional views of the Pacific Ocean.

RECOMMENDED LODGINGS

The Lion and the Rose, Portland

Located in the city's popular Irvington District, the Lion and the Rose is deservedly touted as one of the best bed and breakfast inns in Portland. Ensconced in a fine Queen Anne style home constructed in 1906, the designated landmark building sets the standard for classic Victorian decor.

Enjoy the inn's picturesque gardens from a rear deck or from the lovely gazebo. Looking out, you'll see perennial borders, red brick walkways, and roses, amid the inn's generous greenery.

Stroll the surrounding grounds and enjoy various fountains and statuary prominently placed about the lawn on paved islands. These elements, along with specimen trees such as Japanese maples, add opulent touches to the garden design.

INFORMATION AND DIRECTIONS

The Lion and the Rose, 1810 N.E. 15th Avenue, Portland, Oregon, 97212. Contact Kay Peffer and Sharon Weil, innkeepers. Phone 503-287-9245 or 800-955-1647. Fax: 503-287-9247. Victorian retreat featuring six rooms with private baths; full breakfast served. Rates $95–$120. *Web site: www.lionrose.com E-mail: lionrose@ix.netcom.com*

McMenamins Edgefield, Troutdale

Originally built in 1911 as the Multnomah County Poor Farm, McMenamins Edgefield is now on the National Register of Historic Places. You can expect to find a good deal more than a bed and breakfast inn at Edgefield, where hotel guests and visitors enjoy a vineyard and winery, brewery and pub, restaurant and grill, golf course, theater, and more.

Overall, the atmosphere at the 25-acre estate is ebullient, with original artwork liberally decorating walls and ceilings, fuse boxes, pipes, and staircases. Landscaped within the last decade, a compelling "garden-in-progress" covers $\frac{1}{3}$ of the property. Garden lovers flock to McMenamins Edgefield's gardening seminars, taking the opportunity to investigate the progress and ongoing implementation of the estate's lavish plantings.

Rather than giving the appearance of a commercial enterprise, the Edgefield setting conveys a warm, friendly atmosphere. Here, you'll find lush orchards, herb and container gardens, deep flowerbeds, and bounteous borders featuring unusual annuals and perennials. Head groundskeeper Kim Kincaid mentions other features, such as a beguiling meadow garlanded with perennials and measuring in the vicinity of ten by 130 feet. Kim describes the Edgefield garden style as "informally formal." Visitors have been heard proclaiming it a "gardener's garden."

Visit the Edgefield gardens for yourself and plan to enjoy a meal featuring Northwest cuisine, or to sample one of the fine beers or ales associated with the McMenamins name.

INFORMATION AND DIRECTIONS

McMenamins Edgefield, 2126 SW Halsey, Troutdale, Oregon, 97060. Phone 800-669-8610 for additional information on rates and accommodations. European style lodgings include over 100 rooms. Many rooms feature centrally located shared baths for men or women. Each shared bath offers a sink, toilet, and shower with total privacy. The inn also includes hostel accommodations and a few suites with private baths. Rates range from $20 to $200 for a family room sleeping up to six people. All room rates include full breakfast served in the Black Rabbit Restaurant. *Web site: www.mcmenamins.com*

Located about 20–25 minutes directly east of downtown Portland, off Highway I-84 at the west entrance of the Columbia River Gorge.

Terwilliger Vista Bed & Breakfast, Portland

Terwilliger Vista Bed & Breakfast offers the peace and quiet of a residential area, in close proximity to Portland's bustling downtown. Wonderfully situated in the West Hills of Portland, the inn's half-acre grounds include ivy covered granite block walls, and a lovely terraced lawn and gardens featuring azaleas, camellias, rhododendron, and fruit trees.

Along one side of the spacious Georgian Colonial built in 1941, a superb tulip tree stands sentry. On the front lawn, the lush cascading form of a camperdown elm is glorious when leafed out, yet arguably even more hauntingly lovely in winter, when its leaves are shed to reveal a network of graceful weeping branches. Innkeeper Jan Vatert points out that when the tree's magnificent trunk is exposed, a covering of mosses and lichens impart an ancient quality to the rare specimen.

Exceptional in winter, as well, are views from Terwilliger Vista's inviting windows. Through a host of deciduous trees one can gaze on the Willamette River, the city's twinkling lights, and Mt. Hood's impressive peak, which can be observed changing shape and color as the sky lightens and day breaks.

Just a short walk from the inn, the Chart House restaurant offers majestic views and a fine menu of steak and salmon.

INFORMATION AND DIRECTIONS

Terwilliger Vista Bed & Breakfast, 515 SW Westwood Drive, Portland, Oregon, 97201. Contact Jan & Dick Vatert, innkeepers. Phone 503-244-0602 or 1-888-244-0602. The inn has three rooms and two suites with private baths; full breakfast served. Rates $85–$130. *Web site: www.terwilligervista.com*

Located in Portland's West Hills neighborhood.

Youngberg Hill Vineyard Bed & Breakfast, McMinnville

On a 12-acre vineyard in Oregon wine country, Youngberg Hill Vineyard Bed & Breakfast is surrounded by rolling hills and wonderful views of the Willamette Valley, the Cascades and the Coast Range. The lovely grounds combine the atmosphere of a natural setting with plantings of perennials and annuals.

The inn's farmhouse perches picturesquely atop a hill, on the vineyard estate. Around the estate are more than 800 acres of farmed and forested land. The bed and breakfast Craftsman-style inn promises a convenient resting place for day trips to the area's many exceptional plant nurseries.

From April through September, you might choose to visit the demonstration gardens at Hedgerows Nursery, 20165 S.W. Christensen Road, in McMinnville. Depending on the season, you'll find admirable displays of salvias, penstemons, and other unusual ornamental perennials. Call 503-843-7522 to confirm open hours.

Rose aficionados will want to include Heirloom Old Garden Roses in their itinerary. Located in nearby St. Paul, at 24062 Riverside Drive N.E., this Willamette Valley establishment has extensive display gardens. You'll see fetching fanfares of magnificent old roses, scrumptious modern varieties such as David Austin's English roses, and a 100-foot long pergola that supports 50 kinds of rambler roses. The garden is open year-round; phone 503-538-1576 to confirm weekday or weekend hours.

INFORMATION AND DIRECTIONS
Youngberg Hill Vineyard Bed & Breakfast, 10660 SW Youngberg Hill
Road, McMinnville, Oregon 97128. Contact Kevin and Tasha Byrd,
innkeepers. Phone toll free, 888-657-8668. Fax: 503-472-1313. Seven
inviting rooms feature private ensuite baths; full breakfast served.
Rates $99–$250. *Web site: www.youngberghill.com*

Youngberg Hill Vineyard B & B is about 40 miles southwest of
Portland, approximately a one-hour drive.

WASHINGTON

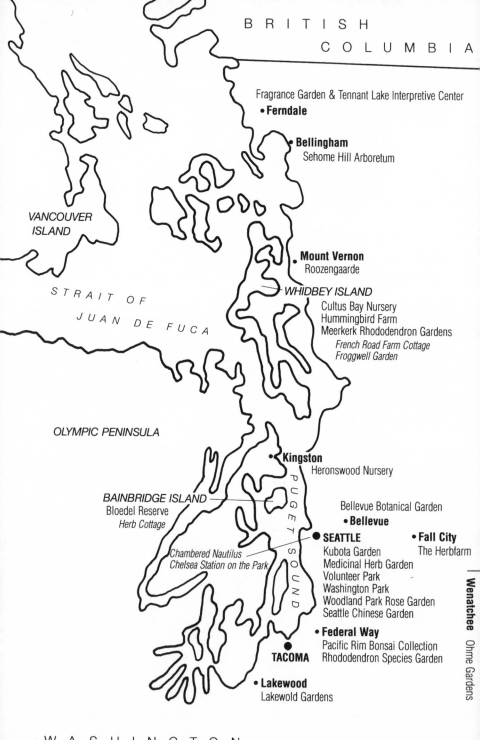

BRITISH

COLUMBIA

Fragrance Garden & Tennant Lake Interpretive Center
• **Ferndale**

• **Bellingham**
Sehome Hill Arboretum

VANCOUVER
ISLAND

• **Mount Vernon**
Roozengaarde

WHIDBEY ISLAND

STRAIT OF

JUAN DE FUCA

Cultus Bay Nursery
Hummingbird Farm
Meerkerk Rhododendron Gardens
French Road Farm Cottage
Froggwell Garden

OLYMPIC PENINSULA

• **Kingston**
Heronswood Nursery

P
U
G
E
T

BAINBRIDGE ISLAND
Bloedel Reserve
Herb Cottage

Bellevue Botanical Garden
• **Bellevue**

● **SEATTLE**   • **Fall City**
Kubota Garden   The Herbfarm
Medicinal Herb Garden
Volunteer Park
Washington Park
Woodland Park Rose Garden
Seattle Chinese Garden

Chambered Nautilus
Chelsea Station on the Park

S
O
U
N
D

• **Federal Way**
Pacific Rim Bonsai Collection
Rhododendron Species Garden

●
TACOMA

• **Lakewood**
Lakewold Gardens

Wenatchee Ohme Gardens

WASHINGTON

14

Seattle Gardens

Kubota Garden, Seattle

The 20-acre Kubota Garden was begun in 1927 by Fujitaro Kubota. A self-taught gardener and Japanese immigrant, Mr. Kubota established a thriving landscaping business in the Seattle area, and designed the extensive gardens surrounding his own home and business. He left behind a significant horticultural legacy that includes designing the Japanese Gardens at the Bloedel Reserve on Bainbridge Island, and another at Seattle University.

A historical landmark, the Kubota Garden evolved over decades as Mr. Kubota installed water features, planted excellent tree specimens, and creatively arranged stone to further proclaim the beauty of the landscape. The cruel internment of the Kubota family in the 1940s resulted in the garden being abandoned during a four-year period. When the war ended, the family returned to their land, and Mr. Kubota and his two sons resumed operation of their company. They proceeded to cultivate pine trees—their specialty. If you consult the garden's self-guided tour map, you'll note an area where outstanding examples of Japanese black and red pines coexist, symbolizing male and female energy.

The Kubota Garden was acquired by the City of Seattle from the Kubota family over ten years ago. Today, the secluded setting is a wonderful respite from the city's more crowded tourist attractions. Garden features include the Necklace of Ponds with Heart Bridge, the Bamboo Grove planted with yellow and black groove bamboo, and the Mountainside with waterfall. On a visit here you'll have an opportunity to see many rare and beautiful plants, including the bamboo, *Phyllostachys nigra* 'Megurochiku.' The Meeting Lawn presents a splendid vignette composed of two unusually expressive trees—a 32-foot long weeping blue Atlas cedar juxtaposed with a 37-foot high weeping Norway spruce.

Within the overall plan of the Kubota Garden, an area known as the Japanese Garden traces back to the 1930s. This serene space is designed in the tradition of Japan's best-known garden style. Presently, Mr. Tom Kubota, son of Fujitaro, remains involved in plans for the garden's future. As this book was slated to go to press, the Parks Department and the Kubota Garden Foundation had recently held a groundbreaking event for the Tom Kubota Stroll Garden. Work on the new garden commenced in the summer of 1999, and a dedication ceremony was planned for October of the same year. According to a foundation volunteer, the garden will allow less vigorous visitors to enjoy the beauty and tranquillity of the garden.

INFORMATION AND DIRECTIONS

The Kubota Garden, Renton Avenue South at 55th Avenue South. Phone the Kubota Garden Foundation at 206-725-5060, or the Kubota Garden Senior Gardener at 206-684-4584, for information or to schedule a guided tour for eight or more visitors. Individual garden visitors are welcome and self-guided tour maps are available. The garden is open to the public every day during daylight hours. No fee.

Located in the Rainier Beach neighborhood of South Seattle.

Medicinal Herb Garden,
University of Washington, Seattle

Extensive paths flow through the University of Washington's beautiful, densely wooded campus. Obtain a map of the campus beforehand, or ask the gatekeeper for directions and you'll soon discover the series of outdoor rooms comprising the Medicinal Herb Garden affiliated with the University's Botany department.

Of particular interest to herbalists and botanists, the medical community, and garden lovers, are the garden's 600 species of beneficial plants. Approximately ⅔ are represented in a fine collection of shrubs and trees, bordering the Medicinal Herb Garden's arrangement of adjacent spaces The remaining species, an interesting assortment of familiar and unusual plants grow in a framework of formal raised beds, emphasized by wooden frames.

The plants are sited in islands of sun, or in the case of shade loving species, shielded by towering trees. Throughout the Medicinal

Herb Garden, precise labels enlighten visitors about the collection in general, and help identify all the specimens. Look, for example, for the rare camphor tree (*Cinnamomum camphorum*).

Dating back to 1911, the Medicinal Herb Garden reaches peak bloom in May and June, but is worthy of a visit during each and every month of the year. Gigantic castor-bean (an annual in Seattle's climate) and masses of Joe-pye weed presented a dazzling exhibition on the summery day when I last visited. Early in the year, look among a host of agreeable plants for the attractive foliage of winter-blooming hellebores. Here you'll see also the interesting branching forms of witch hazels, decorated by delicate clusters of bright flowers.

The Medicinal Herb Garden at the University of Washington holds an important place in the long-standing tradition of utilizing herbs for health purposes, with its wide-ranging, educational displays of beneficial plants.

INFORMATION AND DIRECTIONS

University of Washington Medicinal Herb Garden, Seattle. For information, phone 206-543-1126, or contact the Botany Department at University of Washington, Box 355325, Seattle, Washington 98195-5325.

Located on the campus of the University of Washington in Seattle.

Seattle Chinese Garden (Xi Hua Yuan) at South Seattle Community College, Seattle

In the spring of 1999, a team of Chinese craftsmen—two stone carvers, two carpenters, a stone mason, a painter, a landscape architect and an engineer—arrived in Seattle to assemble the Song Mei Pavilion, a small open-air structure with a flared roof. It is surrounded by a 10,000 square foot demonstration garden displaying rare flora from China. Song Mei will serve as a demonstration garden while the Seattle Chinese Garden Society, which is supported by business, civic, and educational groups, raises funds to begin major construction of a six-acre classical Chinese garden, probably in 2001.

The Seattle Chinese Garden Society's lofty goal is to build a garden based upon a 2,000-year-old tradition. The park-like Sichuan/Chongqing-style garden, highlighted by ponds, rock features, paths, and framed views promises to introduce visitors to a rare, aesthetic beauty, as well as to the symbolism inherent in classical Chinese gardens. The Seattle Chinese Garden will convey the principle of a vast

175

universe, while expressing culturally significant artistic, philosophical, and horticultural attributes.

INFORMATION AND DIRECTIONS

Seattle Chinese Garden: The Song Mei pavilion and garden is located at South Seattle Community College, 6000 16th Avenue SW (north entry), in West Seattle.

For tour information and project updates, write the Seattle Chinese Garden Society, 2040 Westlake Avenue North, Suite 306, Seattle, Washington 98109; or phone 206-282-8040. Fax: 206-282-8194. *Web Site: www.seattle-chinese-garden.org*

Volunteer Park, Seattle

Volunteer Park is a distinctive green space in Seattle's extensive system of parks. Designed by the Olmsted brothers, landscape architects and sons of Frederick Law Olmsted, the park is well-known for its water tower which provides a panoramic view of the city and beyond.

A stunning Victorian-style glass conservatory located at the north end of the parkland is not to be missed! Dating back to 1914 when the Conservatory opened to the public, the elegant and aesthetic building captivates garden travelers. Its layout comprises two opposing wings that hold wonderful collections of bromeliad plants at one end, and cacti and succulents at the other.

As you enter the Conservatory, the Palm House displays such fine plants as orchids, anthuriums, crotons and exuberant ginger plants. Reaching high into the dome of the building, a towering fiddleleaf fig tree is a particularly impressive sight.

In the Seasonal Display House, changing plant exhibitions inaugurate spring, summer, and fall themes. Bulbs and lilies are highlights all through spring, while begonias light up the summer months. Fragrant gardenias and colorful chrysanthemums bring a special beauty to the fall. Holidays are celebrated, of course, with a show of poinsettias guaranteed to brighten any span of gray days. The Fern House features a wealth of exactingly cared for horticultural specimens. Look for fascinating species of cycads, the alluring blooms of angel's trumpet (*Brugmansia*), and enthralling bird-of-paradise.

INFORMATION AND DIRECTIONS

The Conservatory at Volunteer Park, 1400 E. Galer, Seattle. Phone 206-684-4743 for information or to confirm open hours. For details on special tours or plant sales, phone the Friends of the Conservatory at 206-322-4112. No fee charged.

Winter hours 10 A.M. to 4 P.M. daily; summer hours 10 A.M. to 7 P.M. daily.

Located in the city's Capitol Hill neighborhood.

Washington Park, Seattle

Designed by the renowned Olmsted Brothers Landscape Architecture firm, scions of Frederick Law Olmsted, the City of Seattle's fine boulevard plan and park system suggest plenty of reasons to explore neighborhoods throughout town.

Washington Park stands out like a jewel among Seattle's treasure trove of parkland settings, with its well endowed arboretum, and the tranquil landscape of the Japanese Garden.

Washington Park Arboretum, Seattle

In a region where gardening activities are a significant pastime for so many area residents, the beauty of Washington Park Arboretum is maintained by the energetic members of the Arboretum Foundation, a host of volunteers, and the staff affiliated with Seattle's Department of Parks and Recreation and the University of Washington.

Seattle's excellent arboretum deserves a visit (or two or three), whenever you find yourself in the city. Over 4,400 different types of woody plants are cultivated on the arboretum's 230-acre grounds. Among the diverse species, you'll find important collections of rhododendron, cherry, pine, maple, and holly. Every month of the year offers something unique to engage the interest of garden lovers. Pick up a trail map at the Graham Visitors Center and stroll over to the Azalea Way. In April, this ¾ acre features a parade of flowering dogwoods, cherries, and of course, azaleas. The beautiful display here promises to brighten a damp or dreary springtime mood with a sensory assault of the highest order. When bathed in dappled sunlight, this floral arena glistens.

Gorgeous magnolias and lush conifers harbor large-leaved rhododendrons in an area known as Loderi Valley. The collection of "rhodies" blooms from February into June, while the peak exhibition of magnolias spans March through May. The delightful Joseph A. Witt Winter Garden is especially splendid from November through

March. For your tour of the Arboretum Self-Guided Waterfront Trail, look for a special pamphlet distinguished by a lovely line drawing on its cover. As the trail meanders over marshlands and a bridge, you'll have up-close and personal views of Marsh Island and Foster Island, with all the flora and fauna that coexist in a marshland environment. The booklet's delightful illustrations describe plants and creatures found along the way, as well as the evolution of the area's landmass and waterways.

On my recent mid-summer tour of Seattle and the arboretum, I happened upon an extraordinary, horticultural ode to color, installed in a planting area dubbed the Arboretum Signature Bed! An exciting project, the Signature Bed at the Arboretum changes each year when a select group of volunteers takes charge of designing, establishing, and maintaining a special theme planting intended for year-round interest.

The "Bold & Beautiful" project which was thriving during my late-July visit was true to its name. It completely charmed me. Spanning October 1997 through September 1998, this particular Signature Bed display was presented by the Myrtle DeFreil Unit 16 of the Arboretum Foundation, featuring a dynamite design by Richard W. Hartlage, Director and Curator of the Miller Botanical Garden. The plantings conveyed a high drama through the use of plant selections characterized by strong, architectural forms, arresting textural contrasts, and intense colors. The vibrant purples, reds, and yellows of the sumptuous foliage and flowers expressed a joyous energy that was a pleasure to observe.

An A to Z of unusual species and cultivars—*Abutilons* to *Zantedeschias*—starred in the showy extravaganza, distinguished by the fiery, tropical appearance that continues to gain in popularity among many gardening zealots. *Ensete ventricosum* 'Maurellii,' with its huge leaves, towered over coveys of flamboyant cannas, excessive coleus specimens (with wonderful monikers like 'Inky Fingers,' 'Kiwi Fern,' and 'Purple Emperor'), lush fuchsias, and the striking swords of *Phormium tenax* 'Atrosanguineum.'

Based upon the Signature Bed's exhibition during that special July day, I can only imagine the beauty of its earlier permutation in winter and spring seasons. Needless to say, I can't wait to return to investigate the changing designs and witness the creative outpouring of planting ideas in years to come.

INFORMATION AND DIRECTIONS
Washington Park Arboretum, Graham Visitors Center, 2300 Arboretum Drive East, Seattle, Washington 98112. Phone 206-543-8800 for information on scheduled public tours. Individual garden visitors are welcome. Open daily 7 A.M. until dusk. No admission fee. *Web Site: http://weber.u.washington.edu/~wpa/*

Washington Park Japanese Garden, Seattle

Attention to detail is characteristic of the authenticity you'll enjoy when touring Seattle's Japanese Garden. During an early phase of the garden's history, an anecdote serves to sum up the type of efforts involved in creating a garden that would faithfully encompass ancient traditions of Japanese garden design. Juki Iida, the garden's primary designer, initially worked with a number of other designers to produce pages of plans documenting the 3½-acre garden's layout. Upon arriving in the U.S. from Japan, Mr. Iida proceeded to choose 500 massive boulders from their natural mountainous environment, and went on to personally supervise the placing of the formidable, architectural forms which were so essential to the philosophical and artistic underpinnings of the landscaping. Such uncompromising efforts led to the beauty of this garden.

On a self-guided tour of the Japanese Garden, after you pass through the South Gate, follow along the east path past the waterfall. In the exemplary Tea Garden, featuring a Shoseian Teahouse structure, you'll sense the reflective atmosphere associated with the tradition of the tea ceremony. Upon entering the tea garden, visitors pass into a consecrated realm where the world is left behind. Inside the garden's discreet setting, a bamboo fence delineates two areas: an outer area, where guests convene; and an inner area designed to give pause for ritual purification before entering the teahouse. An arbor indicates the garden's waiting area, while the inner section is distinguished by a stone basin for washing.

Walking the Japanese Garden's paths, you'll find a host of lovely features to contemplate. Water elements, which are crucial to the beauty and symbolism of Japanese gardens, abound. Here are the waterfall's soothing intonations, and streams which merge to form the lake. Note the turtle island rising above the lake's glassy surface, with the restrained, sculpture-like arrangement of three Japanese red pines. And on Nakajima Island, which can be reached by either earthen or plank bridge, observe pine trees representing cranes, the symbols of long life.

Viewing the pleasing asymmetry of the lake's outline, the unequal groupings of trees, or placement of outcroppings, you'll discover that what at first appears to be randomness can serve, when studied, to help interpret essential ideals of balance and harmony. The garden's shapes and forms, its arrangements of plants, hardscaping and ornamentation embody deliberate decisions, artfully implying mountains and forests, rivers and plateaus of the natural world.

At the northern reaches of the garden, a handsome arbor with a roof of bamboo trelliswork stands just at the point of the lake's outlet. A mature wisteria supported by the arbor grows forth from a timeworn trunk, suggesting venerable old age. Here, again, you can reflect on how such dissimilarities contribute to the meditative qualities of this beautiful Japanese Garden.

INFORMATION AND DIRECTIONS

Japanese Garden at Washington Park Arboretum, 1000 Lake Washington Boulevard East, North of East Madison Street, Seattle (managed by the Seattle Department of Parks and Recreation). Phone 206-684-4725 to confirm open hours and for further information. Admission fee charged. Open at 10 A.M., seven days a week, from March 1 through November 30. Phone for closing times which vary seasonally.

Woodland Park Rose Garden, Seattle

Roses thrive in Seattle's moderate climate and moist conditions. Under the auspices of the Seattle Parks Department and the Woodland Park Zoo, a fine showcase for these gorgeous blooms is maintained at the Woodland Park Rose Garden. Devoted to the cultivation and exhibition of roses, the 2½-acre Rose Garden opened in 1924. Currently 260 varieties of roses are featured, with some 5,000 rose bushes under cultivation to adorn the lovely, landscaped grounds.

Grass pathways weave through the Woodland Park Rose Garden's appealing layout, ornamented by a handsome bas-relief sculpture designed by Alice Carr, a reflecting pool, and a gazebo. In addition to lavish displays of roses, the garden features a number of rare oriental cypress trees (*Chamaecyparis pisifera* 'Squarrosa'). Known also as Moss cypress or Moss Falsecypress according to common nomenclature, the geometrically arranged trees lend a handsome structure to the garden plan. Pruned in outstanding sculptural topiary forms that accentuate the tree's grayish-bluish foliage that has the appearance of needles, the beautiful arboreal specimens contribute elements of fantasy to the setting.

Within the boundaries of the Woodland Park Rose Garden, one of the 24 All-American Rose Selection Test Gardens is located. You'll be able to peek at the new varieties being considered by growers, while enjoying a wide range of tried and true shrub roses, hybrid teas, and climbers praised for their vigor and radiance.

You may want to keep in mind that peak bloom time for the garden is late June through the end of August. Note, however, that climbing roses start blooming in April, and all the roses continue to bloom until the end of October.

INFORMATION AND DIRECTIONS

Woodland Park Rose Garden, Fremont Avenue North at North 50th Street, Seattle, Washington. For information, phone the Woodland Park Zoo information line at 206-684-4040, or the Rose Garden direct line at 206-684-4863. Open daily from 7 A.M. until dusk, year-round. Individual garden visitors are always welcome. Phone for details on tours for groups of ten or more; two weeks notice required (tours are weekdays between 7 A.M. and 3:30 P.M.). No fee charged, but donations are encouraged.

15

Seattle Vicinity Gardens

Bellevue Botanical Garden, Bellevue

By virtue of its matchless perennial borders, the Bellevue Botanical Garden attracts eager garden travelers much like a beehive brimming with honey draws bears. Established in 1992 through the initiative and creative energy of members affiliated with the Northwest Perennial Alliance, and the City of Bellevue Parks and Community Services Department, the garden quickly achieved national prominence. Operated today by the Parks Department, in partnership with the Botanical Garden Society, the Bellevue Botanical Garden continues to grow in scope and prosper.

The garden occupies a 36-acre segment of Wilburton Hill Park. Over time, the amazingly lush, stunningly designed borders developed along with a number of prominent gardens and special features. A lovely water element—a rill—distinguishes the appealing Entry Plaza and Visitor Center. The flow of water through the rill's narrow channel effectively and appealingly draws attention to the garden's entryway. Wrapping around the north and west side of the center, the Waterwise Garden inspires home gardeners with its exhibition of handsome, drought-tolerant specimens meant to bring beauty to every season.

Installed in 1996, the visually dramatic Alpine Rock Garden features a tiered arrangement, highlighted by rugged basalt outcrops. The agreeably open setting, with its assured hardscaping, provides a perfect haven for a wealth of rock garden and alpine plants. Take a quiet interlude and visit the Yao Japanese Garden, which presents Pacific Northwest and Asian plants in a blend of contemporary and traditional Asian landscape design.

Other collections of flora emphasize fuchsias and groundcovers, while special changing displays highlight dahlias, flowering annuals, and hardy ferns. You'll also have wonderful opportunities for contemplative nature walks along the garden's Loop Trail, which winds gracefully through the Botanical Reserve's woodlands, wetlands, and meadows.

During a midsummer sojourn to the Bellevue Botanical Garden, my great expectations were exceeded. Although I had heard glowing reviews of the garden's famed perennial borders, I found myself unprepared for their spectacular impact when I finally stood before them. I paused to marvel at the exceptional collection of hydrangeas in the Shade Border, then proceeded to traverse the 17,000-square-foot sunny plantings. The diversity of plants found in these voluminous borders are testament to the widespread interest in perennial gardening, and they provide undeniable evidence of the wealth of exciting new plants which nurseries are propagating. What an exciting challenge they present to a gardener who is interested in expanding the repertoire of plant material at home. In the Main Border look for keenly colored groupings that pleasingly jostle the senses. Cerise with chartreuse, for one, surprises both connoisseurs and the average onlooker.

It's impossible to miss the Hot Border! Sizzling in July with bright reds, oranges, and brilliant yellows, the showy exhibition here includes daylilies, branching floriferous crocosmia, red-hot pokers, and the like. You can penetrate the interior of this perennial border by following the hazelnut path, where you'll be enveloped by the intoxicating mix of shrubs, perennials, bulbs, vines, annuals and ornamental grasses. This area is bound to generate a wish list of plants that gardeners will want to grow in their own landscapes.

Plan enough time to savor the borders' tapestry of horticultural rarities—many of which boast sublime variegation, dazzling colors, or lavish bloom. You won't be disappointed..

Note: If you're hoping to locate terrific plants like those established at Bellevue Botanical Garden, see entries for the Heronswood nursery, the Cultus Bay Nursery, and the Herbfarm.

INFORMATION AND DIRECTIONS
Bellevue Botanical Garden, 12001 Main Street, Bellevue, Washington 98005.

Phone 425-452-2750 for further information and directions. Open daily 7:30 A.M. to dusk. Visitor Center open 10 A.M. to 4 P.M. No fee.

Bellevue is located just east of Seattle across Lake Washington. Be sure to avoid the area's rush hour traffic and the drive to Bellevue should take 20 minutes or so.

Bloedel Reserve, Bainbridge Island

A unique, enthralling landscape, the Bloedel Reserve should be at the top of your list when planning an itinerary of Pacific Northwest gardens. Rather than attempting to fully recount the property's history or to encapsulate the reserve's governing philosophy as set forth by Prentice Bloedel, I urge you to read Director Richard Brown's commentary, as printed in the "Self-Guided Walking Tour" pamphlet available at the Bloedel Reserve Gatehouse. Containing informative background material, the pamphlet provides a fitting orientation before one embarks on a tour of the reserve.

Presently, the Bloedel Reserve comprises some 150 acres, featuring approximately 70 developed acres amid the reserve's greater forested grounds. Ties to the timber industry provided the resources when Prentice and Virginia Bloedel first purchased a home and extensive acreage on the northern tip of Bainbridge Island in the early 1950s. Perhaps these same associations inspired Mr. and Mrs. Bloedel, who devoted the next 35 years to contemplating, planning, and ultimately establishing the Bloedel Reserve, a complex, evolving landscape of rare beauty. The Bloedel Reserve is currently managed by the Arbor Fund, a nonprofit foundation set up by the Bloedels.

From the beginning, Mr. Bloedel had a profound sensitivity to the overall site, to conservation issues, the use of space, and other aesthetic concerns. He created one of the country's most lyrical landscapes, and inspired the course of development for the deeply symbiotic environment. Today, the reserve is a place where garden travelers might revel in the majesty of nature, while appreciating the restrained beauty of imperturbable garden scenes.

Upon check-in at the reserve, you'll be given a map delineating all the main and secondary trails. An exploration of the property will shepherd you through settings of picturesque radiance, commencing with a meadow leading to the Bird Marsh. Here, at a point where lovely ponds and plantings culminate in an inviting wildlife habitat,

184

you can view the commingling of natural wetlands with a planned bird refuge. A trestle footbridge farther along leads into pristine woodlands. If you continue on, a boardwalk allows you to observe a forest wetland.

After a relaxed stroll around the area known as the Mid Pond, you'll come upon the stately house that Mr. and Mrs. Bloedel purchased in 1952 and is currently the Visitor Center. During a July sojourn, I stood on the east side of the building looking out toward Puget Sound, savoring the sweeping vista unfolding before me. Lushly planted with St. John's Wort, the contour of the lofty East Bluff effected an ebullient spectacle. At one time lowered 15 feet to enhance the stunning view, the bluff's bright carpet of sunny flowers tempered the setting's formal aspects, and introduced a cheery note of surprise and wonder to the reserve's landscape.

The gardens of the Bloedel Reserve reveal a horticultural panorama of exotic and native species, with sensational varieties of trees, shrubs, perennials, and bulbs. Here, you can admire the lovely garden features, including the Moss Steps and the waterfall areas. Stroll through the Glen, distinguished by its extraordinary array of hardy cyclamen, in bloom from late August through September. Follow the Orchid Trail and soon you'll discover a small secluded spot, underscored by the placement of a bench, and its lovely view of the swan pond. A birthday present from Mr. Bloedel to Mrs. Bloedel, this intimate garden was designed by Geoffrey Rausch.

When you have completed a tour of the Orchid Trail, the harmonious juncture of the Japanese Garden, the Guest House, and the Zen garden emerges. Remembering these gardens, I find that certain details remain vivid long after my visit. One particularly elegant arrangement made me appreciate the expressive quality of unlike elements. In a flawless combination of hardscaping and flora, the Japanese Garden's stone walkway, made of smooth dark rocks set into a field of white concrete, is complemented by the contrasting, somber, and graceful blades of black lily turf planted alongside. This design feature creates a textural cadence that soothes and stimulates the senses at the same time.

Just beyond the stone walk, there is an extraordinary, luminous Katsura tree with its golden autumn color. The tree has a scent that has been compared to hot toffee, and is said to occur when the leaves fall, emitting a sweet fragrance for a considerable distance.

Utterly still, the enclosed realm known as the Reflection Pool suggests a glorious opportunity for repose. I recall pausing to rest there on a pleasant bench, contemplating the unparalleled elegance of the yew hedge, the lawn, and the rectangular pool from my silent vantage point. With its quiet majesty, the Reflection Pool epitomized for me the Bloedels' illustrious legacy. The reserve will deeply nourish the spirit and awaken the imagination of all garden visitors just as it did for me.

Note: The peak period for outstanding displays of blooms at the Bloedel Reserve is April and May for trilliums, magnolias, rhododendrons, azaleas, camellias, anemones, Empress trees, flowering crabapples and cherries, among others. In May and June, you'll enjoy primroses, lungworts, flowering dogwoods, and Solomon's Seal. In September and October, look for *Kirengeshoma*.

INFORMATION AND DIRECTIONS

The Bloedel Reserve, 7571 N.E. Dolphin Drive, Bainbridge Island, Washington 98110-1097. Reservations are required to tour the reserve. Phone 206-842-7631 for information on open hours, or to schedule your visit. Admission fee charged.

Bainbridge Island is located just west of Seattle, about one hour travel time. Ferries leave Seattle approximately every 40 minutes. Crossing time is 30 minutes; driving time on Bainbridge is 15 minutes. You should arrive at the Seattle ferry terminal approximately 45 minutes to an hour before projected departure.

Cultus Bay Nursery, Clinton (Whidbey Island)

How thankful I was that Dan Hinkley of Heronswood Nursery suggested I visit Mary Fisher's Cultus Bay Nursery, on Whidbey Island. A terrific place to explore unusual plant offerings, the Cultus Bay property features exuberant display gardens in the midst of a fine retail nursery. Also here, you'll find Mary's family home—a lovely Victorian-style house surrounded by a luxuriant landscape of charming hedgerows and a profusion of perennials, vines, herbs and shrubs.

In late August, I was astonished by the nursery's densely planted fanfare of blooming herbs, drought tolerant plantings, and the exceptional exhibition of buddleias and hydrangeas. The thriving gardens were complemented by a selection of unusual, one-of-a-kind garden ornaments.

Always on the lookout for variegated specimens, I was thrilled to find both a stunning Porcelainberry vine (*Ampelopsis brevipedunculata* 'Elegans') and the Goldnet honeysuckle (*Lonicera japonica* 'Aureoreticulata') for my new California garden.

INFORMATION AND DIRECTIONS

Cultus Bay Nursery & Garden, 4000 E. Bailey Road, Clinton, Washington 98236. Mary Fisher, proprietor. Open April through September, 9 A.M. to 5 P.M. daily, except for Tuesdays, when it is closed. Phone 360-579-2329 to confirm open hours, for directions and further information. Open off-season by appointment only.

From Seattle, drive north on I-5, and take the exit to the Mukilteo/Clinton Ferry. Cultus Bay Nursery and Garden is located minutes south of the Clinton Ferry Dock, on Whidbey Island—about 1½ hours from Seattle.

The Herbfarm, Fall City

One of the nation's foremost herbal establishments, the Herbfarm is located approximately 30 minutes from downtown Seattle. The company's story is widely repeated, but it's endearing just the same. Twenty-five years ago, Lola Zimmerman placed a wheelbarrow full of herbs under a tree, and posted a sign declaring "Herb Plants for Sale." The rest, as they say, is history.

A genial, family-managed enterprise, the Herbfarm entrances garden travelers with its extensive nursery offerings—more than 600 types and varieties of herbs—and 17 display gardens. You'll find the Victorian, the Moonlight, the Pioneer, and the Good Cook's gardens among a host of theme-oriented plantings that are at their finest from May through September.

The Herbfarm's Edible Eden area features some 300 select species of fruiting perennial shrubs and vines, along with choice heritage trees guaranteed to add beauty to the landscape, and to produce a tasty harvest in the bargain. If traveling far from home prevents you from purchasing living plants, the Herbfarm's delightful country store carries well over 1,000 herbal items from which you can choose fragrant reminders of your visit.

Widely known for its schedule of events and classes that impart good counsel on gardening, craft projects, and all sorts of herbal lore, the Herbfarm has also a well-deserved reputation among those who love fine cuisine. On the premises, you'll find celebrated chefs teaching a wealth of popular cooking classes.

Not long ago, the Herbfarm's nationally acclaimed restaurant met with misfortune when fire struck. I'm pleased to say that plans for a beautiful new Herbfarm Restaurant and Inn were well under way as this entry was being written. In addition to six deluxe suites, the Herbfarm Restaurant and Inn promises once again exceptional adventures of delectable 9-course dinners that celebrate a longstanding tradition of culinary excellence.

INFORMATION AND DIRECTIONS

The Herbfarm, 32804 Issaquah-Fall City Road, Fall City, Washington 98024. Phone 800-866-4372 or 425-222-7103 to confirm open hours, for information on garden tours, or to request a copy of *The Herbfarm News*. Check also for updates on the Herbfarm Inn and Restaurant. The Herbfarm is open year-round: from April through September, weekdays 10 A.M. to 6 P.M.; weekends 9 A.M. to 6 P.M. ; and October through March, everyday 10 A.M. to 6 P.M. *Web Site: www.theherbfarm.com*

The Herbfarm is located 30 minutes east of Seattle. Take Interstate 90 east to Exit 22, "Preston-Fall City". Go through Preston toward Fall City. At the "Y" in the road (about three miles), go left over the green bridge. The Herbfarm is ½ mile farther.

Heronswood Nursery, Kingston

Inaugurated in 1990, Heronswood has achieved national prominence to a degree that owners of other plant nurseries can only imagine in their dreams. The nursery successfully combines the considerable talents of partners Dan Hinkley and Robert Jones. A former horticulture professor, Hinkley uses his expert's touch in the skillful collecting, propagating, and proliferating of unusually regal specimens desired by connoisseurs. Jones, trained as an architect, now applies his acumen to the landscaping and management of the business details.

Appease your lust for rare plants by planning a journey to Heronswood, located in the Arcadian wonderland of Kingston, Washington. The region's remarkable climate allows plants to develop with otherworldly vigor. Avid gardeners from near and far come here to explore the multitude of variegated shrubs and exemplary perennials, the spectacular trees for their fall color and fine form, and the splendid ornamental vines.

At Heronswood's highly touted province of flora, you will find offerings that are unequaled elsewhere. The plant selections include recently discovered rarities resulting from Dan's plant expeditions to places such as Nepal, the Sea of Japan, and South Korea. Tour the lush display gardens and you will see mature plantings that demonstrate endless ideas for beautiful plant combinations. (See details below for information on how you can plan your visit to include a tour of Heronswood's private gardens.)

The woodland gardens are perfection. Look for lovely compositions, like the luminous foliage and graceful, outstretched branches of a golden locust, hovering over a medley of shrubs and herbaceous perennials. Strolling the paths, I was transfixed by the strangely beautiful jack-in-the-pulpits (*Arisaema*), with their startling inflorescences. These popular plants are a fine example of the abundance associated with Heronswood; there were 24 different selections to choose from in the 1998 catalog. At the time this entry was written, 45 species were available from the nursery! Among the exciting choices is one species boasting marbled pewter foliage, and another which stands out for its purple and white striped spathes.

In the Bog Garden, look for the strapping *Rheum palmatum*, an ornamental rhubarb! The billowy perennial borders and luxuriant containers display a range of exciting plants, including "temperennials," a special category found in the Heronswood catalog. While some of these plants are hardy enough to survive cold winters, others are too tender to winter over. These specimens introduce notes of texture and color to the summer garden—from furry, silvery lime leaves, to plummy-purple foliage, and bright golden bronze flowers.

A showcase for skillfully executed garden design, Heronswood's gardens flawlessly integrate lyrical plantings with stunning hardscaping, sparkling water features, and discrete ornamentation. Adorning the gardens are works in stone by Marcia Donahue, metal sculptures by Mark Bulwinkle, and the magnificent "ruin," which was executed by Little and Lewis of Bainbridge Island.

Make sure you get a copy of Heronswood's catalog (if you write for one, don't forget to include $8 for postage). Nowhere else will you glean such erudite commentary mixed with great good humor as in Hinkley's utterly entertaining, instructive, and thought-provoking descriptive notes on plants available by mail-order from the nursery. Forget 99.9 percent of the gardening books you find in bookstores and libraries; this handy catalog is bursting with information that could lead the way to transforming your own gardenscape.

In an area replete with great gardens that are blessed by a climate affording ample moisture and moderate temperatures, the artistry of Heronswood's gardens promises to inspire the designer in each of us to bolder, more inventive plantings.

INFORMATION AND DIRECTIONS

Heronswood Nursery Ltd., Daniel Hinkley and Robert Jones, proprietors.

To visit Heronswood you must first phone 360-297-4172 for an appointment.

Please Note: the nursery is closed for shopping during spring mail-order seasons—late February to mid-May (see catalog or call for exceptions). However, arrangements can be made to pick up orders during that time and you may visit the gardens when doing so.

Guided tours are provided for a $100 fee, one half of which is donated to the local wildlife rehabilitation center in the group's name. The gardens immediately adjacent to the home remain private except during open house dates and paid tours. Each year the public is invited to visit the nursery's grounds and gardens on six "Garden Open Days," as noted in the Heronswood catalog.

Heronswood also offers an excellent schedule of seminars which run throughout spring, summer, and autumn. Phone the number above for further information, or send a fax to 360-297-8321.

Located northwest of Seattle on the Kitsap Peninsula, Kingston, Washington is 25 minutes from the Bainbridge Ferry Terminal; ten minutes from the Kingston Ferry Terminal; 1½ hours from Seattle (including ferry time); and four hours from Portland.

Hummingbird Farm, Oak Harbor (Whidbey Island)

Hummingbird Farm boasts exceedingly photogenic fences and arbors of a distinctive periwinkle blue hue. You may have serendipitously viewed images of the farm's delightful display gardens in magazine articles and on television gardening shows. The Whidbey Island establishment features numerous plants found in the nursery's inventory.

Visit the nursery where you will discover a large selection of new and unusual varieties of perennials, herbs, annuals, shrubs, ornamental grasses and roses. Then take a stroll through the enchanting gardens, which reveal the mature fullness and height of plantings now more than seven years old. In midsummer, hollyhocks and roses lend old-fashioned grace to beds and borders teeming with fragrant blooming herbs and perennials. As new plants are introduced, Ward Beebe explains, the gardens evolve, so a subsequent visit may yield exciting new plants to pique your interest. You'll see especially lavish floral displays in June and July. The ample, textural foliage and handsome forms of bountiful grasses, shrubs, and trees encircling the various garden areas provide year-round interest.

Hummingbird Farm also features a garden store stocked with tools, hand-crafted rustic furniture, and other useful and appealing merchandise. Replete with exquisite dried flowers grown at the farm, including peonies, herbs, and everlastings, Hummingbird Farm's gift shop is also a popular Whidbey Island attraction. Dried floral arrangements include delicate, tiny wall hangings, along with extravagant decorative wreaths.

INFORMATION AND DIRECTIONS
Hummingbird Farm Nursery & Gardens, 2319 Zylstra Road, Oak Harbor (Whidbey Island), Washington 98277. Contact Ward Beebe and Leslie Johnson, proprietors. Open to the public from February through December: Monday to Saturday, 9:30 A.M. to 5:30 P.M.; Sunday, 11 A.M. to 5 P.M.; Closed Tuesday. Also open by appointment. To confirm seasonal open hours, phone 360-679-5044. *E-mail: humming@whidbey.net*

Located on Whidbey Island, between Coupeville and Oak Harbor—about 1½ hours from Seattle, including ferry ride.

Meerkerk Rhododendron Gardens, Greenbank (Whidbey Island)

Whidbey Island is a tranquil and beautiful Pacific Northwest locale, and a popular destination point. Investigate the horticultural richness of the 48-mile-long island located north of Seattle, and you'll understand why it holds such special appeal for garden lovers.

Situated around the island's geographical midpoint, in Greenbank, you'll find the Meerkerk Rhododendron Gardens. At one time the private gardens of Ann and Max Meerkerk, the gardens are currently operated under the auspices of the Seattle Rhododendron Society and with the help of American Rhododendron Society volunteers, Island County Master Gardeners, and local garden clubs. Meerkerk Gardens' ten acres of display gardens thrive within the enfolding Meerkerk Woodland Preserve which stretches over some 43 acres.

Garden travelers are lured here by the thousands of rhododendrons, flowering trees, bulbs, and newer perennial plantings, which create inspiring displays, especially during April to mid-May. By contrast, the forested surroundings (incorporating five miles of nature trails) evoke a reverent admiration for the pristine scenery. The gardens' peaceful atmosphere is perfect for relaxed walks through fine botanical collections. The Asian Garden section highlights exotic species propagated from seed. The International Test Garden for hybrid rhododendrons offers a chance to make comparisons between new varieties and the diverse species and cultivars growing throughout the gardens.

Recently installed, the Rockery Garden features intriguing dwarf specimens of conifers, rhododendrons, and companion plants. And as this entry was being written, plans were in place for a refreshing Meditation Garden. Sited nearby a pond, the garden will have large outcroppings of rocks intermingled with ferns, primulas, and Japanese, Siberian, and German bearded iris.

At Meerkerk Gardens, late March is full with the blooms of early rhododendrons, magnolia trees, dwarf iris and narcissus. The garden's peak bloom time is considered to be from mid-April through mid-May, featuring a brilliant showing of magnolias, cherries, rhododendrons, azaleas and daffodils.

INFORMATION AND DIRECTIONS

Meerkerk Rhododendron Gardens, Greenbank, Washington 98253. Phone 360-678-1912 for information on special events, or to confirm open hours and directions. Gardens open year-round, from 9 A.M. to 4 P.M. daily, with an emphasis on the spring season. Fee charged for adults. *Web Site: http://www.whidbey.net/meerkerk/gardens.html*

Located on Whidbey Island, south of Greenbank, off Highway 525. A visit to Meerkerk Gardens is about a 1½ hours drive north of Seattle, (including a 20 minute ferry crossing). Take the Mukilteo Ferry to Clinton; from Clinton, take Highway 525 north approximately 15 miles, turn right on Resort Road, and left onto Meerkerk Lane (signs are posted).

Pacific Rim Bonsai Collection, Federal Way

A fascinating collection of masterful bonsai specimens is yours to behold at the Weyerhaeuser Company's corporate headquarters campus in Federal Way. The headquarters building is a magnificent example of corporate architecture, and the Weyerhaeuser grounds are notable also for the breathtaking landscape design by landscape architects Sasaki, Walker and Associates, and project leader Peter Walker.

Opened in 1989 as a permanent exhibition, the Pacific Rim Bonsai Collection is appropriately described in the Weyerhaeuser Company's literature as an outdoor museum of living art. The collection is surrounded by a pristine wooded area, highlighted by Douglas-firs. The one-acre display site itself benefits from the handsome design work of Thomas L. Berger, of Thomas L. Berger Associates.

Exhibited in a tropical conservatory and on tables situated outdoors, the Pacific Rim Bonsai Collection is given a partial sense of enclosure by stucco walls, that function as elegant backdrops for groupings of two or three bonsai. Among the exceptional bonsai shown are plants from China and Japan, Korea, Taiwan and the United States. Visitors come from across the U.S. and abroad to admire these remarkable specimens.

Don't miss this collection when planning a travel itinerary of gardens in the Seattle area. Complimentary guidebooks provide visitors with background information about the history of bonsai and the philosophical and artistic concepts upon which it is based. A section entitled "Questions and Answers About Bonsai" explains some of the horticultural principles and technical processes utilized in bonsai design. The guidebook will help those unfamiliar with bonsai appreciate the high level of artistry and technical skill represented in the trees on display.

The Pacific Rim Bonsai Collection presents a unique opportunity to explore a wealth of bonsai imbued with the profound cultural associations of Asian art and society. Quietly experience these bonsai, and you'll become in tune with their rare beauty and symbolic grace. One bonsai of special note (number 102), which displays the best characteristics of two different species, was achieved by grafting or fusing the branch tips and foliage of a Chinese juniper to the trunk and branches of an ancient living Sierra juniper. This masterpiece represents the collection's oldest tree, which is estimated to be between 800 and 1,000 years old.

INFORMATION AND DIRECTIONS

Pacific Rim Bonsai Collection, Weyerhaeuser Company, 33663 Weyerhaeuser Way South, Federal Way, Washington 98003. Phone 253-924-5206 for information, to confirm seasonal open hours, and directions. Individual garden visitors are welcome. For group tours, or program schedule featuring bonsai lectures and special events, phone 253-924-3153 or the number listed above. No fee charged. Open March through May, 10 A.M. to 4 P.M.; closed Thursdays. Open June through February, 11 A.M. to 4 P.M.; closed Thursdays and Fridays.

Federal Way is located about 40 minutes south of Seattle, off Interstate Highway 5, just northeast of Tacoma.

AND IN ADDITION . . .

Fragrance Garden at Tennant Lake Interpretive Center: Ferndale

The Whatcom County recreation complex includes Hovander Homestead Park, a historic farm located at 5299 Nielsden Road, and the Tennant Lake Interpretive Center located at 5236 Nielsen Road, Ferndale, Washington 98248. Phone 360-384-3444 for information. Flower and vegetable gardens are cultivated around the historic Hovander House, where you'll also find picnic areas sited to take advantage of superb views of Mt. Baker. Summer tours are available June through Labor Day, 12 noon to 4 P.M.

The adjacent Interpretive Center features Nielsen House, a natural history facility focusing on the Tennant Lake environment. The facility is open year-round, Thursday through Sunday. Trails, an elevated boardwalk, and tower are stationed to provide observation points throughout the marshland habitat.

Next to the Interpretive Center, a Fragrance Garden features more than 200 choice flowers and herbs designed especially for the enjoyment of the visually impaired. A visit here is best enjoyed from mid-May to mid-August. During the summer only, you may phone 360-384-3064 for Fragrance Garden information.

Lakewold Gardens: Lakewood

12317 Gravelly Lake Drive SW, Lakewood, Washington 98499. Located ten miles south of the Tacoma Dome; Exit 124, off I-5. Phone 888-858-4106 for information. Open April to September, Thursday through Monday, from 10 A.M. to 4 P.M.; except Friday from noon to

8 P.M. Open October to March, Friday through Sunday from 10 A.M. to 3 P.M.. Admission fee charged. *Web site: www.lakewold.org*

This grand estate garden features the design work of landscape architect Thomas Church. The garden's ten acres combine naturalistic areas with an exquisite layout of formal spaces, including an Elizabethan knot garden, a wisteria terrace, parterres, waterfalls, and a rose garden. Collections of Japanese maples and rhododendrons, and a fascinating scree garden featuring gray alpine plants are among the many high points within Lakewold's exceptional landscape.

Ohme Gardens County Park: Wenatchee

Located three miles north of Wenatchee, Washington, near the junction of Highways 2 and 97—approximately 2½ hours east of Seattle. Phone the Wenatchee Valley Visitors Bureau at 800-57-APPLE for information. Season spans April 15 through October 15. Open seven days a week, 9 A.M. to 6 P.M. in the spring and fall; and 9 A.M. to 7 P.M. from Memorial Day weekend through Labor Day weekend. Fee charged. This sublime nine-acre alpine garden, which was created over a period of 60 years by the Ohme family, has hidden pools, an exquisite array of rare flora, and enchanting stone pathways connecting the garden's various levels. Sited on a high bluff, the Ohme Gardens offers splendid views of the Columbia River, Cascade Mountains and Wenatchee Valley.

Roozengaarde Flowers & Bulbs: Mount Vernon (Skagit Valley)

Roozengaarde Flowers & Bulbs, 15867 Beaver Marsh Road, Mount Vernon, Washington 98273. Located approximately one hour north of Seattle, off Highway 5. Phone toll-free 800-732-3266 for information on the company's spring-flowering display gardens that feature a variety of bulbs, or to order a catalog. Roozengaarde also operates a gift store. The garden is open year-round, Monday through Saturday, 9 A.M. to 5 P.M..

Many garden travelers visit the Skagit Valley enterprise to enjoy Roozengaarde's 2½-acre Show Garden, abloom during the first half of April with tulips and daffodils, hyacinths and scillas. As this entry was being written, a new summer cutting garden was in the planning stages. For information on special events throughout the year, check the *Web site: www.tulips.com*

Rhododendron Species Botanical Garden: Federal Way

2525 S. 336th Street, Federal Way, Washington 98003. Phone 253-661-9377 for information. Located between Seattle and Tacoma, on the Weyerhaeuser Corporate Headquarters Campus; adjacent to the Pacific Rim Bonsai Collection (see entry). Open year-round, six days a week from March through May, 10 A.M. to 4 P.M.; closed Thursdays. Open five days a week from June through February, 11 A.M. to 4 P.M.; closed Thursdays and Fridays. Admission fee.

Operated by the Rhododendron Species Foundation, the Botanical Garden features 22 acres devoted to the display and conservation of over 435 species of rhododendron. Several hundred types of companion plants embellish the more than 10,000 plants growing in a woodland setting. To enjoy the peak bloom time, visit the garden mid-March through mid-May. In summer, expect to find late-blooming rhododendrons, lilies, hydrangeas and carnivorous plants. The garden's fall color, and wintry forms of conifers and deciduous trees, are also laudable.

Sehome Hill Arboretum: Bellingham

25th Street, Sehome Hill neighborhood; located above the campus of Western Washington University, Bellingham, Washington. Phone 360-676-6985 for information. No admission fee. This 165-acre preserve has wonderful hiking trails for observation of the native flora and bird population. An observation tower stands as a lookout point over the city of Bellingham, San Juan Islands, Mt. Baker, and surrounding mountain ranges.

RECOMMENDED LODGINGS

Chambered Nautilus Bed & Breakfast Inn, Seattle

Housed in a pretty 1915 Georgian Colonial, the Chambered Nautilus is conveniently situated in the city's university district. The inn sits perched on a high knoll, affording views of the Cascade Mountains. Located close to downtown for easy access to Pike Place Market (a visit there is an obligatory, pleasantly diverting activity on any visit to Seattle), and within walking distance from the University of Washington, the inn has a gracious vintage ambiance—comfortably cozy, yet delightfully unfussy.

Decor at the Chambered Nautilus is just as the inn's brochure states: classic Seattle style. Antiques blend agreeably with other refined pieces to achieve a relaxed look. Expect a warm welcome from innkeepers Joyce and Steve, who exemplify the amiable disposition associated with this appealing city. Successfully combining a casual mood with just the right degree of pampering and personal attention, the Chambered Nautilus promises a perfect home base for your garden travels.

Enjoy the botanical motif of the Garden Chamber room; the romantic Rose Chamber room; or the spacious Scallop Chamber, with a private rear porch and dormer window providing vistas of the Cascades. This lovely inn is in close proximity to the University of Washington's Medicinal Herb Garden and within easy reach (by car or public transportation) of the Washington Park Arboretum and Japanese Garden.

INFORMATION AND DIRECTIONS
Chambered Nautilus Bed & Breakfast Inn, 5005 22nd Avenue NE, Seattle, Washington 98105. Contact Joyce Schulte and Steve Poole, innkeepers. Phone 800-545-8459 or 206-522-2536 for information and reservations. Six rooms with private baths; Garden Chamber room with a detached private bath. Full, deliciously prepared breakfasts served. Rates: $89–$119. Bathrobes, bottled water, private phones with modem access and voice mail, and well-stocked bookshelves are but a few of the amenities provided. Four of the six rooms feature porches affording views of the garden and/or Cascade Mountains.

Located in Seattle's University District.

Chelsea Station on the Park, Seattle

Chelsea Station on the Park Bed & Breakfast consists of lodgings located in two handsome red brick, Federal Colonial buildings. The inn's welcoming atmosphere results in part from the uncluttered beauty of mission style furnishings.

At Chelsea Station you'll enjoy a high level of comfort, terrific breakfasts, and gracious innkeepers who dispense the type of cordial, helpful counsel traditionally associated with bed-and-breakfast inns, although not generally found to be the norm these days. Whether you require directions for your garden visits, dining advice, or help in getting around town on buses, the innkeepers will point you in the right direction.

Chelsea Station is adjacent to the lovely Woodland Park Rose Garden; within easy distance by car or public transportation to the Medicinal Herb Garden at the University of Washington; and not far from Washington Park's fine Arboretum and Japanese Garden.

Just across 50th Street, enter Woodland Park for easy access to the extensive natural habitat of Woodland Park Zoo. Minutes away, the Fremont neighborhood is an artistic mecca filled with bookstores, galleries, colorful shops, restaurants, and inviting cafes which are wonderful for people-watching.

INFORMATION AND DIRECTIONS

Chelsea Station on the Park, 4915 Linden Avenue North, Seattle, Washington 98103. Contact Carolanne & Eric Watness, innkeepers. Phone 206-547-6077 or 800-400-6077 for information and reservations. Nine rooms including suites with private baths; full breakfast served. Rates $95–$135. *Web Site: www.bandbseattle.com Email: info@bandbseattle.com*

The inn is centrally located in Seattle's North End.

French Road Farm Cottage, Clinton (Whidbey Island)

A very special accommodation offering complete privacy, the French Road Farm Cottage is adorned with English and French country antiques, and a fireplace with an Irish enamel pellet stove for cozy evenings.

The cottage's property sets the tone for a perfect getaway, with its warm, eclectic style and irresistible herb garden. If the mood strikes, languish away the day reclining on a chaise lounge. Or roam the surroundings, enjoying a woodland garden and trails through the hayfield into the forest.

Near the cottage, you'll be charmed by the garden's design and the colorful perennial beds with fragrant plantings. Enjoy a relaxing reprieve from touring, but before being tempted to call a halt to your garden excursions, schedule a special visit to Cultus Bay Nursery. Located just south of Clinton and the Mukilteo/Clinton ferry landing, Cultus Bay is fast becoming one of the region's premier gardening enterprises and a glorious garden destination (see Cultus Bay Nursery entry).

INFORMATION AND DIRECTIONS

French Road Farm Cottage, Linda Walsh, innkeeper. Offering private accommodations and an idyllic setting, the cottage sleeps one to three people. It also has a spa bath. On the first morning of your stay, a breakfast basket is provided, just one of many amenities to look forward to when staying at this quaint, quiet retreat. Open year-round. Seasonal rates $135–$165. Phone 360-321-2964 or 360-321-4378 for further information. *Web site: www.frenchroadfarm.com*

French Road Farm Cottage is located near the seaside villages of Langley and Clinton on Whidbey Island, 1½ hours or so from Seattle. Drive north from Seattle on I-5, then take Exit 189 to the Mukilteo ferry. The cottage is a ten minute drive from the ferry dock at Clinton.

Froggwell Garden, Whidbey Island

An exclusive accommodation, Froggwell Garden is the private home of Ralph Hastings and the late Holly Turner. Only recently has it become available during select periods for overnight stays. Booking a stay at Froggwell Garden affords the opportunity to experience the property's enchanted setting firsthand. In complete privacy, guests can come to know Turner's widely celebrated garden, while enjoying the beautifully furnished residence, which was designed and built by Hastings.

Written up in national magazines and highlighted in fashionable gardening books, Froggwell is deservedly recognized by regional enthusiasts as a rare garden retreat. The garden was conceived by the visionary plantswoman Holly Turner, with the benefit and support of her longtime partner Hastings, a skillful, imaginative builder. The garden areas are characterized by a lyrical, romantic layout: level upon level, expanse after glorious expanse are created in an ebullient style that celebrates the nuances of ornamental plantings.

Blessed by the Pacific Northwest climate, Froggwell Gardens ten acres rise up from Whidbey Island's misty mornings like a luminescent horticultural extravaganza. Hidden away within the wild construct of a surrounding forest, Froggwell simply takes one's breath away. Emerald evergreens preside over radiant garden areas filled with the finest specimens. Luxuriant vegetation, bursting forth from unrestrained borders, features distinctive color themes. Striking specimen trees include a weeping pear and a smoke tree, with purple leaves and puffy bloom. Silvery gray artemisias and lavenders are perfect complements.

Lush woodland vignettes seem to heighten the effects of the flowers and foliage thriving in full sun. In the rhododendron glen, common as well as rare varieties comprise the garden's impressive collection. Their blooms light up shady areas, while the scent and texture of their leaves make them fine companions when mixed among small trees, and perennials such as meadow rue, lamb's ears, and Jerusalem sage.

Turner's design plan extends to native trees like the bigleaf maple, *Acer macrophyllum,* and to fragrant shrubbery and clambering roses that perfume the air throughout the year. A garden highlight is the double-white flowering Lady Banks rose: when in bloom, the rose cascades over the residence. Admiring visitors explore the garden's other special features: a moist bog border, and the Gertrude Jekyll Rockery, inspired by the famous English garden writer. In this lively planting scheme, red and purple flowers exist alongside orange calendulas and pansies. Just minutes away from the town of Langley, Froggwell is a gardenscape of startling beauty in a realm apart.

The consummate achievement of a utopian imagination, Turner's Froggwell Garden will provide endless inspiration to all who appreciate the refined art of gardening. Promising a unique adventure for even the most jaded garden traveler, a stay at Froggwell offers an unparalleled bed and breakfast experience.

INFORMATION AND DIRECTIONS

Froggwell Garden, Whidbey Island. Seasonal rates $155–$225; two-night minimum. Discounts available for one week stay or longer. Contact Ralph Hastings directly at 360-321-7308; or phone 360-321-

4378 for reservations, or to obtain further information on midweek and weekend rates. Note: The house at Froggwell features a fully wheelchair accessible north wing on the ground floor. *Web Site: www.froggwell.com*

Located about 1½ hours from Seattle on Whidbey Island, Froggwell Garden is approximately 15 minutes from the ferry landing at Clinton.

Herb Cottage Bed & Breakfast, Bainbridge Island

Herb Cottage Bed & Breakfast is located on a one-acre property on the west side of Bainbridge Island. Innkeeper Karen Day cultivates a bevy of flower and herb gardens outdoors, and is also proprietor of an herbal enterprise, the Herb Basket. The warm environment of Karen's home exemplifies a country cottage style of decor, enhanced by the innkeeper's considerable knowledge of herbal lore. The culinary, cosmetic, and decorative uses of dried and fresh herbs are a part of daily life at this bed and breakfast.

Not only are the inn's morning meals embellished with herbs, but scads of gardening books, magazines and videos are provided for your enjoyment. You'll also find in your room such herbal products as herbal bath bags, dream pillows, herbal soaps, and fresh bouquets of herbs and flowers. These scented delights are the perfect complement to this inviting Bainbridge Island setting.

Located just a short walk from a beach and public pier, the Herb Cottage is a five-minute drive to good restaurants, cafes, and a movie theater. The Bloedel Reserve (a highly recommended stopover on your garden itinerary) is located on Bainbridge Island's northern tip, also just a short drive away. The Herb Cottage is a convenient half-hour by car from Heronswood Nursery on the Kitsap Peninsula (see Seattle Vicinity Garden Destination entries).

INFORMATION AND DIRECTIONS

Herb Cottage Bed & Breakfast, Crystal Springs Area, Bainbridge Island, Washington 98110. Contact Karen Day, innkeeper. Phone 206-842-2625 for information and reservations. Two rooms with private baths; full breakfasts served. Rate $85 for double occupancy. One particularly delightful room, featuring a four-poster queen bed, a private entrance, a garden patio, and a TV/VCR, is highly recommended.

When visiting Herb Cottage Bed & Breakfast, take the Seattle-to-Bainbridge Island ferry, a short ride from Seattle's mainland.

BRITISH
COLUMBIA

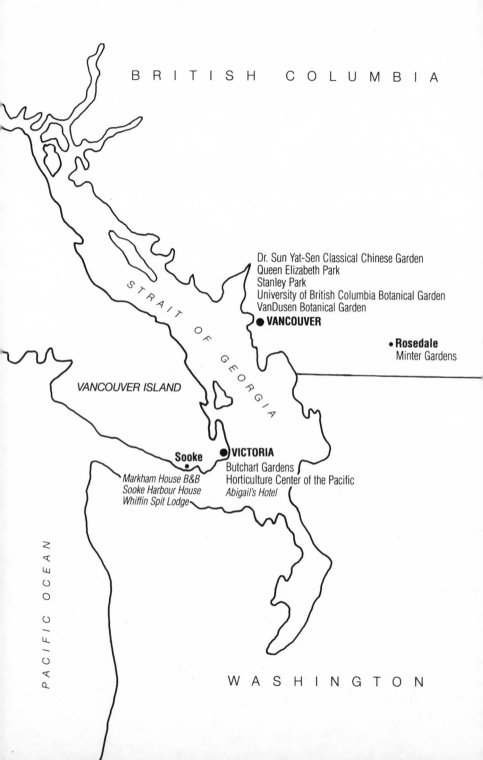

BRITISH COLUMBIA

STRAIT OF GEORGIA

Dr. Sun Yat-Sen Classical Chinese Garden
Queen Elizabeth Park
Stanley Park
University of British Columbia Botanical Garden
VanDusen Botanical Garden
● VANCOUVER

● Rosedale
Minter Gardens

VANCOUVER ISLAND

Sooke ● ●VICTORIA
Butchart Gardens
Markham House B&B   Horticulture Center of the Pacific
Sooke Harbour House   Abigail's Hotel
Whiffin Spit Lodge

PACIFIC OCEAN

WASHINGTON

16

Vancouver & Vicinity Gardens

Dr. Sun Yat-Sen Classical Chinese Garden, Vancouver

Each element in the classical Chinese garden speaks symbolically of human values and philosophical truths. In the context of such a garden, the precise placement of a delicate plant or formidable boulder carries with it layers of meaning. Modeled after the private gardens of the Ming Dynasty (1368–1644), Vancouver's remarkable Dr. Sun Yat-Sen Classical Chinese Garden is believed to be the first authentic, full-sized garden of its kind ever constructed outside China. The garden opened to the public in April of 1986.

The funding for the garden came about through the combined efforts of three branches of government in Canada, and the People's Republic of China. Private monies provided additional support. The building of the Dr. Sun Yat-Sen Classical Chinese Garden was a major project that called upon the expertise of local designers working closely with a large team of accomplished artisans from Suzhou, China's Garden City. Now garden lovers need only to travel to Chinatown, in Vancouver, British Columbia, to have the unique opportunity of visiting a classical Chinese garden.

Attributes of the Dr. Sun Yat-Sen Garden, as in all classical Chinese gardens, demonstrate the Taoist principles of yin and yang. To understand the garden's enclosed environment is to appreciate a balance between contrasting forces: here a motionless pool of water is reflective of yin; a craggy pine grasping a rock's surface is a vignette illustrating yang. Observe softness, and you'll note an opposing hard density, and so on.

The classical Chinese garden traditionally incorporates four primary elements: buildings and rocks, plants and water. At Dr. Sun Yat-Sen Garden, you'll glimpse venerable Tai Hu limestone rocks, their jagged forms connoting the essence of a rough landscape. Oftentimes a rock stands as a sculptural monolith. High walls define the garden's overall space, and make reference to the cosmos itself, with windows opening to embrace surprising views beyond.

The different flora of this Chinese garden symbolizes a range of human virtues. The garden's "Plant Guide" brochure makes clear how the plum blossom, for instance, embodies the idea of rebirth, while winter blooming chrysanthemums are representative of courage. Alluring magnolia trees, spirited climbing hydrangeas, and magnificent tree peonies bearing lavish multipetaled flowers offer their radiant beauty to replenish one's soul. In studying the garden's plants, we are led to examine the deeper implications of carefully arranged pine and bamboo, weeping willow and ginkgo. Once we have gained an understanding of the precepts of the classical Chinese garden, we become increasingly able to decipher the symbolism of the garden and recognize illustrations of such traits as strength and resiliency, grace and courage, a nourished spirit, and a developed mind.

Visit the Dr. Sun Yat-Sen Garden for a unique cultural encounter. Admire the classical Chinese architecture, with its beautiful lattice woodwork, finely crafted, hand-fired roof tiles, and patterned hardscaping composed of cool hued stones. Notice how the repetition of geometric shapes in the stone creates motifs which contribute to the serenity of the setting. Observe the ways in which the garden's aesthetic sensibilities differ from the preconceived norms of Western landscape design, and you'll appreciate the garden's luminous atmosphere, expressing a philosophy that remains as vibrant today as it was hundreds of years ago in a faraway setting.

INFORMATION AND DIRECTIONS

Dr. Sun Yat-Sen Classical Chinese Garden, 578 Carrall Street, Vancouver, British Columbia, Canada V6B 5K2. Phone the information line: 604-689-7133 or 604-662-3207. The garden and gift shop are open daily; phone to confirm hours of operation. Fee charged; group rates available.

Located in the city of Vancouver's Chinatown neighborhood.

Minter Gardens, Rosedale

Majestic mountains provide a stunning backdrop to the Minter Gardens landscape. Rising 7,000 feet, Mount Cheam displays its snow-capped form from mid-September until the brilliant summer sun melts away its frosted mantle. Totaling 27 acres, Minter Gardens presents visitors with flamboyant arrays of flowers and exuberant greenery in the form of emerald-colored lawns balanced by stately mature trees. Its design will delight adults and children, alike.

Located in Rosedale, British Columbia, about 1½ hours by car from Vancouver, these gardens began taking shape in 1979 when Brian and Faye Minter purchased the property after being captivated by the site's beauty. Its fascinating topography is the result of an ancient mountain slide. The gardens were established with rustic buildings designed by architect Peter Thornton. Rock retaining walls made use of the beautiful hard shale found on the land. They exhibit the craftsmanship of Kevan Maxwell, a local landscaper and stone mason. Finally, water was discovered after drilling hundreds of feet into the earth, providing a source for the gardens' streams, fountains, and small lakes.

You'll find 11 different theme gardens at Minter Gardens, a very family-friendly spot. Explore the gardens' Nature Trail, Aviaries, and Vintage Waterwheel and Mill Pond. One of the more compelling displays—the Evergreen Maze, presents its inviting challenge to all who pass by.

The "Largest Floral Flag in Canada," floral topiaries, and a signature flowerbed planted out to highlight the Minter Gardens' name are prominent motifs. Another merry display is ornamented by amusing figures from Snow White and the Seven Dwarfs.

Framed by a regal archway, springtime displays of tulips and flowering cherry trees precede summer's roses in the Rose Garden. An ample courtyard also features a cheery display of bulbs to herald each new gardening year. Not long thereafter azaleas, dogwoods, magnolias, and fine displays of "rhodies," of course, illuminate the Rhododendron Garden.

Lavish annuals abound during the warm summer months, with red and white begonias performing unceasingly before a waterfall that seems to proclaim the passage of melting snows from the surrounding mountains. Dahlias strut their stuff in September, along with heaps of fall crocuses (*Colchicum*). Once in full swing, an autumn spectacle is presided over by brilliant maples, looking down over beds filled with cool-hued flowering kale and cabbage, chrysanthemums and pansies.

There's still more to see here, especially the very recent addition of a thatched roof English cottage, set atop the Hillside Garden. This charming replica won a Bronze Medal at the Minter Gardens' display in Seattle's 1998 Northwest Flower and Garden Show.

INFORMATION AND DIRECTIONS

Minter Gardens, 52892 Bunker Road, Rosedale, British Columbia. Mailing Address: P. O. Box 40, Chilliwack, B.C., Canada V2P 6H7. For information, phone toll-free in North America: 888-646-8377. Or call 604-794-7191 April through October; 604-792-3799 November through March. Meals can be enjoyed at Bloomers Garden Cafe or the Trillium dining room. The Canadiana Shop features handmade gifts. Open daily April through October, at 9 A.M. Fee Charged. *Web Site: www.minter.org*

Located approximately 90 minutes east of the city of Vancouver, or three hours from Victoria, Vancouver Island. To reach Rosedale, take Exit 135 off Highway 1.

Queen Elizabeth Park, Vancouver

Conveniently located in central Vancouver, Queen Elizabeth Park attracts millions of visitors each year who look forward to enjoying the park's immaculately maintained grounds, excellent arboretum, sunken quarry gardens, and ever-popular Bloedel Floral Conservatory.

Encompassing 130 acres, Queen Elizabeth Park inhabits a lovely city garden setting, featuring rolling hillsides planted with a remarkable variety of Canada's native trees and exotic species. Referred to by residents as "Little Mountain," the 500-foot elevation at the park's summit is the highest point within the City of Vancouver, affording wonderful views of the downtown skyline and mountain backdrop.

In the spring, Queen Elizabeth Park is a wonderland of flowering trees and shrubs. This season also yields a tapestry of radiant bulbs that serves to illuminate the encircling greenery. Parading annuals are installed once summer arrives, affording colorful tableaus that enliven the park during those months when many travelers are drawn to Vancouver's picturesque gardens.

Bloedel Floral Conservatory, Queen Elizabeth Park

Should you happen upon rain while visiting Vancouver (but regardless of the weather forecast!), make it a point to seek out the Bloedel Conservatory. You'll encounter a tantalizing, sultry environment within the conservatory's tropical microclimate. North America's second largest single structure conservatory, Bloedel opened to the public in 1969. At present, the conservatory exhibits over 500 species of plants from the rain forest, the subtropics, and the desert.

Beneath the conservatory's impressive geodesic dome, iridescent parrots and free-flying tropical birds find shelter. These beautiful creatures count among a host of more than 50 types of engagingly vocal birds inhabiting the conservatory's magnificent floral jungle. Fine water gardens compel visitors' eyes back to earth, where sleek koi fish swim contentedly amid continuous exhibitions of fragrant blooms.

Perched atop Queen Elizabeth Park, Bloedel Conservatory will charm you with its collections of extravagant flora and exotic birds.

INFORMATION AND DIRECTIONS

Queen Elizabeth Park & Bloedel Floral Conservatory, 33rd Avenue and Cambie Street, Vancouver, B. C., Canada. Phone 604-257-8584 or 604-299-9000, ext. 5055 for information regarding conservatory rates and times. Gift shop. Open every day except December 25th. Fee charged.

Queen Elizabeth Park Arboretum is open year-round. No fee.

Seasons in the Park Restaurant, Queen Elizabeth Park. Open daily. Phone 604-874-8008 for reservations.

Stanley Park, Vancouver

If you come to Vancouver, you must visit the city's vibrant Stanley Park. Named for a former governor general of Canada, the vast parkland was established in 1886 and opened to the public in 1888.

Worldwide there are few park settings to rival this beautiful urban oasis. Occupying 1,000 acres on a spectacular peninsula setting, Stanley Park offers a wealth of recreational activities, as well as a treasure trove for the garden traveler. For a colorful respite during your tour of the park, observe the Ted and Mary Greig Rhododendron Garden's bounteous spring display. If your visit happens to fall between April and September, take in the formal Rose Garden and perennial beds.

Particularly interesting, Stanley Park's overall habitat exemplifies native West Coast rainforest vegetation. Comprised mainly of second growth Douglas fir, Western hemlock and red cedar, the park's coniferous environment includes fragments of primeval old-growth forest—trees that can exceed 250 feet in height. In contrast to the type of planned and installed landscaping you can expect to encounter in most urban parkland, Stanley Park offers a pristine parcel of the natural world within the city's own boundaries. The park's immense area has regenerated naturally after having been logged in the late nineteenth century.

One of Stanley Park's many compelling pleasures is its Seawall Promenade. Affording unparalleled views, the Seawall Path wraps around the park's perimeter for 5½ miles, providing lanes for walking, cycling, and for people on rollerblades. Any segment of the Seawall Path is a rare treat not to be missed.

On the south side of the park, you'll find the Lost Lagoon and Nature House, where many different bird species consort among the rushes and around the watery preserve. The Nature House's seasonal walking tours should prove informative for anyone with an interest in the natural world.

Ferguson Point is located to the north and west of the lagoon, overlooking English Bay. Here you can have a fine meal at the Teahouse Restaurant, seated in the building's lovely conservatory. At the park's north end, Prospect Point offers fine views of the North Shore mountains and the Lions Gate Bridge. You'll also find such other attractions as the Prospect Point Cafe and Gift Shop.

INFORMATION AND DIRECTIONS

Stanley Park, at the north end of Georgia Street, a major thoroughfare in Vancouver. For Stanley Park information, phone 604-299-9000, ext. 4100. For guided walks at the Nature House, phone 604-257-8544. For information and operating times for a free shuttle bus which stops at 14 of the park's popular attractions, visit the *Web site: www.parks.vancouver.bc.ca* and go to "What's New," then to the "Shuttle page." Note: Vehicular traffic proceeds one way counterclockwise in the park. Open daylight hours; no fee.

The Teahouse Restaurant, Stanley Park, Ferguson Point, Vancouver, B.C.: phone 604-669-3281 for reservations and information.

University Of British Columbia Botanical Garden, Vancouver

The University of British Columbia's 70-acre Botanical Garden is a horticultural preserve that has benefited mightily from this Canadian province's climate and coastal conditions. With its fine collections of plants from around the world, the Botanical Garden takes full advantage of a powerful setting overlooking the Strait of Georgia. In an environment where the grandeur of nature largely prevails, captivating plantings pay homage to the beauty of traditional landscaping schemes.

The oldest of Canada's university-affiliated botanical gardens, the University of British Columbia's garden features over 400 species of rhododendron in one segment of many lovely established garden sections. Blue rhododendrons (*Rhododendron augustinii*) are a particularly outstanding feature of the David C. Lam Asian Garden. Here, impressive conifers lend a hushed majesty to the garden's expansive 35 acres.

Focusing on species and varieties of Asian origins and highlighting woody plants specifically, the Lam Garden contains disparate flora such as vines and shrubs sheltered by ancient native trees. Grand fir, Douglas fir, Western red cedar and Western hemlock all grow in the natural habitat of a second-growth coastal forest. Keep an eye out for bald eagles. They are known to rest atop the Botanical Garden's towering canopy, so there's a good chance you'll spot one!

Shift your focus back to the level of "terra firma," and you will enjoy the David C. Lam Asian Garden's diverse understory of plants. Among the graceful maples, fragrant viburnums, and floriferous clematis, you will find specimens of the rare and hauntingly lovely Snake-bark maples. Three distinct species exhibit green and white striped bark. A host of shade loving perennials and bulbs, such as the giant lilies (*Cardiocrinum giganteum*), brighten the warmly-colored bark mulch pathways.

Resulting in part from heavy rainfall, specimens are endowed with a verdant beauty. Search out the yellow waxbell (*Kirengeshoma koreana*), a member of the Saxifrage plant family, with leaves resembling maples and sensational yellow bell-like flowers possessing a rather plush texture. Less statuesque, the Japanese species *K. palmata* grows here too, bearing similar blooms. Himalayan Blue and Nepal poppies, the distinctive Chinese evergreen oak (*Quercus myrsinifolia*), and countless magnolia species stand out among other rarities. In the garden's beneficial microclimate, you'll witness Himalayan magnolias blooming as early as February.

From the Asian Garden, pass through the striking Moongate and Tunnel to the Food Garden. A pivotal design element is created by espaliered apple trees, complemented by a fine collection of fruits, nuts, and vegetables known to grow vigorously in the Vancouver region. Continue on through the handsome arbor. This sizable rustic form provides support for a variety of climbers: *Wisteria, Akebia*, American bittersweet (*Celastrus scandens*), and silver lace vine (*Polygonum aubertii*) among them.

One of the most distinctive gardens here, the Physick Garden was inspired by a sixteenth-century Dutch print. Encircling a bronze sundial mounted on a sturdy pedestal, you'll find twelve differentiated shapes devoted to all sorts of fascinating perennial plants selected for their historical associations and medicinal properties. Signs help to explain ancient usages of these plants. At present, the university remains committed to researching the curative powers of certain indigenous plants.

Stroll the expansive E. H. Lohbrunner Alpine Garden, where plants grouped according to continent are agreeably sited on a west-facing incline to partake of the sun's beneficial warmth. A variety of soil conditions are reproduced here in order to sustain the garden's myriad array of plants. Distinguishing the overall design are enchanting floral interplays of delicately colored, diminutive blooms and showy displays of bulbs. However, this is not to rule out summery showoffs such as red-hot pokers, arising in the African section.

Dramatic foliage contrasts appear to punctuate the garden's rocky paths and outcroppings. The sharply defined shapes of dwarf conifers play off such brilliantly colored specimens as shrubby *Genista pilosa* 'Vancouver Gold.' A popular University of British Columbia Botanical Garden introduction, the cultivated variety of Silkyleaf Woadwaxen boasts golden leaves and bright yellow flowers.

Yet another revealing garden area gives native plants of British Columbia center stage. Here, and everywhere at the University of British Columbia Botanical Garden, you can admire unparalleled beauty during every season of the year. Of course, while touring the garden, plan also to enjoy a visit to Nitobe Memorial Garden, located just three kilometers north of the Botanical Garden.

INFORMATION AND DIRECTIONS

University of British Columbia Botanical Garden, 6804 Southwest Marine Drive, Vancouver, B.C., V6T 1Z4 Canada. Phone 604-822-9666 for general information, to confirm open hours, or to inquire about off-season hours. Or phone the Gatehouse at 604-822-4208. Admission charges vary. Gift shop; ample parking. Open daily 10 A.M. to 6 P.M., with shorter hours during winter months.

Located on the University of British Columbia campus in Point Grey, Vancouver.

Nitobe Memorial Garden

Acknowledged to be one of the finest classical Japanese gardens outside Japan, Nitobe Memorial Garden honors Dr. Inazo Nitobe, a scholar and diplomat who worked to foster a bridge between nations. Highly regarded in the art of garden design, landscape architect Professor Kannosuke Mori of Japan both designed and supervised the actual building of Nitobe Memorial Garden.

In the spring, Nitobe Memorial Garden is aglow with the blossoms of flowering cherry trees brought from Japan to be installed in this serene Vancouver setting. A tranquil spell is cast on all who walk the garden's impeccably groomed paths, with native trees and shrubs growing among thriving azaleas, Japanese irises, and a gathering of maples especially imported from Japan.

Overall, the style of Nitobe Memorial Garden is informal. The Strolling Garden beckons visitors across the portal of its ceremonial gateway. Placed along walkways are perfectly situated benches, together with six distinctive bridges made of wood and stone, aimed at directing wanderers to admire the garden's fertile landscape and aesthetically pleasing views.

The garden's waterfalls, with their pacifying sounds, encourage contemplation and invite repose.

Suggesting nature's perfection is an essential part of the artistry of a Japanese garden. Here such elements as an artificial "mountain," an island and a lake complete this artistic feat.

Stone lanterns ornament the garden. Uniquely designed, of subtle beauty, these lanterns accentuate the forms of plants and their myr-

213

iad shades of foliage, from deep jade to bright chartreuse. Seasonally, the setting's monochromatic plantings enjoy infusions of color. In spring, cherry blossoms and azaleas enliven the scenery with their pleasing palette of many hues, while beautiful blue irises lend cool accents to summer scenes. Sumptuous scarlets and the tawny color of tangerines appear as Japanese maples turn color in fall.

In Japanese culture, tea ceremony and garden art are closely linked. Thus, at Nitobe Memorial Garden you'll find an exquisite Teahouse Rock Garden, with paths of crushed rock surrounding a characteristic teahouse, fabricated of Hinoki cypress. The tea ceremony still takes place, at times, in this lovely building.

A Vancouver sojourn would be incomplete without a visit to this exceptional, authentically designed Japanese garden.

INFORMATION AND DIRECTIONS

Nitobe Memorial Garden is on Northwest Marine Drive, three kilometers north of the Botanical Garden. Phone the Gatehouse at 604-822-6038 for information, directions, and to confirm open hours. Open daily 10 A.M. to 6 P.M.; phone ahead to confirm winter hours. Fee charged; a double entry ticket may be purchased at the University of British Columbia Botanical Garden.

Located on the campus of the University of British Columbia in Point Grey, Vancouver (See UBC Botanical Garden entry for further information).

VanDusen Botanical Garden, Vancouver

Established in 1975, VanDusen Botanical Garden features plant collections representing six continents. Located on a southwest Vancouver site, the garden's luxuriant landscape supports an ensemble of 46 display areas.

Plantings at VanDusen are arranged according to geographical origins, as well as botanical associations. Plant lovers will appreciate fascinating displays revealing a kingdom of flora defined by intriguing relationships. To learn more about the garden's myriad plant communities while touring the various sections, visitors can call upon descriptive signs, a "Visitor Guide" pamphlet, and the *VanDusen Botanical Garden Guidebook*.

Perhaps not obvious to the average garden traveler, VanDusen's lovely lakes, ponds, and streams were originally conceived by garden designers and planners. These attractive water characteristics enhance the landscape. Furthermore, they provide significant habitats for flora, and positively impact on the ecology of the area by attracting a wealth of fauna to the Botanical Garden grounds.

Situated just beyond the garden entrance, a Children's Garden aims to entertain with wonderfully contorted woody specimens, topiary beasts, and a bronze replica of Verrochio's Boy with a Dolphin found in Florence. If you walk north, a formal Rose Garden (especially outstanding during June and July) and a display of ground covers materialize before you arrive at the garden's acclaimed Laburnum Walk. During May, the shrouded arbor is arguably as captivating a sight as you might hope to see on your gardenwalks, with its pendulous, opulent golden clusters creating a sensational exhibition.

After you've passed through the Laburnum Walk, the Perennial Garden appears with its enveloping Irish yew hedge and sandstone wall. Enjoyable in June and July, when the hostas and hardy geraniums are in bloom, this lovely garden of grasses and flowers perhaps shines brightest on into August, when the small space is ornamented by a colorful procession of asters, chrysanthemums and sedums.

For panoramic views of the city, Coast Range Mountains, and the sea, you must explore the Sino-Himalayan Garden, where the nearly 500-feet summit grants all who pause here an overlook of incredible beauty. Predominately naturalistic in style and shielded by woodlands on three sides, the garden is distinguished by rock work and a waterfall. Providing a haven for various *Rhododendron* species that bloom over a period of several months, the Sino-Himalayan Garden presents a gorgeous springtime spectacle of flamboyant flowering magnolias, the fragrant empress tree (*Paulownia tomentosa*), and flashing white bracts of the dove tree (*Davidia involucrata*), looming like fluttery "handkerchiefs" suspended from innumerable branches. In general, February through early March is a period of bright bloom in this garden and the Rock Garden.

Other VanDusen highlights include sterling collections of hydrangeas and camellias, the largest collection of hollies in Canada, radiant tree peonies, ferns, and heathers. Peaceful copses create additional focal points for species and varieties of oaks, beeches, ashes, maples, true cedars, giant redwoods, and conifers such as yews.

A number of commanding visual markers embellish VanDusen Botanical Garden's admirable botanical assemblage. Here are such

215

unique structural elements as the handsome hexagonal Korean Pavilion; the emerald green Elizabethan Maze—a living foliage design fashioned from 1,000 Pyramid cedars (*Thuja occidentalis*); and distinctive stone sculptures placed throughout the gardens. The strong silhouettes of these three-dimensional forms represent yet another exciting aspect of this garden.

INFORMATION AND DIRECTIONS

VanDusen Botanical Garden, 5251 Oak Street at 37th Avenue, Vancouver, British Columbia, Canada V6M 4H1. Phone 604-878-9274 for information on special events, and to confirm open hours. A gift shop features items with horticultural themes. Garden and shop are open seven days a week, except Christmas Day: January through March, 10 A.M. to 4 P.M.; April, 10 A.M. to 6 P.M.; May, 10 A.M. to 8 P.M.; June though mid-August, 10 A.M. to 9 P.M.; mid-August through Labor Day, 10 A.M. to 8 P.M.; Labor Day through September 30, 10 A.M. to 6 P.M.; October through December, 10 A.M. to 4 P.M. Admission fee charged. Guided tours available at specified times; free with regular garden admission.

VanDusen Botanical Garden is located in the heart of the city.

17

Vancouver Island Gardens

Butchart Gardens, Victoria (Vancouver Island)

When Robert Pim Butchart and his imaginative wife Jennie set about transforming Mr. Butchart's Portland cement quarry into the remarkable Sunken Garden that captivates today's visitors, it was nothing less than a stupendous undertaking! If it's color you crave—of nearly unimaginable magnitude, visit Vancouver Island's enchanting city of Victoria to tour the Butchart Gardens.

These impressive gardens stand as a wonderful commemoration of Mr. and Mrs. Butcharts' generous spirit, and pay tribute to the couple's enduring marriage. In this glorious setting, you can feel Mrs. Butchart's boundless energy and Mr. Butchart's enterprising spirit. Mr. Butchart's grandson, Mr. R. Ian Ross remained active as chief steward until his death in 1997. The Butchart Gardens are currently owned by members of the Ross/Butchart family.

Begun in the early days of the twentieth century, the Butchart Gardens encompass fifty lush acres, overflowing with blooms both delightfully commonplace and intriguingly rare. A visit here affords glimpses of such treasures as the coveted Tibetan blue poppy (*Meconopsis betonicifolia baileyii*) that has graced these gardens since the 1920s. At the same time, you'll behold exaggerated vistas, where fastidious lawns surround seemingly endless drifts of familiar summer annuals, put together in rousing rainbows of multicolored zinnias, startling red salvias, and tuberous begonias of all shades and hues. Gaillardias, godetias, and of course, marigolds, as well, grow unrestrained within asymmetrically shaped beds and sweeping borders.

A tremendous source of pleasure for countless visitors from decades past, the gardens continue to draw present-day garden travelers to this lovely region of the Pacific Northwest. As seasons change, the Butchart Gardens reveal a shifting garden spectacle. When snow blankets the ground, expect the subtle fanfare of witch hazels and hollies, heathers and hellebores. The winter appeal of such plants ranges from the refined flowers, to the interesting foliage textures and branching forms. Each year, more than 50,000 new bulbs are imported from Holland to light up the gardens in spring, when blankets of snowdrops are followed by unparalleled exhibitions of scillas, showy daffodils, and grand expanses of tulips from February through April. With the arrival of May, you'll find heaps of anemone and ranunculus emerge. Various rhododendrons bloom from March through June, turning pristine walkways into veritable wonderlands of radiant color!

A summer promenade at the Butchart Gardens should take you past the handsome rose garden, with bush roses, standards, and vigorous climbers drenched in blooms. Roses here start blooming around the middle of June and flower through September. Arresting stands of delphiniums highlight the flowing circular design. Continue exploring and enjoy the gardens' fountains and ponds for a refreshing contrast. A lovely pool anchors the Italian Garden's formal symmetry, while nearby, the Japanese Garden provides a more rarefied setting. Pause here to admire the fine ornamentation and striking bridges, combined with elegant trees, shrubs, and lovely associations of foliage.

The fragile, yet graceful American trout lily, as well as towering stalks of Joe-pye weed (*Eupatorium*) and lovely queen of the prairie (*Filipendula*), are examples of the stunning perennial plantings at the Butchart Gardens. For lovers of the dramatic, nighttime illumination ignites the gardens' great masses of annuals, and such strong vertical elements as tall conifers and the feathery forms of deciduous trees. During the months of July and August, on Saturday evenings, the gardens are aglow with the additional excitement of music and fireworks.

All who favor autumn above other seasons, should come in October and admire the dazzling fall colors of Japanese maples and Liquidambar trees, Boston ivy, purple beech and golden locust.

During the holidays, there is special "Christmastime" entertainment, and buildings are lavishly decorated and lit in festive style for a visually stimulating experience.

INFORMATION AND DIRECTIONS

Butchart Gardens. For information write to: The Butchart Gardens at

Box 4010, Victoria, BC, Canada V8X 3X4. Or phone the gardens at 250-652-5256 for a recorded message; phone 250-652-4422 to speak to the business office. Fax: 250-652-3883. Boasting just over one million visitors yearly, the Butchart Gardens are open to the public every day including holidays at 9 A.M. Gate closing times vary seasonally, so be certain to call or write for a current schedule. Admission fee charged. Restaurants serve light fare at the Quarry Coffeehouse and Soda Fountain. At the Blue Poppy Restaurant, families can enjoy casual meals. For fine dining, phone 250-652-8222 for reservations at the Dining Room Restaurant. *Web Site: http://butchartgardens.bc.ca/butchart/*

Located on Vancouver Island, 13 miles north of Victoria, and 12½ miles south of the Vancouver-Victoria Ferry terminal at Swartz Bay.

The Horticulture Centre of the Pacific, Saanich (Vancouver Island)

Idyll away a day at the Horticulture Centre of the Pacific and you're certain to come away refreshed. Established in 1979 as a not-for-profit society by a group of Victoria area residents, the Centre stands out as a noteworthy resource for gardeners of the Pacific Northwest, as well as a horticultural attraction for garden travelers. Situated in a lovely rural Vancouver Island locale outside the city of Victoria, the Horticulture Centre of the Pacific has more than 100 acres of unspoiled natural areas and demonstration gardens.

Approximately ten cultivated acres are devoted to a variety of specialty gardens, including a substantial trial garden for dahlias; the Doris Page Winter Garden displaying hundreds of plants that thrive in U.S.D.A. Zone 8; and a fairly recent addition, the Takata Japanese Garden. The Centre's principal gardens are found in front of the entrance area, where the landscape and plantings extend invitingly in the direction of a lake. An exuberant collection of shrubs, trees, and borders bursting with perennials and annuals indicate choice selections for Victoria-area gardens. Hardy fuchsias, heathers, and Michaelmas daisies are highlights.

The Horticulture Centre of the Pacific remains committed to preserving a large segment of primarily undeveloped land. Sheltered within the 90-acre parcel of this untouched landscape is an area of wetlands, and a section where native plants such as Garry oak flourish. Dozens of varieties of birds take refuge here, as well.

The Centre engages in and promotes research, and sponsors educational activities such as talks and classes on various garden topics. It also supports a trade school specializing in the training of maintenance gardeners.

Plan to visit whenever you happen to be touring the area. There are always new and expanding gardens thanks to the participation and nurture of 1300 local members from surrounding communities. You can count on memorable garden walks and relaxing vistas at the Horticulture Centre of the Pacific.

INFORMATION AND DIRECTIONS

The Horticulture Centre of the Pacific, 505 Quayle Road, Victoria, British Columbia, Canada, V8X 3X1. Phone 250-479-6162 to confirm hours of operation, for directions, and information on guided tours. Open: April 1 through September 30, 8 A.M. to 8 P.M.; October 1 through March 31, 9 A.M. to 4:30 P.M. Fee charged.

Located east of the Interurban Road in the municipality of Saanich, just north of adjoining city Victoria, on Vancouver Island.

RECOMMENDED LODGINGS

Abigail's Hotel, Victoria (Vancouver Island)

A glimpse of Abigail's striking Tudor facade hints at the comfort and ambiance this jewel of a hotel promises guests. Conveniently located just a few blocks from downtown Victoria and the city's Inner Harbour, the recently renovated and redecorated Abigail's offers an intimate atmosphere on a par with what one finds in any fine European-style hotel.

Canopy and four-poster beds, plush goosedown comforters, refreshing Jacuzzis, and luscious breakfasts—all make you feel that you've landed in the lap of luxury. Abigail's is the perfect place to regroup before embarking on another day of garden outings. Evenings you can nibble on hors d'oeuvres and enjoy a sherry in the library. Around the handsome stone fireplace, you can chat with Abigail's gracious innkeepers and find out more about this registered historic site building.

Keep in mind the city of Victoria's reputation for glorious floral displays, and look forward to the hotel's beautiful landscaping. Handsome heritage gardens afford guests the added pleasure of identifying perennial favorites, while guessing the names of less familiar plants on a walk around the grounds.

Two blocks south of Abigail's Hotel, explore Beacon Hill Park, where naturalized daffodils lend a lustrous glow to a February stroll. One of countless verdant oases in the province of British Columbia, the 120-acre park includes blooming borders and a glistening pond. Ocean walkways, overlooking the Strait of Juan de Fuca, provide spectacular vistas of the distant Olympic Peninsula, good weather prevailing.

INFORMATION AND DIRECTIONS

Abigail's Hotel, 906 McClure Street, Victoria, British Columbia, Canada V8V 3E7. Contact innkeepers Frauke and Dan Behune. Phone 800-561-6565 or 250-388-5363 for information and reservations. Fax: 250-388-7787. Twenty-two rooms include nine "celebration suites" with private baths; gourmet breakfasts served. Entirely nonsmoking. Rates $149–$299 Canadian. *E-mail: innkeeper@abigails hotel.com Website: www.abigailshotel.com*

Markham House Bed & Breakfast, Sooke (Vancouver Island)

Tudor-style Markham House is situated on a ten-acre estate of sloping lawns and landscaped gardens, in a hillside setting graced by mature conifers and a lush tapestry of vegetation. Anyone with a passion for flowers will swoon over Markham House's approximately 100 varieties of tall bearded iris. Blooming from around mid-May through the middle of June, a bevy of irises create a transcendent expanse of color bordering the lower lawns. You'll behold the sumptuous ruffled pink of 'Beverly Sills,' and the extraordinarily beautiful 'Rolling thunder,' of deepest purple. A favorite of Lyall Markham's, 'Peach Picotee,' is distinguished by its salmon-colored fall (the flower's downward hanging outer petals) and pinkish standard (its three more erect inner petals).

Garden areas are both formal and informal. With its woodland backdrop, the trout pond on the house's north side exhibits a wild beauty. Richly planted with spring blooming rhododendrons, the pond is surrounded by rushes, and *Gunnera* (commonly called Dinosaur Food, for its gargantuan leaves). Siberian irises, with their flowers in hues of burgundy and white, add stunning accents to this sensational setting, where nature's random exuberance meets the gardener's guiding hand.

Accommodations are located in the inn's guest wing, featuring three bedrooms with country charm that look out over the picture-perfect scenery. A new Garden Suite features a fireplace, and a double spa tub set in a window overlooking the wonderful pond.

Inhabiting its own secluded nook, Honeysuckle Cottage is found up the garden path. The cottage's woodstove and lovely slate hearth add warmth and beauty to a cozy renovated interior. The cottage is complete with a bedroom, a living area, a bathroom, and an antique pine wardrobe that hides a small, yet serviceable kitchen.

In balmy weather the Markhams serve tea on the patio, where you have a fine view of the genteel landscape with its picturesque trout pond. During winter months a crackling fire indoors establishes an inviting teatime atmosphere.

INFORMATION AND DIRECTIONS

Markham House Bed & Breakfast, 1853 Connie Road, Victoria, British Columbia, Canada V9C 4C2. Contact innkeepers Lyall and Sally Markham. Phone 888-256-6888 or 250-642-7542 for information, reservations, and directions. Four rooms, including the Garden Suite

and Honeysuckle Cottage; all with private baths. Full gourmet breakfast served. Open year-round. Rates $95–$175 Canadian. *E-mail: markhamhouse@victoria.net Web site: www.sookenet.com/markham*
Located approximately 35 minutes west of the capital city of Victoria, ten minutes outside the village of Sooke.

Sooke Harbour House, Sooke (Vancouver Island)

As this entry was being written, Sooke Harbour House was reopening after the completion of a thirteen-room expansion. The inn's premier culinary garden was also being reorganized and replanted. Sooke Harbour House's gardens and the bountiful sea yield important ingredients for the restaurant's regional Northwest Coast cuisine. Drawing diners from around the world, the restaurant has garnered accolades for its imaginative gourmet fare.

Wild native plants figure prominently among hundreds of edible items cultivated alongside leeks and kales, lavender and rosemary. Foods that once offered sustenance to the region's First Nation's People—nodding onion, wild thimble and salal berries, the young light green needles of grand firs, and licorice fern root—contribute to the highly original cuisine enjoyed by the restaurant's patrons.

Menus emphasize the freshest ingredients found locally in season. Seafood and shellfish are especially popular. Dishes may feature sea urchin, gooseneck barnacles, or geoduck. Edible seaweed or a squid ink sauce might appear in an entrée, together with a cornucopia of freshly harvested edible flowers. At Sooke Harbour House, tuberous begonias and johnny-jump-ups are colorful companions in melanges featuring chick weeds, lamb's quarters and wild sorrel for more savory salad flavors.

Set on a bluff overlooking the Olympic Peninsula and Juan de Fuca Strait, Sooke Harbour House offers spectacular views. When you visit the inn, study the attractively planted gardens for a close look at what is surely one of the most fruitful culinary gardens associated with a bed and breakfast retreat.

INFORMATION AND DIRECTIONS
Sooke Harbour House, 1528 Whiffen Spit Road, Sooke, British Columbia, Canada, V0S 1N0. Contact innkeepers Frederique and Sinclair Philip. Phone 800-889-9688, or 250-642-3421 for further information, room descriptions, and reservations. A full service country inn; room rates include breakfast and lunch. Off-season and full-

season rates $175–$465 Canadian. *E-mail: shh@islandnet.com Web Site: www.sookenet.com/sooke/shh*

Located 23 miles west of Victoria, about one mile from the village of Sooke on Vancouver Island.

Whiffin Spit Lodge Bed & Breakfast, Sooke (Vancouver Island)

Innkeepers Al and Sheila Carter provide a warm British welcome at their Whiffin Spit Lodge, located in the charming town of Sooke on Vancouver Island's lovely South West Coast. Acclaimed for its unspoiled natural beaches, beautiful harbors, and stunning sunsets, Sooke also provides easy access to Victoria's gardens.

Just one mile from the center of town, Whiffin Spit Lodge is convenient to hiking and biking trails, salmon fishing, whale watching and art galleries. It's also a short drive to Sooke Harbour House's exceptional restaurant.

Surrounding the Carters' 1918 home is a mature English garden, complete with perennial borders and vivid springtime displays of azaleas and rhododendrons. Graced by a towering weeping willow tree, the gracious ¾-acre property promises a relaxing visit.

INFORMATION AND DIRECTIONS

Whiffin Spit Lodge, 7031 West Coast Road, Sooke, British Columbia, Canada V0S 1N0. Contact innkeepers Al and Sheila Carter. Phone 800-720-1322 or 250-642-3041 for further information, reservations, and directions. Whiffin Spit Lodge offers two rooms on the main floor; one attic suite with a marble Jacuzzi and skylights; and one cozy cottage with fully equipped kitchen. All accommodations feature private baths; full home-cooked breakfasts, and off-street parking. Rates: $85–$135 Canadian.

Approximately a 45-minute drive west of Victoria, just outside the village of Sooke.

Resources for Gardeners

PERIODICALS & WEB SITES

The Bay Area Gardener Web Site: WWW.GARDENS.COM
In the realm of cyberspace, the World Wide Web expands to ever more monumental dimensions with each passing day. Although gardening web sites proliferate, the Bay Area Gardener is undoubtedly among the finest. Brainchild of editor Carol Moholt, an avid gardener with remarkable knowledge of the regions surrounding San Francisco, *www.gardens.com* first appeared to me like a vision. It was memorable encounter.

One evening I sat before my local library's spanking new computer terminal for Internet access, without knowing a whit about computers in general, let alone browsers, search engines, and the like. I was just getting ready to leave early the next morning for a Northern California holiday, and this was the first time I was going on line. Driven by my all-consuming passion for gardening, I typed in the first thing that came to mind: *www.gardens.com*. To my amazement, what I thought to be a generic address led me directly to the Bay Area Gardener's comprehensive listings of Northern California gardens.

I was stunned to happen upon this information-packed, attractively designed web site, and elated to find at my fingertips descriptive listings of gardens located in all the far corners of the San Francisco Bay. Entertaining articles, classes, and lectures are compiled here, offering local gardeners countless opportunities to get connected. The Bay Area Gardener provides an invaluable resource for gardening activities in Northern California, allowing garden lovers like me who intend to visit the area an ideal way to plug into current happenings.

This is the web site where the area's gardeners get the answers to their gardening questions, and where you can experience just what an exceptional resource the World Wide Web can be.
INFORMATION AND DIRECTIONS
The Bay Area Gardener Web Site: *www.gardens.com* Servicing the greater San Francisco Bay Area.

Garden Showcase magazine
If only every state and region catered to its gardening populace with the dedication and panache of Oregon's wonderfully informative magazine the *Garden Showcase!* I highly recommend contacting the folks at Garden Showcase when you're in the planning stages of a trip to Oregon or Washington. Although you may be able to easily locate a copy once you're there, obtaining a copy beforehand will reveal lots of potential places to visit.

Colorful and information-packed, the newsprint-type magazine features articles and stories emphasizing appropriate plant culture, design ideas, and inspirational reveries for Northwest gardeners. Then too, the informed musings of *Garden Showcase's* various columnists offer entertaining, yet sound

PERIODICALS & WEB SITES

227

counsel, along with plenty of particulars with respect to what's going on in the world of horticulture near and far.

Garden travelers will find extensive listings and maps, including a calendar of events with information on tours of public and private gardens; flower shows and happenings; and a compilation of plant nurseries and shops specializing in garden merchandise.

The magazine is packed with alluring ads, so it might be difficult to select from the wealth of garden-oriented establishments you'll find in its pages. Do your best to acquire a copy of this fine periodical. Its practical guidance should benefit your garden forays in and around the Portland area, Southwest Washington, the Willamette Valley and Oregon Coast. In the Greater Puget Sound region of Washington state, look for the new Washington edition of *Garden Showcase*.

INFORMATION AND DIRECTIONS

Garden Showcase, P.O. Box 23669, Portland, Oregon 97281-3669. Contact publishers Jerry and Kathy Chretien. Phone 503-684-0153 or 800-322-8541 to obtain a copy. Published eleven times a year.

E-mail: info@gardenshowcase.com Web Site: www.gardenshowcase.com

Hedgerows Garden Tapestry *Web Site: WWW.HEDGEROWS.COM*

Gardeners in British Columbia with Internet access realize they need only pore over the Hedgerows web site to obtain current news and information on gardening events, together with a wealth of horticultural communiqués. You can find here a monthly calendar detailing what's happening around Canada and England, particularly in the province of British Columbia and the environs of Vancouver.

Consult the "Calendar of Events," which spans January through December, for a listing of special garden shows and festivals that might coincide with your travels. Check out the "Special Features and Garden Information" section for articles; rose links; a horticultural database; and for the latest weather report for south-western British Columbia.

Designed and maintained by Mala Gunadasa-Rohling, Hedgerows also features: "Garden Clubs & Societies" (more than 35 at the time I visited the site); "Commercial Services" (at *eSeeds.com* you can purchase any of the plants mentioned on the web site via secure transactions); and "Gardens Around the World."

Two excellent and altogether irresistible internal links connect you with Vancouver gardens. The University of British Columbia Botanical Garden and VanDusen Botanical Garden can now be accessed directly through *www.hedgerows.com* To take a cyberspace tour, go to the Hedgerows web site, then click on the garden destination of your choice.

To find out what's new on Hedgerows, just point and click on "Sprouts."

INFORMATION AND DIRECTIONS

Hedgerows Garden Tapestry, the Online Gardening Centre for Canada and England. *Web site: www.hedgerows.com* MKG Tapestry International, 115-

5735 Hampton Place, Vancouver, B.C., Canada V6T 268. Phone 604-222-2402 for more information.

Hortus West native plant directory and journal

Hortus West has progressed and prospered over the past ten years, becoming a valuable resource for gardening enthusiasts and professionals. Should you need to locate suppliers of native seeds or plants indigenous to the Western United States and Canada, an updated directory in each issue of the journal details nearly 2,500 plant species and approximately 200 vendors. The directory currently includes nearly 1,000 rare natives listed through single sources.

Whether gardening for pleasure or profession, anyone engaged in the cultivation of native plantings should contemplate using *Hortus West*'s directory as a comprehensive reference for difficult-to-find grasses, sedges and rushes; herbaceous specimens; cacti; trees and shrubs.

Hortus West publishes plenty of material to ponder, as well, from plant profiles and book reviews, to a range of articles covering issues of restoration and preservation, ecology and home landscaping. With the well-being of our environment a subject of ongoing controversy, Hortus West offers authoritative counsel and timely advice, contributing to the dialogue by channeling worthwhile information to its 30,000 readers.

INFORMATION AND DIRECTIONS

Hortus West, A Western North America Native Plant Directory and Journal, P.O. Box 2870, Wilsonville, OR 97070. Phone 800-704-7927 or 503-570-0859 for subscription information. Published bi-yearly, March and September, by Hortus West Publications. Directory of vendors is coded to indicate bare root, container grown plant, rooted cutting, etc. The code also denotes retail, mail order, and wholesale sales. *Web Site: www.hortuswest.com E-mail: editors@hortuswest.com*

Pacific Horticulture magazine

A matchless resource for the West Coast's garden and plant lovers, *Pacific Horticulture* magazine offers quarterly issues, filled with intelligent writing and exquisite photography. Serious gardeners from Vancouver to San Diego can turn to this periodical for stimulating articles on plants, places, and prominent people that inhabit the realms of gardening, horticulture, and botany. *Pacific Horticulture* also updates readers with book reviews, a "Laboratory Report," and calendar listing of events and happenings throughout California and the Northwest.

Count on *Pacific Horticulture* for its dependably incisive and appealing stories. In one recent issue, editor Richard G. Turner Jr. set a thoughtful tone with insightful musings on the critique of landscape design. (He was looking to the awe-inspiring Getty Center, and the new, beautifully designed garden beds situated at the main entrance of San Francisco's Strybing Arboretum and Botanical Gardens). Articles included: "Trees of Golden Gate Park: Silk Oak and Two Lindens," by Elizabeth McClintock; a delightful reappraisal of a once ubiquitous foliage plant—"Coleus"—by Richard W. Hartlage; and an ode to seasonal highlights at the sublime Matanzas Creek Winery gardens, by Julie Greenberg. In this same issue, in a fascinating article on Italy's Landriana Gardens, Joan Tesei traces the development of these spectacular gardens from their creation by renowned gardener Lavinia Taverna. Tesei also gives information on how to visit.

INFORMATION AND DIRECTIONS

Pacific Horticulture is published by the nonprofit Pacific Horticultural Foundation, which is supported by the California Horticultural Society, the Strybing Arboretum Society, the Western Horticultural Society, the Southern California Horticultural Society, and the Northwest Horticultural Society. Issues appear quarterly in January, April, July, and October. To subscribe write: Pacific Horticulture, Circulation Dept., P.O. Box 485, Berkeley, CA 94701. Phone 510-849-1627. $20 per year USA, $23 in Canada and Mexico.

Pacific Northwest Gardening Web Site: WWW.NWGARDENING.COM

Marie McKinsey's excellent web site, *www.nwgardening.com*, covers the world of gardening spanning the region west of the Cascades from Medford, Oregon, north to Vancouver, British Columbia. An excellent web site to frequent before embarking on a sojourn through Seattle or the greater Vancouver area, Willamette Valley or Portland environs, Pacific Northwest Gardening (*www.nwgardening.com*) will acquaint you with upcoming events and happenings of special interest. You can select from a wealth of gardening activities at any time of the year—from symposiums and plant sales, to open garden tours and talks by garden writers.

INFORMATION AND DIRECTIONS

Pacific Northwest Gardening *Web Site: www.nwgardening.com*, Direct your Internet browser to *www.nwgardening.com* for a valuable on-line resource with links to plenty of garden-related websites in the Pacific Northwest and the world.

GARDEN SITES, SHOPS,
BOOK STORES & SHOWS

CALIFORNIA

Garden Statuary, Tarzana
While exploring the Los Angeles area, plan an excursion to Tarzana, hometown of Edgar Rice Burroughs. Direct your car toward Ventura Boulevard, one of the town's main thoroughfares, and you'll notice the vast courtyard of Garden Statuary, filled with examples of more than 2,000 styles of garden ornaments the company manufactures.

In business since 1946, Garden Statuary displays its primarily concrete merchandise beneath an inviting gathering of pine trees and palms. Under the cool shade of the trees, you'll find among the offerings numerous fountains large and small, planters and pots of all sizes, statues, benches, and garden furniture for patios. The prices range from $8 to $30,000.

A full service business, Garden Statuary accommodates customers by supplying unique castings (in fiberglass or concrete) of special one-of-a-kind items, in addition to their own ever-expanding line of garden items. European, Asian, and Mediterranean styles and designs are represented among the company's extensive inventory.

INFORMATION & DIRECTIONS
Garden Statuary, 19130 Ventura Boulevard, Tarzana, California 91356. Phone 818-343-4321 for further information and detailed directions. Open Monday to Saturday, 9 A.M. to 5 P.M.; Sundays, 12 A.M. to 5 P.M.

Tarzana is approximately 30 minutes northwest of central Los Angeles. Garden Statuary is located on Ventura Boulevard, running along just south of Highway 101, about midway between Topanga Canyon Boulevard to the west and Sepulveda Boulevard to the east.

Lompoc Flower Fields, Lompoc
The blooms may change from year to year, but if you're planning to travel through the Lompoc Valley during the high season of May through September, you can count upon 19 miles of glowing flower fields. Larkspur, lavender, and lobelia, stock, statice, and sweet peas are some of the luscious flowers you'll most likely behold.

For nearly one hundred years, commercial growers have cultivated colorful blooms in the Lompoc Valley, where crops thrive in the mellow climate with cool, moist summer conditions. Not only are impressive amounts of flower seeds produced in these fields, but also beautiful cut flowers are harvested for sale to florists and for use in dried arrangements across the western United States.

During the annual Lompoc Flower Festival held the last weekend in June, the Alpha Literary and Improvement Club presents its annual flower show.

231

Admission fee is charged. At other times, enjoy your own self-guided tour of the flower fields by contacting the Chamber of Commerce and requesting a map.

INFORMATION AND DIRECTIONS

Lompoc Flower Fields. Write the Lompoc Valley Chamber of Commerce, P.O. Box 626, (111 South I St.) Lompoc, CA 93438-0626. Phone 800-240-0999 for more information. Fax: 805-737-0453. During the Flower Festival, guided bus tours journey through more than 1,000 acres of flowers in the valley, ending up with a short tour of the city's extensive collection of outdoor murals painted by noted muralists from the U.S. and Canada. A fee is charged.

Web site: www.lompoc.com

Lompoc is located about one hour north of Santa Barbara (three hours north of Los Angeles). Approach the town from Highway 101, exiting onto Highway 246 West in the direction of the Pacific Ocean.

San Francisco Flower & Garden Show, San Francisco

One of the country's premier gardening extravaganzas, the San Francisco Flower & Garden Show dazzles showgoers! The show's 13th year was 1998, and it heralded the move from a downtown Fort Mason location, to the spacious Cow Palace. This affords visitors freeway access and plenty of parking, and provides exhibitors with the boundless space they yearned for in the past.

The '98 show's three acres of exhibits featured inspirational vignettes for urban garden settings; an orchid show and botanical art exhibit; a children's gardens competition; droves of seminars hosted by Sunset Publishing; a marketplace with 250 booths featuring the latest and best in all sorts of gardening essentials (and nonessentials); a plant market; and, of course, sensational display gardens to please visitors who possess the fortitude to cover all that ground.

In 1999, the show featured 24 beautifully landscaped, full-size display gardens. New areas at the '99 show included the Garden Living area, which demonstrated how California gardens are enjoyed as living space; and the Orchid Pavilion. The pavilion's impressive 20,000 square feet of space delighted many who attended this elaborate exhibition of orchids.

The San Francisco Flower & Garden show is regularly held in springtime, around mid-March. Each year, the show offers visitors more to see and do than in the previous years. Those of us from other climes may visit upcoming shows for the breathtaking rush of ushering in a new gardening year amidst the exceptional sights and spectacles of these events. The show's lovely, if fleeting gardenscapes can be counted upon to illustrate imaginative elements appropriate to the numerous microclimates within the greater San Francisco Bay Area, and to lend ideas for designs and plantings that gardeners everywhere will appreciate.

Every year, the San Francisco Flower & Garden Show's opening gala (along with a portion of the gate proceeds) benefits the Friends of Recreation and Parks of San Francisco.

INFORMATION AND DIRECTIONS

San Francisco Flower & Garden Show. Phone 1-800-829-9751 for show dates, general information, a preview of the show, and to confirm location. During office hours, call 415-771-6909. *Web site: www.gardenshow.com*

To approach the Cow Palace from San Francisco take Highway 101 south to the Cow Palace/Third Street Exit. Travel south on Bayshore Boulevard, then right onto Geneva Avenue.

Smith & Hawken, San Francisco / Berkeley / Mill Valley / Palo Alto

No other enterprise equals the high visibility and panache associated with Smith & Hawken's ever expanding line of accouterments—from useful, well-made tools for maintaining a garden, to aesthetic embellishments that tickle one's fancy.

With its classic garden furnishings and comfortably cosmopolitan apparel, Smith & Hawken has been at the forefront of the gardening blitz that's sweeping the country. Whether you wish to create a personal garden sanctuary outdoors, or to introduce a decorative botanical theme indoors, you'll find a wealth of furnishings and accessories at Smith & Hawken.

When I first entered the Berkeley Outlet Store, I felt I'd died and gone to heaven. There are a slew of shops dotting the greater Bay Area now, so if you find yourself in the neighborhood of any Smith & Hawken store, pay a visit and see if you can resist not buying something for yourself or a special friend who gardens.

In Marin County, stop by the original Smith & Hawken Mill Valley nursery located at the foot of Mount Tamalpais, to see where it all began.

INFORMATION AND DIRECTIONS

Smith & Hawken stores:

Berkeley (Store & Outlet), 1330 Tenth St.; phone 510-527-1076.

Mill Valley, 35 Corte Madera Ave.; phone 415-381-1800.

Palo Alto, 705 Stanford Center; phone 650-321-0403;

San Francisco, 2040 Fillmore St.; phone 415-776-3424.

Call before visiting any of Smith & Hawken's Bay Area stores for hours of operation.

Avoid San Francisco's early morning or late afternoon commuter traffic. From San Francisco drive north on Highway 101 to Mill Valley in approximately ½ hour. Plan on approximately 40 minutes going east across the Bay Bridge to Berkeley, or when following Highway 101 south to Palo Alto.

Sonoma County Farm Trails, Northern California

An organization of family farms, specialty growers, and wineries, Sonoma County Farm Trails produces an informative yearly map listing dozens of member establishments who invite your visit, and certainly will not turn away your commerce. Do fresh raspberries, delectable culinary condiments, and fine wines pique your interest? Maybe you'll be traveling with a child who would enjoy petting a llama or observing an emu up close? By devoting a day to sampling the fresh produce and diverse fare at a few select destinations, you can begin to explore the fertile dominion that is Sonoma.

Surveying participating businesses can be fascinating and fun, especially if the thought of shopping for hand-spun yarns or hand crafted herbal gifts sounds tempting. Even exotic cats and birds number among the pets available for purchase or adoption. You'll also find Christmas tree farms, places to picnic, and wonderful purveyors of fresh and dried flowers.

Gardeners flock to the area to buy manures, worm castings, and mulches from various Farm Trails merchants. So what, you might ask, could top the discovery of serviceable essentials like quality fertilizers? Well, Sonoma lures horticulturally-oriented tourists from across the country with a mind-boggling array of specialty nurseries, many of which feature irresistible display gardens filled with rare plant species. Usually there are specimens for sale, as well.

In order for a nursery to become a Farm Trails member, the vast majority of plant stock must be propagated, not purchased from other growers. You'll find here wonderful varieties of native plants, scented geraniums, bearded iris, orchid hybrids, rhododendron and azaleas, daylilies, camellias, bog plants, Japanese maples and carnivorous plants. When purchasing plants directly from one of these growers, you'll be able to ask an expert on the premises for advice on what conditions a particular species requires in order to thrive.

INFORMATION AND DIRECTIONS

Sonoma County Farm Trails. To receive a map write: P O BOX 6032, Santa Rosa, CA 95406. Or request a map via *e-mail: farmtrails@farmtrails.org*. For further information phone Farm Trails at 707-571-8288. *Web Site: www.farm trails.org*

Sonoma County Convention and Visitors Bureau, 5000 Roberts Lake Road, Suite A, Rohnert Park, CA 94928. The bureau offers an information-packed guide to the area entitled "Sonoma County's Vintage Views." To obtain a copy, phone the bureau at 800-326-7666 or 707-586-8100. Web Site: *www.visitsonoma.com*

Note: Before embarking on a trip, be sure to phone ahead to confirm business hours for each participating member of Sonoma County Farm Trails you wish to visit. To learn the dates of the one weekend set aside each year for a festive celebration, contact Farm Trails directly. You'll need to purchase tickets for that weekend's special events including activities such as hayrides, spinning demonstrations, and garden tours.

Sonoma County and its countless attractions are located just one hour north of San Francisco and the Golden Gate Bridge. Take Highway 101 to the Highway 37 exit, proceeding north on Highway 121 to the historic town of Sonoma. Or stay on Highway 101 and travel northward to explore Petaluma, Santa Rosa, Geyserville and Cloverdale. The Sonoma County Farm Trails map presents a detailed view of the county's streets, backroads, and members' locations.

Sullivan Goss Books & Prints, Ltd., Santa Barbara
Discovering Sullivan Goss and its adjoining Arts & Letters Cafe qualifies as a Santa Barbara highlight. Specializing in fine and applied arts, Sullivan Goss Books & Prints maintains an inventory of 30,000 new, out-of-print, and rare books, including a fine selection on landscape architecture, and countless volumes on art, architecture, and design.

Be sure to peruse the establishment's selection of both vintage and contemporary botanical prints. Well represented here are also landscape painting and landscape photography.

Once your appetite for visual enchantment is satisfied, take just a few steps and you'll cross the threshold of the Arts & Letters Cafe. A year-round patio and ornamental fountain create a charming setting for the cafe's exquisite menu. Choose delicacies such as a prosciutto and persimmon appetizer, peppered ahi loin with thyme oil, exotic mushroom risotto, or herb crusted fillet of beef for a satisfying dining experience.

INFORMATION AND DIRECTIONS
Sullivan Goss Books & Prints, Ltd., 7 E. Anapamu Street, Santa Barbara, CA 93101. Contact Frank D. Goss, proprietor. Phone 805-730-1460; Fax: 805-730-1462. *Web site: www.sullivangoss.com E-mail: sales@sullivangoss.com*

Sullivan Goss Arts & Letters Cafe. Phone 805-730-1463 for reservations, and to learn more about the cafe's schedule of evening entertainment featuring a variety of musical programming.

Located in central Santa Barbara.

VLT Gardner Horticultural & Botanical Books, Santa Barbara
In business for the past fifteen years, proprietor Virginia Gardner offers a treasure trove of 8,000 new and vintage books. Specializing in regional gardening, Southern California specifically, Virginia carries a range of books on horticulture, botany, and gardening of all persuasions.

A botany major in college, Virginia also studied art and landscape design, and completed a Master of Library Science degree. A founding member of the California Garden and Landscape History Society, Virginia has served on the board of the Southern California Horticultural Society and *Pacific Horticulture* magazine, and currently conducts docent tours at Ganna Walska Lotusland and the Santa Barbara Botanic Garden.

Before starting her own enterprise, Virginia sold books as a volunteer for the Southern California Botanists, which was established in the 1920s. Engaging, opinionated, and refreshingly unconventional, Virginia conducts business by appointment only. If you're a book lover or gardening enthusiast, and you'd like an opportunity to pore over a marvelous collection of gardening tomes, contact VLT Gardner Books in advance to arrange a date.

VLT Gardner's offerings include a suite of ten selected Mattioli botanical engravings (also sold separately), printed from original woodblocks. Also available are numbered limited edition copies of *California Gardens*, by Winifred Starr Dobyns, and *Lotusland: A Photographic Odyssey*, a colorful chronicle of Ganna Walska's fantastic Santa Barbara gardens, with text by Theodore Roosevelt Gardner II.

INFORMATION AND DIRECTIONS

VLT Gardner, 625 E. Victoria Street, Santa Barbara, CA 93103. Contact proprietor Virginia Gardner. By appointment only. Phone 805-966-0246 to schedule a visit. Fax: 805-966-9987. *E-mail: vltgbookss@aol.com*

OREGON

Powell's Books For Cooks & Gardeners, Portland

Powell's enormous "City of Books" store at 1005 W. Burnside Street, in Portland, is a book lover's paradise. One of the nation's great bookstores (if not the largest!), Powell's main store occupies one entire city block.

Powell's specialty store, "Books for Cooks & Gardeners," is located in the trendy Hawthorne neighborhood. There is always a good selection of gardening remainders and sale books to pore over here. Rare and collectible volumes are available for those of us with a penchant for the beauty of aged illustrations, fragile vellum, or flowery prose. Browse through reprints of early gardening literature and you might find it as fascinating as I do to ruminate on the concerns voiced by garden writers of years gone by.

Depending upon when you travel to Portland, you can attend special events like the Powell's Books for Cooks & Gardeners Annual Open House for gardeners, which takes place around March. This event includes appearances by gardening authors. Nursery representatives offer a range of plants for sale.

As if gardening books were not temptation enough, garden ornaments and other essentials are enticingly displayed here. You'll find anything from large pots, planters, and birdbaths, to herbal hand creams and gardening gloves.

INFORMATION AND DIRECTIONS

Powell's Book for Cooks & Gardeners, 3747 SE Hawthorne Blvd., Portland, Oregon 97214. Phone 503-235-3802 for directions and further information. Open daily; Monday through Saturday 9 A.M. to 9 P.M., and Sunday 9 A.M. to 8 P.M. *Web Site: www.powells.com*

WASHINGTON

Flora & Fauna Books, Seattle

Botany, horticulture, ornithology and all fields of natural history are specialties at David Hutchinson's fascinating bookshop, Flora & Fauna Books. The stock includes new, out-of-print, rare and antique books from all over the world.

Flora & Fauna is the sort of shop that invites serious browsing, and one that can offer helpful advice to both experts and beginners. Business can be done by mail order, phone, or fax, and you can meet the books and staff at various horticultural and related shows around the country. Do visit if you are traveling in the Seattle area.

INFORMATION AND DIRECTIONS
Flora & Fauna Books, 121 First Avenue South, Seattle, Washington 98104.
Contact owner David Hutchinson. Phone 206-623-4727 for further informa-
tion. Fax: 206-623-2001. Open Monday to Saturday, 10 A.M. to 6 P.M. Pacific
Standard Time.
Located in downtown Seattle.

Herban Pottery, Seattle

Herban Pottery carries a cornucopia of terra cotta vessels and garden ornaments from around the world. Classically styled Italian urns, colorful one-of-
a-kind hand-painted pots, decorative birdbaths and handsome benches
were some of the treasures I found when I perused the wares at this lively
Seattle shop.

Herban Pottery's delightfully diverse inventory intermingles elegant Renaissance forms with casual South-of-the-Border motifs. Flower boxes,
hanging planters, and pottery of every shape, size and design are displayed,
along with jumbo Tuscan olive jars and impressive lion fountains I could
easily envision colorful annuals spilling over the robust rim of a lovely
Barcelona basket weave pot.

Whether you tend a low-maintenance patio, pamper a backyard cottage
garden or rural woodland retreat, go on a shopping expedition to Herban
Pottery and pick from the vast range of planters, water features, and garden
accoutrements.

INFORMATION AND DIRECTIONS
Herban Pottery, 3220 First Avenue South, Seattle, Washington 98134. Contact
Alison Rae Bockus & Daniel Bockus, proprietors. Phone 800-618-4742, or
206-621-8601, for information, to confirm open hours, and to obtain directions. Open Tuesday through Saturday 10 A.M. to 6 P.M.; Sunday noon to 5 P.M.

Lucca Statuary—European Garden Ornaments Ltd, Seattle

Unique cast stone and concrete pieces are among Lucca Statuary's treasure
trove of Italian and English inspired garden ornaments. Overflowing the establishment's indoor showrooms and outdoor patio areas is a lavish presentation of planters and urns, benches and fountains, birdbaths, pedestals, and
statues for both indoor and outdoor environments.

Bringing together an extensive collection of pieces with a range of appealing finishes, Lucca Statuary offers sensational possibilities for various
stylistic sensibilities. I found myself responding to pots displaying raised
acanthus motifs, and the Montecarlo urn, with its fluid, curvilinear design.
For a distinguished addition to all sorts of garden settings, I suggest the classically elegant lines of the Roma Urn or Vaso Paladino planter. A more formal landscape would be enhanced by the Della Robbia wall fountain or
Spanish lion pond.

If you're thinking of adding something special to your garden at home,
plan a brief detour from your itinerary of garden destinations to visit Seattle's
Lucca Statuary. Be prepared to spend time pondering over the shop's huge
selection of garden adornments.

237

INFORMATION AND DIRECTIONS

Lucca Statuary—European Garden Ornaments Ltd., 7716 15th Avenue NW, Seattle, Washington 98117. Contact Francine Katz & Peter Riches, proprietors. Phone 206-789-8444 for further information, and to obtain directions. Open seven days a week: Monday through Friday 11 A.M. to 6 P.M., Saturday 10 A.M. to 5 P.M., and Sundays noon to 4 P.M.

Northwest Flower & Garden Show, Seattle

For the last ten years or so Seattle's Northwest Flower & Garden Show has presented increasingly tantalizing garden exhibits on its five acres. The Northwest region's top-notch exhibition draws garden lovers from near and far to revel in beautifully produced show gardens, and a plethora of retail exhibitors catering to every imaginable gardening niche.

An exceptional yearly event held during February, the Northwest Flower & Garden Show presents an international roster of trend setting designers and horticultural visionaries offering ongoing garden talks. Audiences are entertained and motivated by a wide range of topics, from container gardening and craft projects, to selecting and designing with bulbs, grasses, and perennials. These seminars offer a wealth of inventive possibilities and suggestions on how to transform the garden design at home into a landscape of uncommon beauty. You can look forward to the promise of a satisfying horticultural adventure, if you coordinate a journey to the Seattle area with a visit to the next Northwest Flower & Garden Show.

INFORMATION AND DIRECTIONS

Northwest Flower & Garden Show, Phone the SHOW HOTLINE at 800-229-6311 for show dates, and information. In the Seattle area, phone 206-789-5333. Or direct your Internet browser to: *www.gardenshow.com* to access location information, directions, descriptions of displays, a schedule of seminars, etc.

The Washington State Convention Center where the show is held is located on Pike Street and 8th Avenue, just off I 5 in downtown Seattle.

GLOSSARY

Allée: a formal element in garden design such as a long pathway, connecting road, or avenue running between queues of symmetrically planted trees.

Arbor: a structure that may serve as an entryway or focal point within the garden, often providing support for climbing vines or roses.

Arboretum: a site dedicated to the cultivation and study of trees.

Bog: a consistently wet garden area; a habitat specifically designed to remain waterlogged in order to grow plants known to thrive in damp conditions.

Bonsai: an art form encompassing venerated techniques for growing dwarf trees or shrubs in ornamental shapes; also refers to a plant pruned and trained in this way.

Bromeliad: a large family of primarily tropical plants, many of which grow on trees or rocks in natural settings and derive moisture and nutritional sustenance from the air. Some types of bromeliads grow in terrestrial environments where porous plant matter accumulates, such as the forest floor.

Copse: a gathering or small grove of trees or shrubs.

Craftsman style: spanning 1876 to 1916, this style was inspired by nature and craft traditions. The craftsman bungalow appears to hug the earth, with a distinctly horizontal design: interiors exhibit a rather open floor plan. Local materials such as stone for fireplaces, decorative wrought iron, and simple but abundant woodwork—ceiling beams, built-in shelves, wainscoting, and the like, are common.

Cycad: primitive, cone-bearing evergreen plants; palm or fern-like in appearance.

Epiphyte: a type of plant that grows on another plant for support, but not for its nutrients; examples include nonparasitic plants such as certain orchids. Also known as an air plant because it does not grow in soil.

Espalier: a method whereby fruit trees, roses, etc., are trained to grow on a single, planar surface such as a building wall or a fence, using wires to support particular branches; designs vary from elaborate crisscross patterns, to a layout of horizontal or vertical lines.

Garden room: a separate, enclosed area within a larger garden, designed to celebrate a unique idea or character; boundaries may be created with hedges, walls of brick or stone, or changes in elevation.

Gazebo: a pavilion-like structure placed for viewing the garden; early examples were traditionally designed as six-sided buildings, commonly incorporating filigree metalwork as decorative embellishment; contemporary gazebos often feature airy designs of open latticework.

Hardscaping: refers to hard materials used in a garden plan, adding definition and substance to the landscaping; in addition to decorative garden structures such as arbors, examples include paved brick paths, ornamental fences, stone walls, rock work encircling ponds, or wooden frames surrounding raised beds.

Herbaceous: nonwoody plants differentiated by top growth that generally dies back to the ground in winter.

Italianate gardens: a style inspired by Italian architecture and garden design; may incorporate elaborate roofing tiles, intricate stonework, classical statuary, lavish urns, or formal plantings of shrubbery clipped into geometric shapes, archways, or a window-like opening framing a particular vista.

Knot garden: herbs and/or low hedges such as box planted in a decorative knot design; a garden style dating to the sixteenth century.

Orangery: citrus trees cultivated in a greenhouse setting; or orange trees planted outdoors in a decorative manner, as in a courtyard where the trees are arranged according to a particular design.

Outcropping: a rocky formation that supports alpine types of plants; in a garden setting, may allude to a rock of outstanding shape or color set in place to achieve a natural appearance.

Parterre: garden beds shaped in pleasing configurations; may be outlined by shrubs such as boxwood and feature ornamental flowers or herbs planted within.

Pergola: a garden structure much like an elongated arbor, with vertical posts and a horizontal framework or latticework overhead to support climbing plants.

Peristyle: a type of courtyard surrounded (or enclosed) by columns; an arrangement of evenly spaced columns encircling a building.

Pollard: the technique of severely cutting back the branches of a tree to its trunk: either to restrict growth, to promote dense foliage, or more traditionally, to produce straight new shoots for garden usage such as stakes.

Riparian: along the banks of a river or other watercourse.

Rill: a formal water feature, often constructed in concrete or stone; a rill is generally designed as a straight, narrow channel which moves water from one level or terrace, to the next. A rill's function as an element of garden design is to direct the eyes up or down a slope, or across an expanse

Scree: a garden habitat that has been implemented with a combination of rocks, gravel and sand in order to simulate the type of drainage and overall growing conditions found in natural settings where alpine plants thrive; an accumulation of rock and rubble found on a slope, or at the base of a mountain.

Secret garden: a secluded area within the overall plan of a garden, meant to please and surprise visitors, and to function as an intimate retreat.

Tableau: a conspicuous garden scene where plants and design components come together to produce an especially delightful scene.

Vignette: the successful combination of various garden elements into a unified point of interest or tableau; may include alluring plant associations, attractive garden structures, or take in a picturesque view.